When The Garamuts Beat—

A memoir of fifty years in Bougainville by Franz Miltrup SM

and tales of adventure faith and peril

Second Edition

Translation by Fr Harry Moore SM
Edited by Christine Leonard

Praise for the previous edition

'Just finished reading your book. You've done an absolutely brilliant job. I'm very impressed with the amount of research you've had to do. A Great read. Thank You.' Ken D. J.

'I have finally started reading Franz Miltrup's memoir....and now I sit up late at night. It is a fabulous story and wonderfully edited. I am now finding reasons to pick it up and continue.' Dennis D.

'Great news that it's now there for the younger generations to read!!'

Pat D.

'In the early hours of this morning, I finished the wonderful book that you spent so many months organising. It is a real credit to you Christine. Franz would be thrilled with what you and Harry have done. I found it hard to put down and read it in a few days. So thank you so much from the bottom of my heart.' Margaret T.

'It was a mighty good read, especially concerning his relationship with various Japanese officers who treated him with respect...The other thing that hit me with the book was the dedication of so many people to their mission for their whole life. I knew many such people from my time as a 'didiman' around New Britain and New Ireland, so the catalogue of those who spent their lives on the mission was very interesting. Miltrup seems to have lived in a degree of poverty, maybe a Marist habit.' Jack B

'For all of us who are familiar with Bougainville and with mission life, it is indeed a fantastic read. I hope it is a best seller. Once more congratulations.' Edmund D.

Second edition published 2025 by Christine Leonard

Copyright © 2025 Harry Moore SM and Christine Leonard

All rights reserved regarding the translated and edited version of Fr Miltrup's memoir. Apart from any fair dealing for the purposes of private study, research or review, as permitted by the Copyright Act, no part of this edition may be reproduced by any process without written permission from the publisher/editor and translator

Translation by Fr Harry Moore SM

Edited and published with additional content by Christine Leonard

ISBN: 978-0-6453256-5-2 paperback

E: leonardstories01@gmail.com

www.leonardstories.com

Cover photo: Koromira mission church, Leonard family collection

CONTENTS

CONTENTS	vi
Maps	x
Foreword	xii
Preface	xiv
Acknowledgements	xvi
Marist background	xviii
Timeline of key events	xxii
Introduction	2
1 Leaving my home	4
2 Bougainville	14
3 Settling in	18
4 Piano mission	24
5 Kastam—Tradition	46
6 Build up to war	60
7 Bougainville at war	64
8 Peace time	102

9 Return to Bougainville	128
10 Turiboiru mission	134
11 Tubiana mission	146
12 Arawa parish	158
13 Panguna—my last parish	176
14 Leaving my home Bougainville	182
Marist confrères	186
Marist consœurs	212
Afterword	224
Appendix	226
Abbreviations	282
Glossary and added notes	284
Maps and selected photographs	294
Bibliography	296
Index	300

Maps

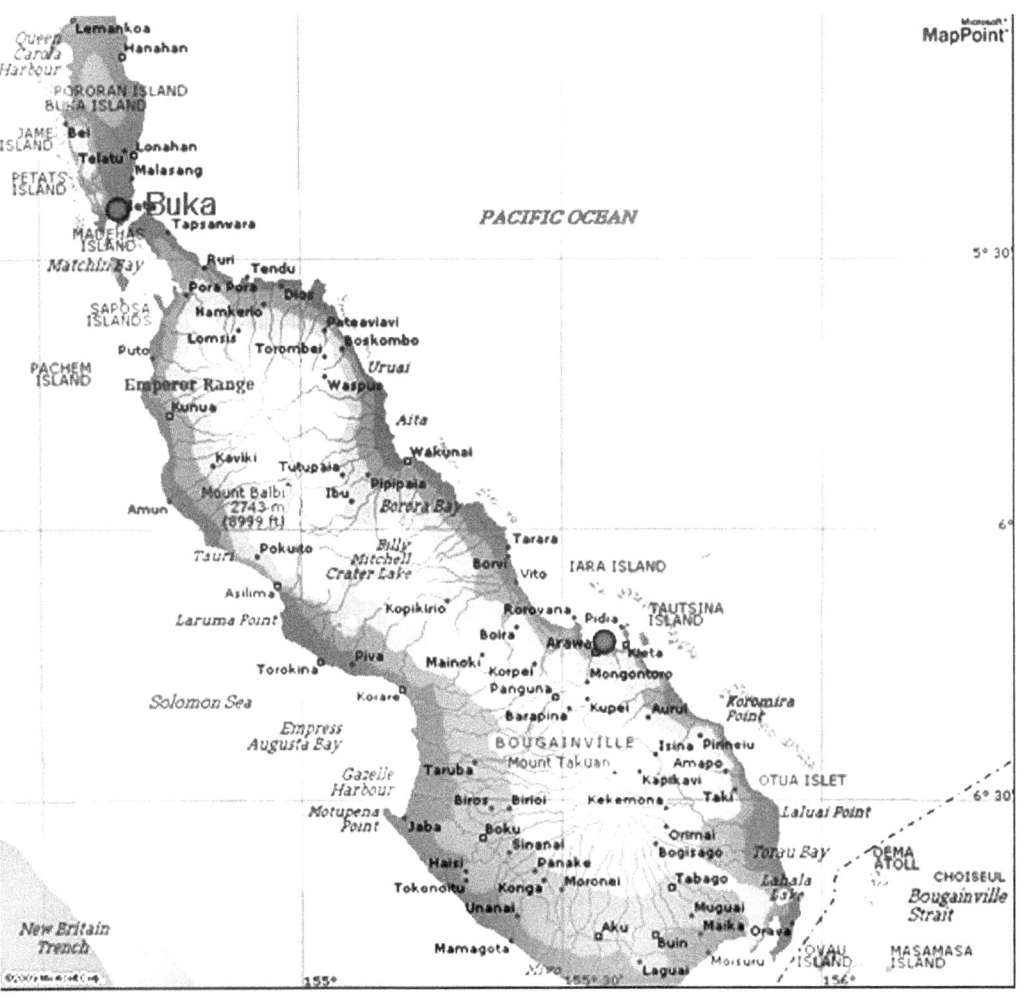

Lemanmanu 1922
BUKA
Hanahan 1922
Burunotui 1910-22 1924-32
Gagan 1922
Gogohe 1962
Hahela 1932
Tsiroge 1946
Hantoa 1947
Tarlena 1933
Teop 1924-31
Chabai 1932
Tinputz 1920
Tearouki 1948
Simba 1956
Asitavi 1935
Sipai 1934
BOUGAINVILLE
Mabiri 1958
Kuraio 1941
Manetai 1948
Tunuru 1929
Kieta 1901
Piva 1947
Deomori 1960
Koromira 1908
Moratona 1949
Sovele 1930
TERRITORY OF PAPUA & NEW GUINEA
BRITISH SOLOMON ISLANDS PROTECTORATE
Piano 1937
Haisi 1961
Tabago 1947
Sirovana (Tambatamba) 1920 25 1931-56 1914
Monoitu 1922
Katuku 1931-38
Turiboiru 1922
Patupatuai 1905-22, 1934
CHOISEUL
FAURO
SHORTLAND ISLANDS
Poporang (Nila) 1899
MONO

2

TOROKINA I
CAPE TOROKINA
MISSION TRAIL
Counterattack by 3d Rdr Bn, 9 Nov
Continuation of attack by 3d Bn, 9th Mar, 9 Nov
Coconut Grove, First delaying action by 23d Japanese Inf. 13 Nov
Piva Forks, third delaying action by 23d Inf 17 Nov
Japanese retirement toward high ground to
PIVA No. 1
3d Rdr Bn trailblock hit on 5-7 Nov
Japanese 23d Inf's original position, 7 Nov
PIVA No. 2
Piva River
PIVA TRAIL
EAST WEST TRAIL
ACTION
1943
succeeding actions
500
1000

3

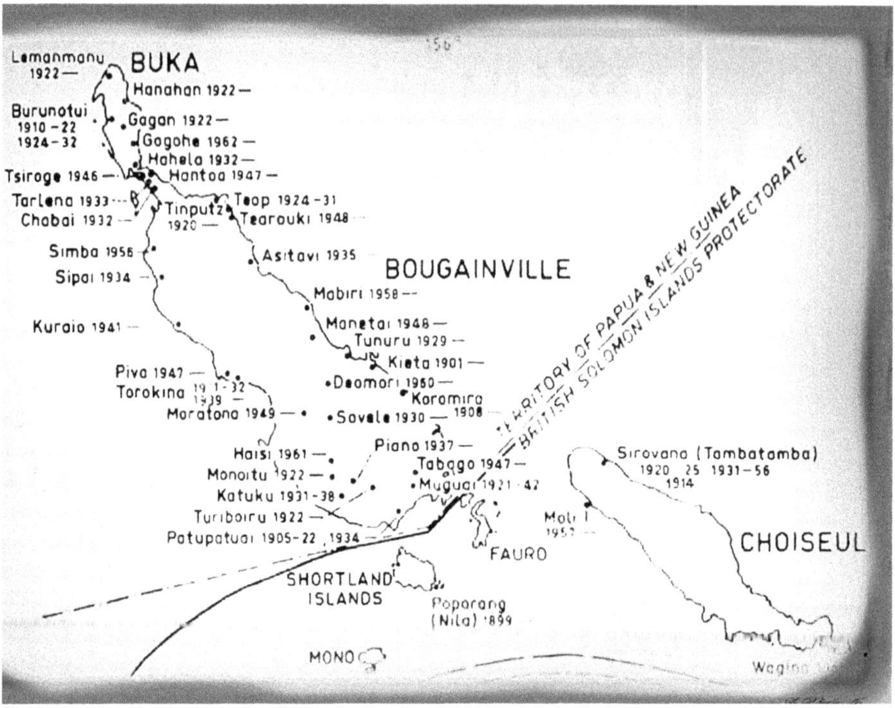

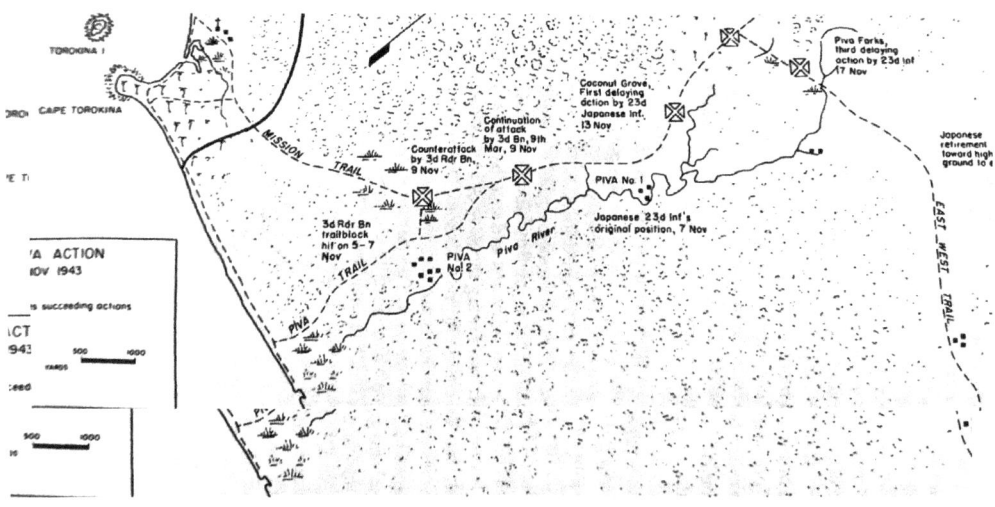

Foreword

Fr Franz Miltrup laboured for nearly 50 years of his life in 'God's vineyard', serving the people of Bougainville. His memoir tells us in his own way of his love for the people of Bougainville and of his untold rich personal experiences, some very informative, some very funny, and some very painful and sad.

His memoir is a great reminder of the life he and all the other missionaries, sisters, catechists, and lay people endured and sometimes enjoyed, in the service of the Church.

Friedel Miltrup
Darlington Western Australia
24th November 2021

When The Garamuts Beat

Preface

When the young Franz Miltrup left Germany, the land of his birth in 1937, to realise his destiny as a priest in remote south Bougainville, he would live through turbulent times, from Australia's early colonial period through to a world war, living under guard in captivity by the Japanese. Fr Miltrup SM returned to Bougainville for its post-war. peace and reconstruction phases, up until Papua New Guinea's (PNG's) independence and beyond.

Immersed in the lives of his parishioners and his faith, Fr Miltrup SM was a fluent speaker of Telei, the Buin language, and *Tok Pisin*, albeit when he spoke, it was in is own unique style. *Tok Pisin* does not boast a vast vocabulary, leading to ideas and arguments being described metaphorically, or in a round-about way that potentially takes the speaker and listener on an oral dance of discovery. Since the 1930s when Fr Miltrup first learned Pidgin, the *lingua franca* has changed significantly.

When I read Fr Miltrup's *Tok Pisin* memoir, an abiding question stayed with me; how would Franz Miltrup write this in English? His war diary was in English, but I do not know who transcribed it.

Fr Harry Moore SM, translated Fr Miltrup's memoir into English by drawing on his personal knowledge of the man and his own missionary life in Bougainville. This text is not always a literal translation of the *Tok Pisin* version, but Harry and I have tried to bring Franz Miltrup's voice to the page, so that readers can enjoy the memories of a humble man who lived in an extraordinary land through extraordinary times. There are terms in the memoir that would not be used today, but were retained as an honest portrayal of what Fr Miltrup and others said, in line with the social norms of the times.

Sections for selected biographies and background articles on the Marist priests, brothers and sisters, whose lives intersected with Fr Miltrup's are included to broaden readers' understanding of Fr Miltrup's Marist community. Articles written by eyewitnesses, whose accounts are attributed, and who lived through the tumultuous events of the Second World War, are included in the Appendix. All reasonable attempts have been made to ensure any inclusions meet with copyright standards.

Fr Miltrup mentions many villages, hamlets, and river, and despite maps and other source material offering varying spelling options, every effort was made to ensure they bore the accepted and correct spelling. Fr Miltrup also wrote of events in detail as to place and dates. Confirming the veracity of all these incidents was not possible, as we appreciate that Fr Miltrup wrote according to memory, in the latter years of his life, in a land far away from his beloved Bougainville.

Christine Leonard

Throughout the text Franz refers to the Japanese as Japs: normal enough in the 1940s, but now seen to be offensive by some. I have not taken the liberty of changing Jap to Japanese, but I hope this story will not cause offence.

Harry Moore SM

Acknowledgements

When Harry Moore asked me to edit this memoir, he entrusted a *Tok Pisin* copy of Fr Miltrup's manuscript into my care. I am grateful for his patience, trust, and the confidence he placed in me to make Fr Miltrup's memoir more accessible to a wider readership.

Harry provided me with Marist reference books which, whilst not conclusive, proved invaluable and the key source for biographical data. They did not however include details on the Bougainvillean and Papua New Guinean diocesan clergy. Information on these individuals is limited.

Information on The Missionary Sisters of the Society of Mary (SMSM) was provided by the sisters' archivist, Sr Jennifer Clarke SMSM. Thanks go to Sr Margaret Tisch SMSM for connecting us and to Sr Jenny for digging into the Society's records and providing the background I was looking for as well as a wonderful collection of rare digitised photographs. Her efforts to secure the SMSM General Council's permission to include the war stories of some of the sisters makes the contributions in the Appendix all the more interesting. The General Council is aware that too little is known or understood of the lived experiences of the SMSM in Bougainville in the early years.

Much appreciation also goes to Monica Larcombe and the Buin community in Queensland for checking on the Telei words. It was a revelation to us all as to how the language has changed over the years.

Appreciation also goes to Bill Brown MBE for clarifying some village names, and details of his role and that of Des Ashton's, in the administration.

Posthumous thanks and appreciation go to the Late Fr Kevin Kerley SM who ensured Franz Miltrup's typed document survived.

Last but not least thanks go to Fred Miltrup. Fred visited his Uncle Franz in Bougainville, and he also travelled with him to Europe when Fr Miltrup returned to Germany on holidays. Fred was happy for this project to proceed.

Christine Leonard, Editor

Marist background

The first Marist mission was established in Papua New Guinea (PNG) by a group of young French priests and brothers led by the charismatic young Bishop Jean-Georges Collomb SM, who came with doctorates from the University of Milan, in civil law, canon law, and theology. These Marists landed on Woodlark Island (known by locals as *Muyua*) on 15 September 1847.

In less than a year, they established another mission on Umboi Island (also known as Rooke Island), with plans to start a new foundation on Buka in Bougainville. Malaria intervened however, and Bishop Collomb succumbed to the disease on Umboi, on 16 July 1848. The bishop was buried on the beach, and his grave has long since been covered by the sea. The venture was abandoned and it would be another 50 years before the Marists returned to PNG (Moore: 2021).

In the last years of the 19th Century, Cardinal Jean-Pierre Broyer, the Marist Vicar Apostolic of Samoa, spearheaded the move to establish the Order in the Solomons. Frs Eugene Englert and Karl Flaus, acting as envoys for Cardinal Broyer, arrived in the Shortland Islands in the Bougainville Strait in March 1899, per the advice of Herr Fritz Rose, the German Consul of Samoa. This was the only area settled by Europeans, hitherto part of the German Protectorate, but soon to come under British control.

When The Garamuts Beat

In July 1899, after meeting Rudolf von Bennigsen, the newly appointed and first official Governor of Deutche-Nueguinea, Broyer was: 'authorized, in writing to acquire in the Solomons all the land reasonably necessary for the mission.' Englert paid Chief Ferguson six gold sovereigns for some land on Poporang Island. The chief was the son of the renowned warrior 'King' Gorai, whose warring raids up and down the east coast of Bougainville have been written about extensively. After visiting Poporang and seeing 'the extraordinarily active agricultural work' the Marists had achieved, Governor Bennigsen urged them to expand northward to Bougainville. In 1900, he wrote:

> I am disposed to cede to the mission, in the port of Kieta, a piece of land...from 400–500 hectares on condition that, work is done there not as a mission but that it be agricultural work, as is being done in Poporang (Laracy: 1969. P.106).

Sisters Claire and Ignace arrived at Poporang from Samoa in April 1901. By September of that year, a newly established school boasted seven female students, all from Bougainville, plus 52 youths, all but four also from Bougainville and Buka. From 1902 to 1909, the next governor of Deutche-Nueguinea, Dr Albert Hahl, offered the Marists more land, holdings the Marists increased due to their negotiating directly with village chiefs. Some of those acquisitions are as follows:

- In 1900, an initial 35 hectares were acquired at Kieta, on the east coast of Bougainville, from Sarai, chief of Pok Pok Island.

- The price was ten axes, ten work knives, 20 lengths of cloth, a box of beads and a six-oared whaleboat. Sarai's arrangement was subsequently disputed by Apotu, the leader of Rigu, (the site next to where Tubiana mission was eventually established), and others. When Fr Englert and his curate, Pierre Meyer, arrived in Kieta in October 1901 to establish a station, they did not find harmonious relations amongst their Bougainvillean neighbours.

Marist background

- In 1902, land at Patupatuai on the Buin coast was acquired from the villagers of Kahili, who sought protection from attacks by warring tribes from the Shortlands. The establishment of a station at Patupatuai in 1903 initially failed, when J.B. Perpezat died of blackwater fever just three weeks after his arrival. In early 1905, Frs François Allotte and John Rausch made a second attempt to establish a station at Patupatuai. Within seven months, the German administration established an outpost at Kieta.

- By 1913, the Marists held 500 hectares of land in Kieta, 1,000 hectares in Buin, 120 hectares in Koromira, 200 hectares at Torokina, and 125 hectares on the island of Buka. This was in addition to land at other locations.

Establishing stations on these lands was fraught with challenges, largely due to the effects of malaria on the early settler priests. Prefect Apostolic, Joseph Forestier, moved his headquarters from Poporang to Kieta in early 1910 (Laracy: 1969. Pp 100, 105, 107, 110, 113).

When The Garamuts Beat

Timeline of key events

5 Jun 1909	Franz Miltrup was born in Osnabrück Germany
13 Apr 1932	Professed as a Marist in Glanerbrug Netherlands
29 Jun 1935	Ordained in Fürstenzell Passau Germany
Mid-Jul 1937	Studied tropical medicine in Würzburg
14 Oct 1937	Farewell party held in Meppen Germany
Early Nov 1937	Departed from Naples Italy on MV *Viminale 2*
Mid–Dec 1937	Arrived in Sydney Australia
24 Dec 1937	Departed from Sydney on MV *Malaita*
11 Jan 1938	Arrived in Kieta Bougainville
mid–Jun 1938	Appointed to Piano mission in south Bougainville
25 Dec 1939	First Christmas in Piano
Early Apr 1942	Japanese forces landed in Buin south Bougainville
19 Sep 1942	Japanese soldiers take missionaries from Muguai as prisoners of war to Kahili
21 Sep 1942	Japanese soldiers take missionaries from Turiboiru to Kahili

When The Garamuts Beat

01 Oct 1942	Ten missionaries, four from Muguai, and six from Turiboiru (two priests, a brother, and seven sisters), were transported from Buin by ship to Rabaul.
25 Dec 1942	Last Christmas in Piano south Bougainville
2 Feb 1943	Departed from Monoitu (Siwai district) in south Bougainville with three priests and travelled north to Kieta to be interned by the Japanese
Mid-Feb 1943	Arrived in Kieta and imprisoned by the Japanese at an internment camp at Tubiana
6 Jul 1943	Taken to Buin by Japanese soldiers
1943	Held at Bogisago in the mountains of south Bougainville in a Japanese camp
1 Nov 1943	US 1 Marine Corps landed at Torokina Empress Augusta Bay Bougainville
10 Dec 1943	As a result of an American bombing raid, Japanese forces behead the American priest Fr John Conley in Kieta. Fr Florent Waché died during that bombing raid
New Year 1944	Fr Miltrup was escorted back to Japanese HQ in south Bougainville
28 Jun 1944	Travelled from Buin to Nagovisi with Fr Schlieker
Oct 1944	Returned to the Japanese camp at Bogisago
16 Apr 1945	Escaped from Bogisago under the planning and guidance of Lt Paul E Mason RANVR, by walking over the mountains to Torokina. Fr Miltrup was to be beheaded the next day
7 May 1945	Departed from Torokina on MV *Katoomba* for Australia
May 1945	Fr Wilhelm Weber executed by Japanese soldiers near Tarara, east coast Bougainville
2 Jun 1945	Fr Miltrup arrived in Sydney, taken to Hunters Hill

Timeline of key events

6 Aug 1945	US Army Air Force drop an atomic bomb on Hiroshima Japan
14 August 1945	Japan agrees to surrender, bringing about the end of WWII in the Pacific
Mid-Jun 1946	Fr Miltrup returned to Bougainville, and Piano mission after spending some time in Torokina
Mid-Jul 1949	Transferred to Torokina as Director of the Major Seminary
Mid-Dec 1953	Ordination of Bougainvillean priests; Fr Alois Tamuka at Turiboiru and Fr Peter Tatamas in Hahela, Buka
Early Mar 1954	First holiday. Departed on MV *Malaita* for Sydney. Departed from Sydney on MV *Viminale* for Naples
Mid-Apr 1954	Arrived in home town Osnabrück Germany
Early Dec 1954	Returned to Australia on MV *Johan van Oldenbarnevelt*, spent six weeks in Sydney
Early Feb 1955	Returned to Bougainville, stationed at Turiboiru in Buin district for ten years
1959	Bishop Thomas Wade retired
1960	Fr Leo Lemay appointed as Bishop of Bougainville
Early Jun to mid-Aug 1960	Fr Miltrup's nephew, Freidel (Fred) Miltrup, visits Bougainville
29 Jun 1960	Fr Franz Miltrup's Silver Jubilee as a priest
1964	Appointed to Tubiana mission near Kieta
Aug 1969	Rorovana villagers protest against enforced land acquisition for Conzinc Riotinto's mining lease
Early Apr 1971	Fr Miltrup returned to Germany on leave
1972	Appointed to Arawa parish for ten years
24 Nov 1974	Bishop Gregory Singkai consecrated at Tubiana
1977	Fr Miltrup took leave and returned to Germany

1982	Fr Miltrup took leave, returning to Germany. Appointed to Panguna parish
13 Apr 1982	Fr Miltrup's Golden Jubilee for belonging to home parish of Steinbeck
Early Apr 1985	Took early leave to Germany
13 April 1985	An early celebration of his Golden Jubilee in Germany as a priest
Jan 1986	Left Panguna parish, retiring to assist Fr Herman Wöeste at Koromira mission
Oct 1986	Left Bougainville for the last time due to ill health
1 Nov 1989	Finished writing the memoir
3 Nov 1996	Fr Miltrup passed away aged 87 years in Lathen Germany - RIP

Timeline of key events

Tok i go pas

Patere George Lepping na mi i bin stap long Bogenvil longpela taim tumas, bipo taim long pait namba tu long graun. Nau mi lapun long ol. Bipo long taim mi stap iet long Bogenvil, ol i askim mi long raitim daun ol samting i kamap taim mi no stap iet. Tasol pastaim mi no laik. Nau mi stap long ples, mi bin kirap na raitim daun ol samting mi ken tingting bilong ol dispela krismas mi bin stap long Bogenvil.

Tasol me laik tok pastaim; dispela em i no buk bilong ol man save, na em i no buk bilong antropologi. Em tu i no dairi, tasol em i buk long ol samting i bin kamap na mi ken tingim bek long em.

Sapos mi rait long ol kastam bilong ol man-meri, mi tok long ol man bilong Buin. Mi hop ol man-meri riddim dispela buk ol i kisim liklik hamamas long em.

Lathen, Germany, 1 November 1989, de bilong Santo Martin[a]

Introduction

Fr George Lepping and I were in Bougainville long before the Second World War, and now we are both the oldest of them all. When I was still in Bougainville, I was asked to write about my experiences, but I was not interested. Now that I am in my homeland, I have started to write what I remember of those years I lived in Bougainville.

I should say firstly, that this is not a book for intellectuals, nor is it a book for anthropologists. It is also not a diary. It is a book of things that happened as I remember them.

When I write about the customs of men and women, I refer to the Buin people. I hope whoever reads this book receives some enjoyment from it.

Lathen, Germany, 11 November 1989, St Martin's Day

When The Garamuts Beat

1 Leaving my home

Mama bilong mi tok olosem, 'pikinini bilong mi, yu stap hia long ples. Na taim mi dai pinis yu i nap long go.'

Farewell to family and friends

I was ordained to the priesthood at Passau, Germany, on 29 June 1935. If Marists wish to join a mission overseas, they must first get permission from Marist head quarters in Rome. The Marist Mission centres in Oceania are at Wallis and Futuna (where Saint Peter Chanel was killed in 1841), Fiji, New Caledonia, Samoa, Tonga, Vanuatu, and South and North Solomons.

When I received the Sacraments of Ordination, I applied to the Superior General in Rome to join the missions. It was the Society's custom for Marist priests and brothers who applied, that a response would be received on 28 April, the anniversary of St Peter Chanel's death. The first time I applied, the response was 'no'. They advised that I should wait a while, but my feelings about going out to the missions remained strong, and when I applied a second time, the Superior General agreed that I could go. I would be sent to Bougainville.

In the summer of 1937, I took a course in tropical medicine at Würzburg. One lesson I recall the doctor telling us students was, if a patient could not breathe, to roll a piece of paper like a cigarette, cut a hole in the person's windpipe, insert the paper tube, and the person could breathe again.

When The Garamuts Beat

The custom at this time for missionaries was to let their beards grow so I let mine grow, but I really did not like it, and ended up shaving it off. I fitted myself out with white trousers, a white hat, and white shoes, and said my goodbyes to family and friends. My mother pleaded, 'Franz, don't go until I am dead.' She lived for another 18 years, by which time I would have been too old to join the missions. My father had other thoughts. He said, 'Franz, you are safer in the missions than you are here.' It was good advice.

One of my biggest concerns at the time was that I needed a passport and visas to travel to Australia and Bougainville, remember this was 1937 when the Nazis were running Germany. They did not like people leaving the country, so I told officials I wanted to visit Holland. I was granted a passport. If I was completely honest and told them about Australia, I would never have been granted one. I did travel to Holland though, to visit an aunt who was a nun.

As the date of my departure drew near, I called on our parish priest Theo Bledendiek, to say goodbye. He was so upset he turned away and wept. He could not bring himself to shake my hand, but he promised to call on my parents. I never saw Fr Bledendiek again, as when I returned to Germany for holidays after more than 15 years, he had died. My brother and a priest, Heinrich Lahrmann, drove me to Meppen, where on the 14 October, my family and friends put on a farewell party for me. After the party we all went to church in Meppen to pray for a safe trip. With me was Else Faulois, a doctor, who was leaving for Africa.

After the prayer service, I went to the station and caught a train to Rheine and Osnabrück. The train conductor was known to me as 'Uncle' Potter. He was a family friend who often stayed with my parents. At Osnabrück, I was met by my brother, Fritz, and his wife, Angela. He did not tell my mother in case she wanted to say another last goodbye. I never saw my brother again as he was killed during the war on the Russian Front, near Riga in Latvia.

Leaving my home

I then travelled to Magdeburg where I stayed with Fr Martin Reinhardt's sister. I made a quick visit to my old seminary at Fürstenzell before taking another train to München. I arrived in Rome without a toea (PNG currency meaning 'a cent'), as at München station, after asking a porter to help me with my bags, I ended up giving him all the German money I had. Thank God there were no problems with Customs at the German Italian border. I finally arrived in Rome with no money, but was made welcome by Fr Dubois, who took care of all the missionaries leaving for Oceania.

At the Marist house I found other priests waiting to go to missions in the islands. There were two Dutchmen, seven French, one from Luxemburg, and myself, a German. Of this group, two were going to New Caledonia, two to New Hebrides (now Vanuatu), two to Fiji — one who was newly ordained, the other, an elderly priest returning from leave. One priest was heading to Futuna, and then there was me, for Bougainville.

We spent two weeks together in Rome with Fr Dubois urging us to explore the city. One day we saw Pope Pius XII. A regrettable issue that came up for me was that all the priests spoke French, and I could not, and while they could speak a little English, they chose not to. A rule in our Society was that priests ordained in the same year, sat at the same table, this meant that I sat with the French. Fr Dubois noticed I was feeling isolated and homesick so he moved me to join the two Dutchmen.

A few days later, we went to St Peter's Basilica, and the Pope gave his address in German. I was so happy, my spirits lifted and I was no longer thinking of my parents and the home that I left behind. The French-speaking priests however could not understand what the Pope said.

After two weeks in Rome, Fr Dubois took our group on an early morning train to Napoli, as our ship was due to leave the city that afternoon. But the *Viminale's* departure was delayed so Fr Debois found us a place to eat and sleep for the night. The next day we visited Pompeii, returning in time to board the *Viminale* in the afternoon. As our ship sailed out of the harbour, we sang the *Ave Maris Stella* in keeping with Marist tradition when missionaries left their home country for stations abroad. It was early November 1937.

Napoli to Sydney

After some days I began thinking of the ship as our home on the ocean. We passengers enjoyed an inexpensive bottle of wine shared between two people with our evening meal. In the dining room we were assigned to a large table that included a Greek Orthodox priest. After docking at Aden and clearing Customs we were free to go ashore, but the ship's doctor tried to give us injections, to which I said that I was given all the necessary injections in Germany. I think he was trying to make money out of us.

On the *Viminale* there was a man with a large shipment of animals for an Australian zoo. He went ashore to a beach to buy *me me* — goats, as fresh meat for his animals on the ship. We got talking later, and when he heard that I was going to Bougainville he told me that Bougainville had many species of birds, and that he would pay well for any birds I sent him. Later I found out that missionaries had shotguns and called on local men to shoot birds and chickens, as they were the only source of fresh meat. Later on, as people bred pigs and cattle, villagers would share some of their fresh pig meat with the mission in times of special celebrations or a funeral.

Colombo was our second stop. It was a large city with busy roads and markets full of people selling all kinds of things. When I was with the Dutch priests, Frs Henk Oude-Engberink and Alois van Houte, wandering around we noticed a man following us, trying to sell us things. When he spoke to us in English we pretended not to understand him, so he switched to French, which I could not follow. Then when he heard my companions talking in Dutch he switched to Dutch. We eventually bought some curried meat that was so hot it burnt our mouths. After the three of us had seen enough of Colombo we returned to the ship.

Leaving my home

Now began what seemed a long journey across the Indian Ocean to Sydney. We ditched our black clothing for tropical whites, and to kill time during those two weeks of hot sunny days we played all kinds of games. During the day passengers could dress as they liked, but everyone was expected to dress neatly at night especially in the dining room. On week days we held Mass in our cabins, whereas Sunday Mass was celebrated in one of the saloons, with soldiers and officers sitting near the altar. Everyone seemed to be Catholic.

As we drew closer to Australia, a man pointed out stars we would not see in Europe, including the Southern Cross. We also noticed a black cloud in the heavens, a sure sign of Australia —smoke from bush fires. I was told that fire doesn't always destroy the Australian bush, and that eucalyptus trees can rejuvenate after a fire. The early European settlers who came to Australia had cut down so many trees, selling the timber without replanting, and now Australia has dust storms.

Our first port of call in Australia was Freemantle. It was December 1937, and as we walked down a road, we came across a man selling cherries. This was a real shock to us, as in cold climates, one never sees cherries in December. We had forgotten where we were and that Australia had longer summers than winter.

The next day we arrived in Perth, a beautiful city which got me thinking it must be the most attractive city in Australia. Everyone was most welcoming. On leaving Perth, Australian wine with German names like Riesling appeared on the dining tables. The wine was very good but it was stronger than European wine so we had to go easy.

The next stop was Melbourne. Unlike Freemantle, it was much larger, like most of Australia's other populated cities along the east coast. *Why was this so?* I asked myself. It turns out the centre of Australia is extremely hot. There is low rainfall and not much forest, but the country has plenty of resources in the ground.

Finally, our last day on MV *Viminale* saw us entering Sydney Harbour. Fr Élie Bergeron, charged with looking after us missionaries was down at the docks to meet us. He was also in charge of any personal effects, including cargo arriving later. When we collected our luggage, it was soon evident that one or two pieces were lost or stolen. Fr Bergeron took us to the Marist Mission Centre at Hunters Hill, where missionaries rested or waited for a ship to take them to their allocated place of work.

After our evening meal, we noticed priests going outside to light up pipes or cigars. We presumed to join in as new men, but Fr Boch, the House Superior, said we needed permission from our bishops to smoke. I was very surprised to hear this as I thought the Superior General in Rome had granted his approval.

Some days later, Henk Oude-Engberink, Alois van Houte, and I, caught a tram from Hunters Hill into the city of Sydney, to buy things useful to our missions. Hunters Hill is not close to the city's centre. Sydney which has a population of some millions, is divided by a large bridge which its citizens fondly refer to as 'our Harbour Bridge'. Near this bridge is St Patrick's, a large Catholic church considered the oldest church in Sydney, and operating under the care of Marist parish priests.

The sun was hot so we looked for somewhere to have a beer. I couldn't find anything until a man directed us to a nearby hotel. On entering the establishment I was struck by the lack of tables and chairs. There was one table with a couple of chairs so we sat down and waited for someone to take our order, but no one came over. I walked over to the bar where a woman took my order for three beers and I returned to our table. After waiting some time, it was clear nobody was bringing them, so I went back to the bar and collected them.

Not long after, three men approached us. At first I thought they wanted me to buy them a beer, but they returned with more beers and sandwiches for us, and seemed keen to know where we were from and where we were going.

Leaving my home

They noticed we were Catholic priests and explained the rule put out by Cardinal Gilroy forbidding priests from entering a public bar, a situation we knew nothing about. The cardinal also forbade priests from travelling in the same vehicle as a woman. 'What about our mothers?' asked a priest apparently. The Cardinal responded, 'they should hold up a sign in the car window — THIS WOMAN IS MY MOTHER.'

The next day Father Bergeron accompanied us into Sydney. Being another hot day, Henk declared, 'Miltrup would love a glass of beer!' to which Bergeron let it be known he knew how Germans loved their beer. Bergeron took us to a hotel with a saloon, and on sitting down we shared what had happened the previous day. Fr Bergeron explained that it was permissible for priests to have a beer in a saloon as long as it was furnished with tables and chairs.

Bound for the islands

We did not stay long in Sydney. On Christmas Eve of 1937, Frs Henk Oude-Engberink and Alois van Houte, Sister Fabian from Ireland, and I, boarded the MV *Malaita*. The Dutch priests were destined for the South Solomons, while Sister Fabian and I were travelling on to the North Solomons, or Bougainville, as it eventually became known. Our voyage took three weeks.

At midnight we celebrated Christmas Mass in the ship's saloon, attended by Catholic passengers and the ship's Irish doctor. The saloon was decorated with many balloons and things, but there was no Christmas tree or candles. The only carol everyone seemed to know was 'Silent Night, Holy Night'. I looked across to the long table set for the food and thought about how different Christmas was celebrated in Germany compared to Australia.

The following day the doctor came to see me. We could not hold a daily Mass in the saloon as it was against company rules, but he offered the use of his cabin. Sr Fabian and I went to the doctor's cabin everyday where I held a private Mass. On Sundays we celebrated Mass with the Catholics in the large saloon. The captain conducted a Sunday religious service for non-Catholics. Not all Catholics were permitted to attend Sunday Mass however. I observed some of the crew pretending to polish shoes near the saloon door while Mass was celebrated.

After Sydney, the *Malaita's* first stop was Brisbane in Queensland, and we three priests found our way to the Marists at Ashgrove, who gave us a warm welcome and showed us around nearby sites. I regretted our visit was short, but we had to be on board by nightfall as the ship was sailing up to Cairns, our next stop.

In Cairns, the captain recommended everyone take a train trip which stopped at a few places, I forget their names. I remember we picked up some mangoes and really enjoyed eating them, but by the time we returned to the ship our white clothes were a mess. Thankfully for us, Sr Fabian got busy cleaning our clothes.

We enjoyed a few good days on board before arriving at Tulagi, a major centre in the South Solomons, where Fr Eugene Courtais, a French priest, welcomed us. After having our passports checked by the Customs officer, we were free to leave the ship and go ashore.

We didn't waste time there as we were keen to visit Tulagi mission station which meant getting into a smaller boat for the journey. By the time we reached the mission it was seven o'clock at night and very dark. Some people had lit a large fire on the beach to guide the skipper in to shore. This area was called Visale. People helped us carry our luggage and cargo ashore.

This was the end of the journey for the Dutch priests. The Japanese would later kill Henk during the Second World War. Alois stayed on Tulagi for many years before moving to Australia where he worked at St Patrick's in Sydney. I stayed at Visale while the *Malaita* called into other islands, dropping off cargo and picking up copra (dried coconut meat).

Leaving my home

Thinking back to my visit, I remember sleeping very well even though it was my first time to sleep under a mosquito net. The net hung from above the bed while its side dropped around all sides of the bed to the floor, to prevent mosquitoes getting in under the net to bite us with infected blood from someone else. This is how the vector transfers the malaria parasite. We took quinine and other medications to prevent getting malaria.

Breakfast was a light meal and my first time to have pawpaw and banana for breakfast. The bananas were so sweet, tasting better than any I had ever encountered. The main meal was in the evening when it was cooler and eating was more enjoyable.

After a few days at Visale, Fr Daan Stuyvenberg took me back to the *Malaita*. We were together at St Olaf's minor seminary in Holland and later at the major seminary at Fürstenzell, Bavaria. Daan worked on many islands in the Solomons eventually becoming Archbishop of Honiara, the capital of Solomon Islands.

I can't recall the small places we called into on our way back to the *Malaita,* but by the time we arrived the captain was a little annoyed with Daan, as he was waiting for me and Sr Fabian to return to the ship so he could depart.

On this last leg of our journey the ship stopped at Shortland Island, which was still part of the South Solomons. At that time the country was under British control, but as a parish, Shortland was part of the Bougainville diocese — two countries, one diocese.

If the bishop was in Buin and wanted to visit Shortland on church matters, technically he was supposed to travel all the way up the east coast of Bougainville to Kieta, to apply for permission and pay a fee should any local persons wish to travel with him. On his return to Bougainville, if he brought everyone back, he could apply for a refund of the fee paid.

The government was not keen on black people travelling freely between the two countries but the Buin people didn't care. There was much intermarrying and strong customary links between the Shortlands and the people of Buin and Siwai, so they mostly travelled at night.

We arrived at Nila, the district capital, very early in the morning. I was finishing up Mass when Fr Joe Lmarre knocked on my cabin door to take me to Nila. There I met Fr Albert Binois, who looked after the mission station on Choiseul Island. Later, when the Second World War started, Fr Binois moved into the bush on Choiseul, and neither the Japanese nor the Australians could find him. He emerged from the jungle when the war ended.

Long midde mi lusim Nila na mi go long Kieta, bikpela ples liklik long Bogenvil. Mi stap long sip na lukim bigpela maunten, na ol pipol bilong Bougainville, em niupela hom bilong mi.

Taim mi tingting nabaut, em wanpela man bilong kru bilong sip i kamap long mi na askim mi: "yu bai i go we?" Na mi tokim em, "mi go long dispela ailan. Mi misionari na mi laik wok long dispela ples." Em i bekim tok bilong mi na tok "yu laik go long dispela ples? Em ol pipol bilong dispela ailan ol i no man, ol i animal tasol."

It was around midday when we left Nila, heading for Kieta, a sizeable station on Bougainville. I studied its high mountains from the ship's deck, thinking about its people and what would be my new home.

As I was taking all this in, a ship's crewman walked up beside me and asked where I was heading. I pointed to Bougainville and said that's where I was going, that I was a missionary and looked forward to working there. He questioned why I would really want to work there, describing the people who lived there not as human but as animals.

Klostu 4 kilok long avinun Malaita i kamap long haba long Kieta em 11 Januari, 1938. Em ples bilong me klostu long paipela ten krismas.

2 Bougainville

Stori liklik

French navigator, Louis Antoine de Bougainville, named the 9,300 km² island after himself when he 'discovered' it, while circumnavigating the globe from 1766 to 1769. He even has a flower named after himself. Bougainville is the largest of the islands in the Solomons group.

Within the Catholic diocese of Bougainville, there are several smaller islands, Buka, Nissan, Carterets, Fead, and many more. It has seven volcanoes, one active — Bagana, and a high mountain range running down the middle of it.

In Halia, '*buka*' means 'what did you say?' or 'I didn't understand what you said.' The story goes, a white explorer asked a man, 'what is the name of this island?'

The local man, not understanding, replied '*buka*?' and so the large island off the northern tip of Bougainville was called Buka.

Missionaries first went to Tubiana from the Shortland Islands, but at first the locals were not keen on white men moving in, so the missionaries returned to the South Solomons. But establishing a Bougainville mission was still in their minds, and when they returned, they developed a better understanding with the villagers and were allowed to stay.

Before the First World War, the only Christian missionaries on Bougainville were Catholics, but when the Australian government took over

When The Garamuts Beat

The government headquarters in south Bougainville was at Kahili, a mosquito-infested place on the beach. The administration approached Fr Maurice Boch, the priest in charge, for a block of land on Kangu Hill, indicating it wanted to grant the Catholic missions freehold land at Turiboiru, Muguai, Monoitu, and Sovele.

As time went on, the administration gave or sold the land on Kangu Hill to *ol Talatala* — people of non-Catholic faiths. This move enabled the Methodist Reverend Voyce, easy access to *wokabaut* and evangelize in many villages in Siwai, and the mountains behind Koromira and Kieta.

The custom was that if any *Talatala* wished to enter a village, it had to be with the full agreement of all *papa bilong graun*. An objection by one individual was enough to block entry. The same applied to Catholics and *Sevende* (Seventh Day Adventists) if they wanted to enter a village where a faith group was already established.

When I arrived in Bougainville, the population was about 60,000, and the roads were terrible. The German government had started a road-building program, but it was interrupted by the First World War. When the Australian forces won the Battle of Bita Paka, six miles from Herbertshohe (now Kokopo) on New Britain Island, the German administration in Kieta put its bullion and important documents on a ship and scuttled it near the point off Tunuru.

After the First World War, Bougainville came under the Australian administration remaining that way, until the new nation of PNG was granted Independence on 16 September 1975.

Bougainville does not have many life-threatening animals. They have sharks and *puk puk* — crocodiles in the sea, and large lizards on land, but the island has many beautiful birds and butterflies. There is a small creature, the centipede, whose bite can be very painful. To ease the pain we rubbed black soot on the bitten area.

Bougainville

Nearly everyone on Bougainville is afraid of snakes, although none is poisonous. There is one type of snake that people allow in their houses, the python, because it eats rats and mice. A young *kiap* started a rumour that tinned fish was snake meat. It sent sales of tinned fish right down.

There are several volcanoes on Bougainville, Bagana, the most well-known and not far from Torokina, constantly belches fire, smoke, and ash. The other widely known and larger volcano is the dormant Balbi.

4

When The Garamuts Beat

3 Settling in
Makaki, Kieta

After clearing Customs, I was welcomed by Frs Anton Klöster and Wilhelm Weber, who brought me to Makaki hill, where I met Bishop Thomas (Tom) Wade, parish priest Charles Seiller, and Frs Florent Waché and Gabriel Lebreton. The manager's house was down on the beach at Tubiana.

Fr Karl Flaus, who built a house in Meppen, organised the brothers to flatten the top of Makaki hill and dig a cellar. The belief was that there were fewer malaria mosquitos on hills where the temperature was cooler. It was brutal work in the hot sun, but the new house had cool underground rooms for eating and storing food. The rooms above-ground were for bishops, the resident priest, and visiting priests. A verandah surrounded the building, which had a special annex for resting. The Americans bombed the house during the war.

Bishop Tom Wade and Wilhelm Weber went to Kieta to conduct a marriage, and while they were away Charles Seiller and I started singing some German songs. The following morning, Sr Wendelina, a German speaker from Alsace, said she could hear us and sang along from her room. In the early days, these missionaries never returned to their homelands for holidays or for any reason, no matter how important.

Most priests brewed beer, but Fr Seiller constantly experimented with the recipe, making some of his brews undrinkable. After the midday meal, most priests and brothers had a siesta or holy hour. If you didn't want you were expected to keep quiet. I couldn't sleep because it was too hot, and the goats would come around the house and go *'me me me.'* At night, the church and house doors were kept shut, otherwise the goats hopped up on the chairs and altar, drank the holy water and ate the flowers. During the war, the goats died out. They were either killed by bombs or ran frightened into the sea.

As I had not yet received a permanent appointment, I remained in Kieta. One day the bishop asked, 'would you like to go to Buin?' The next day Fr Klöster and I took the small mission ship *Raphael*, and seven hours later, we arrived in Buin.

The sea was calm when we set out so I did not get seasick, but it was very rough on the homeward run, so Kato, the captain, decided to shelter in Koromira harbour. Klöster wanted him to press on, but Kato insisted it was too dangerous.

The unexpected detour allowed me to visit Koromira mission, where I hoped to see the Luxembourg priest, Fr Nicolas Goedert, but he was away visiting villagers. We slept in his house and left the following morning for Kieta. Fr Goedert was very sorry he missed us, when he learned we'd called in while he was away.

The surf at Koromira is tricky, it can sink a dinghy coming ashore. The second time I called into Koromira, I learned something new; if you need to get ashore, you must watch the waves for a break. There was a pattern. After the seventh wave a break appeared, when the crew rowed with all their strength finally landing us safely ashore.

Some days after returning from Buin, I told the bishop about the disagreement between Klöster and Kato, and the bishop explained that Kato knew the sea. The sea in Kieta was boiling at the time, so it would have been very dangerous to proceed.

Settling in

Tunuru mission

After a short stay at Kieta, I travelled north to Tunuru mission by boat, where I visited Fr Klöster, Fr Wilhelm Weber, and my old friend Br Xaverius Koch. While there, I felt constantly tired, hot, thirsty, and sweating. One morning after breakfast, I was forced back to bed when I overheard Klöster say to Weber, 'all this man does is sleep,' to which Weber replied, 'leave him alone. He hasn't been given an appointment yet, and he is still adjusting to the climate.' Fr Weber and Br Xaverius made very good wine from pineapples, pawpaw, and bananas, but sometimes it turned to vinegar, and excellent vinegar it was too.

Tunuru was a large parish then, but over the years, two more parishes, Deomori and Manetai were created. Tunuru's first parish priest was a New Zealander, Emmet McHardy, who started a catechist school there. Unfortunately, he contracted Tuberculosis (TB), returning to his homeland after three years, to die at a young age.

In those early days Bougainvilleans did not live in large villages, but in small hamlets scattered through the jungle. Emmet was forever trying to get the children to come to his school. Wilhelm Weber took a different approach, focussing instead on instructing the adults so that they could teach their children. Before an important celebration such as Christmas or Easter, Wilhelm instructed the adults, and if they passed their test, he baptized them. If they failed, they had to wait.

North Bougainville

I was asked to go to Tarlena to hold a retreat for the German brothers. Our first stop on the mission boat was at Asitavi, a new parish run by the American Fr Albert Lebel, who welcomed the bishop and me.

Our next stop was Tinputz. The mission buildings were sited on a plateau above a good harbour where Br Gregory ran a sawmill. After a few months, a large engine and other sawmill equipment were delivered to the mission by ship. The mill was set up in the jungle and with the help of locals, materials were cut for buildings in other parishes. World War Two destroyed everything.

We were welcomed by two older priests, Frs François Allotte and Paul Caffiaux. Many years previously, Allotte was based in Buin with the then young Fr Jean-Baptiste Poncelet. Poncelet was a butterfly collector who identified a new variety that he named after Allotte. Fr Poncelet also discovered a new species of tree rat, which the scientific community called Ponceletti.

We left Tinputz in the morning, arriving at Tarlena that afternoon only to find the place in the grip of a drought. There was no water for washing or drinking, so we bathed in the saltwater and drank *kulaus*. Walking from Tarlena to Chabai took an hour, where the American priest, Fr James (Jim) Henessy from Boston, was based. Hennessy, a friend of Bishop Wade, conducted a minor seminary there. During the Second World War, the Japanese arrested Jim on Buka Island near Lemanmanu, taking him to Rabaul.

In July 1942, Jim was put on the MV *Montevideo Maru,* bound for Hainan Island. An American submarine fired on it with four torpedoes, causing the ship to sink with more than 1,000 military and civilian prisoners on board. Fr Jim Hennessy dedicated his life to missionary service and to his country. Two of his students joined the priesthood, but I will say more about them later.

When the retreat was over, Fr Adam Müller arrived in his small boat, the *Miva*, to take me to his parish in Kunua on the west coast. "I have plenty of rainwater in my tanks. You will be able to have a good wash", he told me. The *Raphael* was anchored offshore when we arrived, ready to take on freshwater for Tarlena.

That night the drought broke. The rain fell and the rivers rose, cutting us off completely. So we spent the time reading for mistakes in the proofs of

Settling in

Adam's catechism that was sent by the printers in Sydney. Adam Müller took me back to Tarlena on the *Miva* when we finished. I remained on board, as we visited the island parishes of Nissan and Carterets that came under the control of the priests from Buka.

Missionaries were not allowed to visit the atolls such as Mortlocks, Feads and Tasman Islands. The story I heard was that during the German time, Doctor Bruno Kroening, who was based in Kieta then, did not want missionaries visiting the outer atolls.

While I was still in north Bougainville, Fr Paul Montauban invited the bishop and me to lunch at Ieta, one of two villages on the beach near Buka Passage, before returning to Kieta. As we sat down to eat, we were surprised to be waited upon by men in white *laplaps* with white serviettes draped over their left forearms, much like waiters in Sydney. Buka people had a much longer experience in the ways of white people, both good and bad, compared to elsewhere in Bougainville.

At this point, I still did not know where I was going to work, but on our return to Kieta, the bishop advised me that in the near future I was being sent to a new station near Buin called Piano.

When The Garamuts Beat

4 Piano mission

Piano was to be my new home for many years. I was told a story about the days of tribal fighting. Long before the white man came, there was a battleground called Piano, right in the middle of what is now Piano station. The battleground which can still be seen is slightly elevated.

After battle, people held a *singsing* and cried for their dead. In the old Telei language this ritual of grieving was called *piarei*. Warriors fought with axes, spears, and clubs. No one had guns. After the fighting, chiefs took the widows of their dead warriors; this was how big chiefs ended up with so many wives. I have more to say about Piano, things I learned after living there a while.

Before I left for Piano, I mentioned to Florent Waché, in Tubiana, that I was expecting a large box, and I asked him to send it to me at Piano. Brother Joseph of Meppen warned me that good timber for building things was hard to come by. When it arrived, Waché wanted to keep the planks from the box to make coffins, but I insisted that I needed them for an altar. Inside the box was a small motorbike, to make it easier for me to travel over the bush tracks.

The mission ship brought supplies from Kieta to Buin four times a year. When I left Tubiana on the *Raphael,* to take up my appointment at Piano, Bishop Tom Wade and Br Xaverius accompanied me. Xaverius was to build a catechist school in Patupatuai station, located near Buin.

When The Garamuts Beat

The government required that anyone over the age of 17 had to pay a poll tax, but people were exempt if they were still attending school. When the tax collectors arrived, there would be a surge in enrolments of the older boys, but when the tax collector left, so did the big boys.

Bishop Wade was shuffling the priests around. After 22 years at Monoitu, Fr Joseph Grisward, from Alsace, was to take leave in America. Fr Josef Schlieker, my teacher during my youth in Meppen, and who was stationed at Katuku, was to replace Grisward in Monoitu. Both stations were in Siwai. Previously, Fr Jim McConville ran the main catechist school for all of Bougainville from Katuku.

Our journey to south Bougainville was calm, and as we passed Muisuru in Buin district, we saw three priests on the beach, Pierre Schank, Josef Schlieker, and Joseph Grisward. Bishop Wade said, 'if Pierre Schank comes out to the *Raphael*, I will pretend to be drunk.' Sure enough, Pierre came out to the ship, and Bishop staggered around as though he had drunk too much beer, and spoke as such to him. Schank claimed he wasn't fooled but I am not so sure. Joseph Grisward and Josef Schlieker, who remained on the shore, walked to Patupatuai while we continued by sea.

Arriving at Patupatuai, I met Jean-Baptiste Poncelet, the naturalist priest stationed at Turiboiru for many years, including during the Second World War, before retiring to his homeland in Belgium.

The following day Josef Schlieker and I rode bicycles to Katuku; my rear end was not in good shape. We stayed two or three days in Katuku, allowing Fr Grisward time to pack and leave Monoitu. When we reached Monoitu we went straight to the sisters' house, to find two French nuns, Sr Martial, who looked after the small hospital and orphans, and Sr Domitilla, who ran the school, teaching girls to read and write. Domitilla also worked with her students in the food gardens.

Piano mission

Josef Schleiker advised them of his appointment to Monoitu. It was the first the sisters had heard of it. Joseph Grisward had not told anyone in the parish. Very early that morning he simply got on his bike and left.

One of Sister Martial's orphans, a seven-year-old boy, became her 'right-hand man' in years to come, and as an adult, he travelled to Sydney to become a brother. Later on, he joined the seminary at Bomana near Port Moresby, but did not see it through. After leaving the seminary, however, he was a great help to me in instructing new converts at Arawa.

Fr Henry Fluet, an American, was stationed at Piano for 12 months. He later went north to Asitavi, to wait while Xaverius finished the catechist school at Patupatuai.

The first time I walked around my new parish, I observed the *haus garamuts* displaying plenty of skulls of warriors who died in battle. When colonial governments outlawed tribal fighting, these human skulls were gradually replaced with pig skulls — *dispela taim govenmen i tambuim pait, ol i putim het-bun bilong pik long ol haus garamut.*

Haus garamuts are meeting houses for men, where large wooden slit drums — *garamuts,* are kept. Men beat the *garamut,* calling people to a meeting or to send messages. Women were forbidden to enter these houses.

§

Piano started as an outstation of Turiboiru mission station, which meant that parishioners from Piano walked a long way to Turiboiru for Sunday Mass. When I arrived, Piano had a church made from bush materials, a priest's house, and school buildings.

The priest's house stood on strong wooden stumps. If termites didn't eat the posts they still lived in the ground, so they were always a problem. The floor of the priest's house was cut from split palm wood — *limbum.* We swept the dirt and dust into the gaps to fall onto the ground, making it cool and easy to clean.

White ants were our *nambawan pren no gut!* Should they decide to climb out of the ground and along one of the posts, they can destroy a house in *kwiktaim* — a short time. We found poisoning their trail was a reliable solution. Another way to keep them out of the house was to put sheet metal on top of the house stumps. Ants were a constant plague; they charged into the house when it rained, and they loved the light at night.

The bedroom consisted of a canvas stretcher, a blanket, and a mosquito net. There was one more room with a table and chairs and a lantern and candles for nighttime. There was no such thing as electricity, but a priest might purchase a pressure lamp if he could afford it. After the rain, hundreds of insects flew in attracted to the lamplight, and soon the table would be covered in dead insects.

A corner of the verandah was the designated washroom — *rum bilong waswas*. A bucket of warm water would be hung up for the priest or visitor to wash. Just like the dirt, water ran away through gaps in the floor. There was no such thing as plumbing.

I am reminded of a story about bathing. A French priest on Bougainville, was looking around his new parish when he came upon a plantation, where the planter insisted he stay for the night at his house.

The planter's *haus boi* — man servant, told the visiting priest he would *mekim redi wara bilong patere*, to which the priest said, 'thank you,' that he would be along directly. But the priest was drawn into conversation with the planter. The *haus boi* came again to remind the priest '*wara i redi.*' 'Yes bai mi kam,' assured the priest, but the *masta* and *patere* kept talking. The *haus boi* interrupted them a third time. Now the planter grew *kros liklik* —annoyed, exclaiming, '*olosem wanem? Yu no save ol patere i no save waswas!*'

Piano mission

This brings me to thinking about a moral law of Bougainvilleans. They are very particular about bathing and enjoy it immensely. No matter where you are in Bougainville, men have their special places for bathing, as do women, and men are forbidden to go near the places where women bathe. Villagers often caught pneumonia though. They didn't have sheets and blankets, and in times of strong winds and lots of rain, nights could be cold, but people still liked to wash and swim in the cool rivers and streams.

Back to Piano; near the priest's house, there was a *haus kuk*, equipped with a wood stove. Firewood was collected from nearby gardens or the big bush. Wood fires create a lot of smoke, making the *haus kuk* inside black with soot. I don't need to talk about hygiene.

§

When Josef Schlieker brought me to Piano, it was mid-June 1938. I had no Pidgin, no Telei, and no English, so I could not communicate well with the American, Henry Fluet. Xaverius and I were both from Osnabrück, so I visited him regularly at Patupatuai while he built the school.

On one of my visits, I passed a man sitting on the steps of a house. I stopped to ask, 'can I help you?'

He replied, '*kaikai tounoke.*' I heard the word *kaikai*, which I knew meant food in Pidgin, so I assumed he asked for food. It also means 'speaking' in Telei. What he said was, 'I have nothing to say to you.'

One day Henry Fluet sent me to a hamlet to baptize a baby, but when I got there I found that the infant's father, who was still pagan, was not in favour, so there was no baptism. I later discovered that every priest had to submit his annual statistics to the bishop by 30 June. I suspect Henry wanted to boost his numbers.

Parents brought their babies in for baptism, and it was customary for the priest to give the child a Christian name. The babies were always naked but anyway I still asked one mother, 'is this a boy or a girl?' The mother held the baby up and said, '*nkio! lukim nkio!*'

On 1 July 1938, Henry Fluet left Piano for Asitavi with Albert Lebel; I was now left alone in the middle of nowhere. I couldn't speak English, Pidgin or Telei. Bougainville has at least 20 distinct languages, but there were no vocabulary or grammar books to help me. Once I became fluent in Telei, I realized it has similarities with Greek. One wise man told people they originated from Siberia.

I was often asked how Pidgin came about, as the language has English, German, French, and various local words. It seems that it evolved from traders trying to communicate with the native peoples. After the Second World War, Pidgin English became the *lingua franca* of PNG, being used by the government and church.

Bishop Wade was an American of Irish parents. He understood Bougainville customs and traditions very well, but there was one time *em i girap no gud* — he got very cross. He was on a *wokabaut* in Monoitu, and I was to meet him at the Mivo River to bring him to Piano station.

So we met at the river and on the way to Piano, we passed Aku village. I had been asking and asking the Aku villagers to fix up their church as it was close to falling down, but no one took any notice, so I suggested we call in so the bishop could see it.

When the bishop entered the church, a dog lay under the altar with a litter of pups, and as Bishop drew closer, it attacked him. He stormed out of the church and let *Waitpus* Makis know how angry he was at the state of the church. Makis got the message; it wasn't long before Aku had a church to be proud of.

Piano mission

§

Not long before the Second World War started, a strange sickness spread through many villages in Siwai, and places further away such as Turiboiru and Muguai in the Buin district. So many people died, particularly in these areas. If anyone spent time close to someone with the sickness, they caught it. Many thousands in Siwai died of this sickness.

I told *Waitpus* Makis that people must be stopped from leaving the villages, and not go anywhere near places where sick people had died or where bodies were burnt. His people listened, and the villages under Makis' control had fewer deaths than other areas.

One Saturday during the epidemic, I wanted to visit Morula as people there were asking for me. On the way I passed through Kakarikiru, where I learned that a woman was close to death. I anointed her with Sacraments for the sick, and on my way back on the Sunday, I heard she had died. I sent word to the government doctor at Kangu station, who met me at the *kiap's* house in Aku.

The doctor sent word to our catechist in Kakarikiru to bring the dead woman's body to the *haus kiap*. The doctor asked if I could lend him a small saw and chisel to open up the woman's skull. The catechist, who was from the same village as the dead woman, assisted the doctor, putting him very close by during the autopsy.

Afterwards, the woman's body was brought back to Kakarikiru for cremation, and it didn't seem long after that, the catechist fell ill and died. He died carrying out his duties. Piano did not suffer many deaths as they listened to the *waitpus* and me.

Many people died from tropical ulcers and TB when the first missionaries came. If someone got a cut and flies and dirt landed in a wound that wasn't cleaned quickly, a sore soon developed into an ulcer with a terrible smell. If I had to enter someone's house who had an ulcer, I could not stay long inside. Even at church, if worshippers had sores, the smell was very strong. At least the church was not like houses; they were open around the sides, so the wind carried the smell away.

In later years we found a very effective medicine, I forget the name, but it was a red mixture that you added to water, packing it on the sore. It ate away the white puss leaving the sore clean, but the pain was excruciating if you accidentally put it on good skin. Once an ulcer started clearing up, we treated it with other ointments. If people got sick or had an ailment, it was common to ask for an injection of NAB: it was regarded as a miracle drug.

Malaria was the biggest killer. *Ol waitman*, sisters, and priests had quinine and other anti-malarial medicine but villagers had nothing. I checked the parish records and it seemed every year, going by baptisms, we might have 80 to 90 babies born, but about 40 to 50 deaths, so there was not much population growth.

In Piano, Henry Fluet planted banana trees around the priest's house, but during my medical training at Würzlurg in Germany, I learned that mosquitoes love banana trees. They lay their eggs in water trapped where the leaves grow out from the trunks, so I asked my staff to remove them.

Unbeknown to me, with help from the students, they transplanted them to their gardens. Six months later they brought me bunches of bananas. This variety tasted like apples and bananas. There are so many varieties of bananas; some are only for cooking. When edible bananas mature, the bunch is cut down and hung in the house until it ripens, ready for eating.

§

One year Bishop Wade held a retreat for the priests at the cathedral at Tubiana in Kieta. In one of his talks he spoke about possessions. 'We mustn't talk about this is mine, that is yours', he said. Later on, Bishop came down to Piano to hold confirmations. We were going to Morula in the afternoon as

Piano mission

Bishop was holding more confirmations there. As we gathered our things together, he called out to me, 'Father, have you seen my alb? I can't find it.' I responded, 'I thought everything was ours?' Bishop was not impressed. It seemed he had forgotten about his talk at the priests' retreat in Kieta.

A Superior General from Rome visited all the priests on Bougainville one year. The priests invited the most senior *kiap* to Tubiana, after which he invited everyone for lunch at his house. Most of the priests said they didn't have time as they needed to travel back to their stations.

As the others left the *kiap's* house, it was nearly *bello* — midday, and the Superior General was feeling the heat. He then announced to us priests that we could do away with wearing the black talars (priest's vestments). From that time on, our priests did not wear them except when in church.

Sr Crescentia was born in Vechta in Germany. She came to Bougainville with the very first group of sisters *taim bip*o. In all the years of her missionary life she had never taken a holiday. When the sisters came to Bougainville they were never permitted to return to their homeland or take a holiday. Sr Crescentia died in Kieta, aged 96.

I was at Piano for nearly two years when Sr Crescentia received a parcel from Germany, which included a white priest's soutane that she thought would fit me, and I liked the idea of wearing white instead of the usual black. Wearing the white soutane or vestment made me stand out as everyone else had only black ones.

§

About three years before the Second World War broke out, Bishop Wade came with the news that the sister's house at Sovele had caught fire and burnt to the ground. He asked if the people of Piano would like the sisters to come to their parish. If so, they had to build a house for the sisters and the girls who assisted them. The sisters would also need a *haus kuk*.

When The Garamuts Beat

I put it to the *waitpus*, Paramount Chief Makis of Aku, who called a meeting of all the *luluais*. They were all in agreement that the sisters should come to Piano.

Makis advised them that some villagers must bring timber to build the houses, others should bring *limbum* for flooring, others to bring *saksak* fronds for roofing and walls, and carpenters to build the houses. Bishop gave me some floorboards.

While the sisters' houses were being built, they stayed at Turiboiru. When it was ready for work to start, a great crowd of men gathered, ready to work. The houses were completed in four days, a record achievement. The only building left was the *haus kuk,* but this was *samting nating* – nothing to worry about, as it was finished in short time.

It is always best if the missions can work in cooperation with the *waitpus*, and the *waitpus* works with in the *luluais*. I witnessed this level of collaboration over many years, as in years later when we built a *haus sik* — health centre, with funds donated by Misereor.

In preparing for the house building, it was custom to hold a big *singsing* with *kaikai*. It was up to every catechist to find a pig, and the mission would pay for the *kaikai*. The day of the *singsing,* I was given another lesson in *kastam* - culture. I assumed we could sit back and enjoy the proceedings, as we had paid for the food.

The *ekio* —month, arrived, when I learned that I was expected to offer a pig to Makis, *waitpus bilong ol*, as a way of saying 'thank you' to everyone who helped out and contributed to the project. Makis then divided up portions of my pig amongst his *luluais*.

When it came to killing pigs, men did not use the tools of white men but struck a blow to the heart with a large stick. The animal is then placed on a fire to burn its hair off. Butchering starts at the head, working down to the tail. Meat is cut into long strips for people to take home to cook and eat later. The meat looks very black, but it tastes good when cooked again.

Piano mission

Whenever the church held an important celebration, I was expected to give a pig to *Waitpus* Makis, who then shared it with the chiefs who put on the *singsing*. A few days after the *kaikai* and *singsing*, I invited the sisters and their girls to Piano, as they were waiting in Turiboiru.

§

Josef Schlieker was a good friend. He was stationed at Monoitu, a station within Piano parish. He would ride his *wiliwil* across to Piano, and the two of us went *wokabaut*, visiting all the villages and hamlets throughout the parish. When Josef rode to Piano, he took a narrow bush track that ran through the middle of Monoitu and Piano, and I often rode the same way back. It was through Josef Schlieker that I came to really know the place. He also showed me how to correctly record parish baptisms, marriages, and deaths.

I wish to especially thank him for instructing me in these matters, because if we did not enter the details in the beginning, it caused a huge amount of work later. We were not taught this in the seminary, and as a result, many early priests were careless in filling in these books.

§

One of the biggest dangers of living in the bush was the rivers. I could leave the station in the morning with the sun shining, but come to a river only to find it in flood. If it rained in the mountains during the night, I could find myself at a river up to four hours waiting for the level to drop. Rivers also change course. Many times I left Piano only to find at the first river there was nowhere to cross, leaving no choice but to go back.

Piano sits between Patupatuai and Monoitu. There was a road between Buin and Patupatuai and one between Buin and Siwai that I could ride the bike on, and while the road wasn't very good, it was alright for a motorbike. When the bishop told me I was going to Piano, I wrote to my brother in Germany to send me a small motorbike, and after some months, the Miele bike arrived. When people first saw and heard it, they took off with fright, some climbing the nearest tree.

It wasn't an easy ride to Monoitu, as there are two big rivers between Piano and Monoitu and if I wanted to go south to Patupatuai, there were two more rivers. I took two of our strongest students on the back of the bike to help carry it across the rivers. They helped me across the first river, but when we came to the last river I would give them an estimated time to expect my return. My students did not wear watches; they relied on the sun to gauge the time we agreed upon.

Sometimes I reached the river and the students weren't there. If big rains had flooded other rivers it would prevent them from coming back. In this case I returned to Siwai or Patupatuai, sometimes making good time, but often not.

Josef Shlieker also purchased a small motorbike, so we sometimes travelled together on our bikes. We were at the Silivai River one day when we noticed a huge tree. I commented that if the tree ever fell, it could form a natural bridge to help us get across. Well it did fall down, but the tree was nowhere to be seen, it must have been carried away in the rushing waters. So we were left with carrying our bikes across the river.

I can't begin to talk about the many times I fell off my bike. My legs had burn marks from the exhaust pipe until I bought a suitable pair of boots. Wilhelm Weber was visiting from Tunuru one time and he advised me to cut the pipe off close to where it joined the motor. It solved the burnt leg problem, but our workers could hear me coming from miles away, and were always hard at work when I arrived. I have other scars on my legs from those years of walking through the bush and abandoned food gardens.

When it rained and the grasses grew long, there was a particular seed that stuck to my legs, causing infection. I talked to someone about this, and he suggested I brush the seeds off as soon as possible. It worked. If I removed the seeds quickly sores did not come up.

The Second World War had started but the Japanese had not yet reached Bougainville. The administration had a curfew enforced, meaning when the sun went down, everyone was supposed to be back at their home station. I needed to see Josef one day, so I calculated the time I needed to leave Piano and when to leave Monoitu so I could get back to Piano before dark, but I had to pass the *kiap's* house on the way.

This day he happened to have *wanpela masta* staying with him. I didn't want to see him on this occasion, but he must have spotted me as his native cook caught up with me, handing me a message to call in. By the time I left and reached the Mivo, the river was up.

I lifted the bike up on on one shoulder and above my head to keep it out of the water, but halfway across I couldn't carry it any further. Faltering in the middle of the river, I tripped over a stone and fell into the water with the motorbike coming down on top of me, pinning my two hands. It took all my strength to push the bike off. By the time I freed myself I was struggling to stand up.

With the bike submerged in the river I walked back to Piano, three hours in the dark. The next day I sent the students to the Mivo to look for my knapsack and bike, but the flood had carried them out to sea or buried them under tons of sand.

One good thing about rivers in a hot country is that you don't need to worry about catching a cold or falling ill if you washed in the river. The sun soon dried you off, including your clothes.

One day when I was visiting Patupatuai, I needed to return to Turiboiru. I was deep in the bush and a long way from villages, when I fell off my bike flying over the top. I lost a lot of blood when I lowered my head. I knew no one was around, so I asked myself, what now? A man eventually found me on the road. He ran to Turiboiru to inform Sr Sevarina, who sent an old car to pick me up and bring me back to the station, where she patched me up. After the war, I gave up riding motorbikes.

§

Piano parish didn't have land of its own, so it was up to the priest-in-charge to approach *papa bilong graun,* for somewhere nearby where the mission's school students could grow food. If the landowner allocated an area, the priest must offer an appropriate gift of appreciation. Should the priest not understand local customs, they could find themselves dealing with many problems in a very short time.

Another complication that can arise is when other landowners learn that the priest has been granted certain land, they may assert that they are also *papa bilong graun,* And they would be right, as land ownership in Bougainville is not granted to any one individual.

I recall the first time I visited Nakorei. As with all villages, it had a small chapel where villagers came together for daily prayers morning and night. The chapel was where catechists instructed parishioners. It was also where *ol lapun* came should they decide to convert. When I visited Nakorei, I joined everyone for evening prayer and heard confessions for those who wanted. After this I talked things over with the men, and as was *kastam,* the catechist showed me to a house to sleep.

There must have been a large fire in the house earlier, as by late evening it was full of smoke, and the catechist's dog kept barking and running in and out all night. The house must have been where the catechist kept dry firewood, as he also came in during the night for firewood. When the sun rose I was so happy to go outside to get some fresh air and wash up.

I remember a catechist named Kauro. In the beginning, he was a good catechist who worked for Fr Poncelet, taking charge of the area. Believing his wife could not bear children, Kauro took a second wife who soon fell pregnant. When Fr Poncelet learned of this, he explained to Kauro that he would have to give up his work as a catechist.

The child of the second wife was born with an enlarged head, *na em i longlong liklik* — mentally disabled. Everyone put it down to a punishment from God. Kauro persuaded his family to join *ol Talatala* — people of non-Catholic faith. Some of Kauro's uncles on his father's side, who lived on Shortland Island, came across to see him and his father.

After some discussion Kauro's father agreed to return to the Catholic faith. The new catechist called on Kauro's father to return to his community's church, which he did. One night after evening prayer Kauro's father came to me for confession, and his people in the mountains soon heard that Kauro's father had returned to the Catholic faith, but Kauro's mother, his sister, and second wife did not.

Kauro's father returned to Mass at Piano the following Sunday and took communion. He was making it known he had returned to the Catholic faith even if the women in his family had not. Some years passed, and Kauro's child could be seen walking around, but one day his body was found in the river.

A child is not named until after its birth. This can take some days, but if something happens and the child is thought to have offended the spirits, the family will quickly change its name, so evil spirits don't recognize the child with its new name and stay safe.

Infants are often named after an event or situation connected with their birth. For instance, if a child is born on the road, they might be called *Monale* which means road in Telei. I asked one little girl her name, and she said '*Missis*'. She was so named because at the time of her birth, a white woman visited her village. Some parents named their children after Japanese officers during the war, but they soon changed them when the war finished.

Sometimes parents named children after their priest, as a way of saying 'thank you.' if the priest had helped the family in some way. A catechist from Morou asked me if I could say a Mass for him because he and his wife were desperate for another child. Their last born was 13. I held a Mass and God blessed them with twins. One of the twins died very soon after birth and the surviving twin was named Francis Miltrup. But little Francis got diarrhea, and his mother could not get him to the aid post in time, so the child died in the village.

The mother, Elizabeth Ntuga, bore another son, who she also named after me, and he is still living. Francis III wanted to go to a seminary but was unable to, becoming instead an assistant to Fr Herman Wöeste at Koromira. When the bad times erupted in Bougainville, Francis Jnr returned to Buin with his mother and sister.

I've spoken about death, but I want to talk about visiting someone who was very ill. After one Sunday Mass in a village the catechist came to tell me about a man who was very sick. When he was young this man was a well-known catechist. I returned to my house to gather some things when I found Wallis Brown, a white planter, waiting for me. I said I would have liked to invite him in for *liklik kaikai*, but apologized as I needed to visit a sick man, so he left.

On my way, I passed the *haus kiap* in Aku where Mr Brown was staying. He called out as I rode by, offering me a cup of tea. A short while later I continued on my way, arriving at Kakarikiru, the village of the sick man. After being shown where he lived, I prepared oil for anointing the sick, and then he died. He was waiting for me. The next morning we held a Mass before burying the old catechist.

Three times a year, the mission ship brought supplies of flour, sugar, salt, kerosene, and material for *laplaps* to the stations. If the boat had cargo for Piano, it anchored off Tokuaka around five o'clock in the morning.

Men from the surrounding villages made their way in the middle of the night to meet the ship and wait for the cargo to come ashore at Tokuaka. If the sea was so rough that the boat could not anchor offshore, they might return home, only to walk back again another time.

Piano mission

The carriers looked for items not so heavy to hoist upon their shoulders for the long walk to Piano mission. Heavier items such as bags of salt were lashed to a long pole and carried by several men. The sound of men singing told us the carriers were coming. There was always a leader who sang with his team, and as they unloaded their burden at the station, he would announce what was in the various boxes.

The priest paid each man with American-made *stik tabak* — a stick of tobacco, laced with some kind of molasses, a piece of *laplap*, and a meal of rice and *bulmakau* — tinned meat.

§

Villagers did not smoke like *ol waitman*. They wrapped their *tabak* in a sheet of newsprint which burned only when you drew on it. The 'cigarette' was quite long due to the length of plaited *stik tabak*. Smokers rarely finished their *simuk* in one go. A good place to keep it for later was behind the ear, handy to light up later or share with a friend.

This seems a good place to *stori liklik* about tobacco. I asked people what they smoked before *waitman i kam*. Everyone said dried banana leaves. One man told me; when the Buin people travelled to the Shortland Islands, they noticed the tobacco of *ol waitman,* but were forbidden from bringing seeds back to Buin.

One enterprising man collected some of these seeds, hiding them in his hair. After reaching Buin, as he combed his hair the seeds fell out. This is how real tobacco came to Buin.

The Buins take a dried leaf and roll it into a long 'stick'. Afterwards, they hang it in the *haus paia* — smoke house. Missionaries bought a lot of tobacco from the locals.

The people of Kieta are *Nasioi*. They produced better quality tobacco than in Buin. The *Nasioi* harvest the leaves, bind them into long thin bundles and hang them in a warm dry place for a few months to cure. The Buins did not grow a lot of tobacco except in small plots near the village.

When I first arrived in south Bougainville, as I travelled through the parish, people often asked me if I had any tobacco, as the *lapun* missionaries produced their own. If someone asked me for something I didn't have or didn't wish to share, I was taught to respond, *'noke kogu'* — 'I have only shit'. I only needed to say it once, and people laughed and would not ask again.

Christmas 1938 - 1939

I will never forget my first Christmas in Bougainville. I was in Piano. Firstly, I should say it is a very hot place to celebrate Christmas. No sooner does the sun rise than the daily temperature remains a warm 30 degrees celcius all year round.

That first Christmas was nothing like what I experienced in my homeland and I was looking for a reminder. My mother baked a Christmas cake every year when I was young, so I decided to do the same. I mixed flour, syrup, lemon juice, and sugar. When I took the cake out of the oven it was flat and hard like a discus; I forgot to add yeast. I was not meant to enjoy reminders of Christmas at home.

Leading up to Christmas, the village catechists brought people to the station who they had instructed for baptism and first communions. The priest would ask the catechist if they understood the faith sufficiently for communion, and if they said 'yes', they received their first communion after being baptized.

In those days, the church required parishioners to fast, and not even drink water from midnight before taking communion. I worried about the people who walked down from the mountains, after seeing they did not bring much food with them. I thought I was helping by giving them some rice, but this was before these mountain people had ever seen rice. Naturally, they did not know how to cook it let alone eat it. Despite walking a very long way, they still did not care for the rice, preferring to follow the doctrine. I was still learning.

Piano mission

After baptizing people in small groups, I heard their first confessions. When we finished, I asked everyone to tell me their names. I came to a young girl and asked for her name. She replied, *'Missis'*. I turned to the catechist to check if I heard right. This was the girl I mentioned earlier when talking about names. I heard confessions through the night until midnight when the beating of *garamuts* started — *long midnait ol garamut i krai*. Men, women, and children entered the *haus lotu* — church, to sing *Misa de Ángeles* in Latin, followed by many of our Christmas hymns in *Tok Ples*. After Mass followed Benediction.

My work rarely finished before 2 am. But I would take a lantern and walk into the big bush with some students to visit Morula, a sub-station of our parish. We reached Morula just on daylight to find many people waiting for me to hear confession. There were also children to baptize, then another Mass and Benediction.

Only after talking with all those who needed to see me, could I have a cup of coffee and get some sleep. At dusk the next day, *garamuts* started up again, and I returned to the *haus lotu* for evening prayer, signalling the end of Christmas Day.

§

To show you how ignorant I was, one day a *lapun* came up to me with an English gold coin he said was worth ten shillings (Australian). He wanted to exchange it for ten shillings, but I wasn't interested as I suspected he was trying to trick me. When I next visited Turiboiru, I spoke to Fr Poncelet who said, 'why didn't you take it? It is good money!'

Some weeks went by and the *lapun* approached me again to change his gold coin, so I swapped it for ten shillings. The *lapun* explained that when he was young he worked on Shortland Island, and *ol masta* paid *ol wokboi long ol, long gold mane* — paid native labourers in gold coin. I ended up changing his coin with a Chinese trader.

When I was at Laguai and about to go to sleep, a young man

approached me to change his gold coin for ten shillings. This time I didn't hesitate. Some days later I went to Patupatuai, and Fr Wally Fingleton from Nila was there. I shared my gold coin stories with him. He was keen to buy some so I said, 'I'll bring you one next time I return to Patupatuai.'

When I returned to Turiboiru, a *lapun* was waiting for me. He said, 'I want my gold coin back, the one you bought in Laguai. The young man you bought it from stole it from me while you were there.' The *lapun* said that the young man had not only stolen his gold coin, but he then lost the ten shillings I paid him in a card game. I wanted to hold onto the coin but the *lapun* became very agitated so I gave it to him. I lost not only my Australian money purchasing the coin, but I had now lost the gold coin and had nothing to give Wally Fingleton.

5

Bougainville's two most well-known volcanoes are Mt Balbi and Mt Bagana. Bagana throws out a lot of smoke and ash, whereas Balbi is quiet, and said to be extinct. Bagana isn't far from our station at Torokina. I can't say our *gurias* — earthquakes, are due to these volcanoes. No, the source of our *gurias* was always someplace else, but we felt them strongly on the island.

Around midday one day in Piano, the ground started shaking. My house bucked and shook sending everything onto the floor. My motorbike fell over, bending the handlebars. I straightened the bike out and got ready for the inevitable call-outs, such as when a group of men turned up to tell me a man had died. Fortunately, the bike started so I rode off to attend.

When I returned, another man was waiting. Again I rode out as the road buckled and shook all over the place.

Returning home the second time, I found the catechist from Nabaku waiting to tell me a woman had died in childbirth, but the infant was still alive. The village was deep in the bush, but could I ride there to give the mother her last rites and baptize the newborn he asked. When I got home I felt ill, I knew it was malaria.

Writing about *gurias* reminds me of New Zealander Sr Kevin. When the earthquake hit and the ground shook, she ran to me singing out, 'Father, give me your blessing, please!' Maybe she imagined the ground opening up and pulling her in. There were places where the ground did open up.

Before any roads were built, I visited a village high up on a mountain, and on the way I had to jump over a large deep hole where the ground split open. If a *guria* was making a gradual advance we would hear leaves shaking in the trees first. Many people were killed by falling trees and branches as they worked in their gardens. I could say a lot more about earthquakes but this memoir would be too long.

§

There is a lake in the mountains of Bougainville called Loloro. People from Siwai and Kieta could go there, but not if you were from Buin. Buin people believe that Loloro is where the soul goes when they die.

One day Josef Schlieker and I took some students from Piano up to see it. We left Piano early one morning and slept the night at the last village closest to the lake. If you are in the mountains when it rains, clouds come down so low you can't see a thing. As we left the village we could see some areas but others were hidden in cloud.

The next day Josef led our group down to the water's edge. If the students were on their own they would have been too afraid, but as Fr Schlieker was with them, they swam in the lake and I drank the water.

When The Garamuts Beat

5 *Kastam*—Tradition

Bilong wanem bilong luluai i no moa stap?

Buin people are very proud. If a person is accused of something they did not do, they cannot forget or forgive. An example is a situation that happened; a man on a mission station was falsely accused of prowling around the sisters' house one night and the sisters and priest believed the story. The man who was falsely accused would not accept any amount of apology, until the sisters and priest gave him a present and formally shook hands. Only after these formalities would the threat of unresolved grievance finish.

Before the war, the *luluai* punished people for wrongdoings. Not long before the Second World War started, plantation labourers were paid in cash, which is how money theft started. I never locked my house when I lived in Buin. I could leave my house in the middle of the night and no one would ever take anything, but after the war, things changed. Thieving became a common occurrence.

You might wonder what happened to the influence of the chiefs. *Bilong wanem strong bilong luluai i no moa stap?* The Australian government took away the power of the chiefs.

In the days of the *luluai*, they had the power to punish or kill. But it wasn't the *luluai* who carried out punishments, they had their own law enforcers. If an enforcer was given a 'kill order,' he would search out the condemned man and say something like, 'friend, I really need a *kulau* to drink. Could you climb up and get one for me?' As the victim put his arms around the tree to climb, an axe was driven into his skull killing him instantly.

If a man or woman was suspected of wrongdoing and refused to admit it, they were made to stand in the middle of the village in the hot sun until they confessed. Women were not allowed to go into the bush on their own, otherwise people assumed they were up to something *'no gud'*, and might receive a severe punishment.

The men and women of Buin feared their *luluai*. One day a man from Tualagai came to me with a complaint; his wife had run away to her village Lukauko. 'I want you to go and see the *luluai* in Lukauko and bring my wife back,' he said. The deserted husband was a hunchback, and the village women were saying bad things about his deformity.

When I arrived at Lukauko, I found the *luluai* and told him about the man's problem. He went looking for the woman whom he soon found, ordering her:'get your things together, follow the priest and return to your husband.' The woman followed the *luluai's* orders, and together we returned to Tualagi where she rejoined her husband.

Before the Japanese arrived there was an incident. A large group of men were walking through the station and I asked them where they were going. They were going to fight the men of Tugiogu, because a man called Tome, of Nabaku village, had taken a girl without her parent's permission, and had not paid any bride price. Needing to know more I walked with them to see if it could be straightened out. Halfway between Piano and Tugiogu, I heard the men of Tugiogu shouting, and as they came closer I saw them cutting tree branches to make clubs. *Waitpus* Makis from Aku, Ekio my head catechist, and I, joined hands across the path separating the two groups. I shouted that they should talk not fight.

Meini, who was also a catechist, threw a spear, hitting me in the hand. When Makis spoke, the two groups listened, finally agreeing not to fight. No blood was spilled and nobody died. Tome became a problem for me later.

Kastom - Tradition

§

Nobody believed people died from sickness. Death was caused by evil spirits making poison. Late one night I was woken by people calling out for me. A catechist in a distant village was dying and I was asked to come quickly. I grabbed my bicycle, holy oil, blessed Sacrament, and lantern. When I arrived at the sick man's house I was told he was doing well, as the *mekai* — medicine man, had driven the poison out. I was very frustrated, but there was nothing I could do except return to Piano. *Bel bilong mi kros liklik, tasol mi go bek long Piano.*

Early one morning long before we held Mass, a man came to tell me that *Waitpus* Makis was very ill and near death. I grabbed my bicycle and hurried as fast as I could to Aku.

On reaching Makis's house I found it full of people crying; some were even throwing Makis's possessions out the window onto the ground. My first concern was to find the cause of his illness. I learned that it was pneumonia and that he had been ill for nine days. I gave Makis the Sacrament, telling him I was returning to the mission to say a Mass for him, and then I would come back to check on him.

When I returned to Makis's house the next day, people were still crying and wailing. I threw everyone out — *mi rausim ol,* and gave Makis some of my medicine. Actually, it was wine. I knew that if he got through this day, he might survive.

I stayed with Makis all day, returning home that night. The next morning a messenger came, 'Father, you win! Makis is fine and asking for tea and biscuits.' After that my reputation in everyone's eyes had grown widely.

Some months later, I was called out to a place called Mouakei. A woman was suffering from pneumonia. When I gave her the Sacrament of the sick, she spoke to me and told me her name. She also told me a medicine man had told her she would die, as he had seen her spirit leave her body. I told her not to believe him and, that she must listen to me, and she would be alright. The woman did listen and made a good recovery.

Another incident involving medicine men was at Tugiogu. While in the village, I wanted to check on a sick child whose parents had assured me was improving. As I left the family's house, I noticed a man hanging about nearby, and he asked me how the *pikinini* was. I told him the child would get better. After leaving the village, he went into the family's house saying he had expelled the evil spirit, and then asked them for payment for his good works. I did not realise that the man I spoke to was a *mekai*.

If a man, woman, or child became sick, the family usually called for the *mekai*. Some would rub the person's skin spitting betel nut juice over them or something like that. They might also throw betel nut or tobacco on the ground, chanting, 'the evil spirit is gone, and you will be well again.' After some years I came to know all the *mekai* in my area. I offered each of them five pounds if they could prove to me they had made a sick person well again. They did not like my offer, as they knew *ol i giamanim ol man* — they were tricking everyone.

§

Bougainville follows strict segregation of the sexes. In church, men sit on one side and women on the other. In school, girls sit on one side of the classroom, boys on the other. When the sisters sent food to the priests or wanted to convey a message, they always sent two girls, never one on their own. I thought this was a good practice. Gossip and rumours are so easily started and can ruin a priest's reputation.

If a priest sent a catechist on an errand, the catechist had to take care. If he asked a village woman for some tobacco or some other thing, even if it was for the priest and she provided it, her community would likely think the catechist was up to no good, and his work in the area would be finished. *Taim bipo* — in the old days, before I went to Bougainville, this sort of interaction between a man and a woman led to a death sentence.

Kastom - Tradition

This brings me to the women and girls in Buin. One day I went to Turiboiru to look through the parish records of baptisms. Priests started the mission at Patupatuai first, not far from Turiboiru. As I looked through the pages I noticed that over several years, no girls or women were baptized at all. A few names came up here and there, where the sisters baptized an infant girl close to death.

It was nearly ten years since Turiboiru started in Buin, when a *luluai* from one of the coastal villages sent some girls to be educated by the sisters, and to be baptized. They learned to read and write and how to cook for the priests.

When I arrived at the missions, parents were starting to send their daughters to school, but only if they wanted to. Once parents got to know the sisters, they felt confident that their daughters would be well cared for.

Buin people followed a strict moral code for male and female youth. The sexes were forbidden to come too close, including when working in the garden, attending school, or going to church.

Husbands and wives usually had sex in their gardens. If a woman was pregnant she could not speak of it to her husband, but would break the news first to her husband's brother, who then told the husband. As the time drew near for the birth, the husband built a hut in the bush, where the woman, her mother, and possibly a *lapun* woman stayed until the birth. The husband could not go anywhere near the hut.

I was living in Piano for several years when a man came to see me. His wife had given birth but there were complications with the placenta. All the sisters were away on retreat, and the man insisted I go with him. The rain was pouring and it felt cold. The woman and her baby were under a small shelter on the ground. I worried about how many customary laws I was breaking but I knew that I had to cut the placenta to save the baby. I baptized the infant and anointed the mother with Sacraments for the sick.

The sisters returned the next day and went to see the woman. The infant had died but the woman survived. I thought about how the family allowed me into such a *tambu* place. Maybe *ol kastam bilong ol* was not as strong as *bipo*?

When The Garamuts Beat

Sometimes mothers lived secluded in the bush for a very long time; it was up to them. When they felt ready to return to the village they sent word to their husband. Preparing the feast was women's business. When the *kaikai* was ready, word was sent for the mother and baby to enter the village. The child was then formally accepted into the clan.

It was strictly forbidden for a man to have sex with his wife during her pregnancy. Sometimes during this period, men visited *meri pamuk* — women with multiple sex partners. One time I went to Muguai to see Fr Pierre Schank. I wanted to talk to him about a catechist who was in some trouble. The first thing Pierre asked was, 'is his wife pregnant?' This was *'nambawan bisinis long dispela graun'* — the main issue of concern in the district, he said.

In Buin, there is a word for infertile women — *uale*. These women did not live in special houses like in other countries, but when there was a special *singsing* and *kaikai*, the *luluai* sent for *uale* to attend to the invited men.

Having children was very important to men, but as I looked through parish records I noticed a woman might only bear a child after a two-year gap, but in cases where a child died, another child was born the following year. I asked my catechist, Ekio, about this.

He explained that sometimes a woman wasn't interested in having sex with her husband until the infant could walk. There was a reason behind this. If women had other small children still not at walking age, and the men were not helping with the care of their children, the women did not want to sleep with their husbands. It took many years for this pattern to change.

Now, more fathers support their wives in child-rearing. I knew of a woman who, year after year, bore a child. She came to see me, asking if I would counsel her husband to help her with the children. She was sick of his *wokabaut nating*.

Taim bipo governments and missions, one infant of a set of twins was killed, as people considered one was possessed by a bad spirit. When the missions began, and sisters were established enough to care for orphans,

Kastom - Tradition

parents brought one of the twins to them to raise. When the girls grew up and were ready to marry, the family turned up asking for their daughter back. Why you might ask. They saw the girl as a means of getting bride-price.

When a young man reached an age to marry, his parents started looking for a suitable wife. If they were impressed by a girl, they approached her parents to see if they would agree to the match. Assuming both sides were in agreement, they settled on the bride price, and the parents of the man paid the first installment.

The girl then lived with the young man's parents while he lived in a *haus boi* — house with other single men. The girl was observed for her skills in looking after the pigs, the food gardens, and anything else relevant to the household. If either party decided they were not keen to proceed, the girl was free to return home. If everything went well, the families sorted out the bride price, such as how many pigs, how much *mimis* and *aputa* — shell money they must offer to the girl's parents.

Shell money is made on one of the islands of South Solomons and is measured in lengths of about one and a half metres. A standard string starts at the fingertips extending across the neck and outstretched arms to the opposite fingertips. *Mimis* is highly prized, and costs a lot more than *aputa*, and is often wrapped around a baby's belly. The white shell of *aputa* is much more common than the small red shell, *mimis*. *Aputa* can be used to purchase a pig and other things. I'm speaking of Buin *kastam*. Other parts of Bougainville have their own *kastam*.

Sometimes young people chose their own partners, despite their parents being against the match. This was the case with Kaitsi, a *boss boi* — *foreman* on the mission station, who fell in love with a girl from Tualagai. She was the daughter of a *luluai* and attended school at Piano. Kaitsi asked me for help, so I approached *Waitpus* Makis who agreed to speak to the girl's parents, but they did not want to hear the *waitpus*'s message.

The young couple still insisted they wanted to marry, and the girl's parents eventually accepted the match. It was now up to Kaitsi to somehow find enough money to buy the necessary *mimis*. They married and had a child, but happiness was not to last.

The Japanese sent Kaitsi to Ballalae Island off South Bougainville, to work on the airstrip they were building, and he was killed in an American bombing raid. After the war, I heard Kaitsi's widow married the man to whom she was first promised.

Getting back to *kastam marit long Buin*, when a man is about to marry, he must build a house that he and his bride will live in. The man's relatives help with construction, as well as coming up with the money to meet the bride price. Sometimes bride price can be very costly and the prospective groom struggles to find the money. The man's parents and grandparents pay for the *kaikai* and pigs. On the wedding day, a *lapun meri,* washes the bride, anoints her with scented oils, and decorates her body in *mimis* and *aputa*.

If the girl is not marrying a *luluai* she will walk to the new house, where she prepares food and calls her husband to eat. Once they have eaten together, the couple is considered husband and wife in the eyes of the community. Sometimes the couple will stand on the back of a pig, and if it squeals it is an omen of a long and happy life. If the bride is the daughter of a *luluai*, more importance is placed on the ceremonies, for instance, the woman is carried from door to door. Her feet do not touch the ground.

In the early 1960s after the Vatican Council, we tried to include local *kastam* into the church. When a couple married, everyone from the village brought the *kaikai* from the *singsing* in baskets into the church, placing them around the altar. The couple stood together near the altar during Mass and were blessed by the priest, and when it came to communion, the bride and groom offered each other the Host. The priest blessed the food and after Mass everyone ate together outside the church. This way, we felt they were married in the eyes of God and the eyes of the community. Rome was not keen on these ideas, and we returned to the old ways.

When I first went to Buin, I found it very difficult to get people to adopt a Christian-style wedding in church. I invited the intending couple to come and see me at the church, but they did not want people to see them walking into church together. The prospective bride would come to the door where the women usually entered the church, while the man with his witnesses and the catechist, stood at the door where the men entered the church. Only once inside did everyone move in closer.

One of the main reasons people were hesitant to marry in church, was the importance they placed on bearing children. The church expected a married couple to stay together for all time, whereas the man needed assurance that his wife could bear children. If they followed a Christian marriage, then it was permanent even if children did not follow. In the case of a woman already pregnant, it was much easier for couples to agree to marrying in church, but there were still reservations.

When a couple decided to marry in church, the catechist brought them in with their witnesses. Once inside the church, they shut all the doors to prevent people from hearing what was being said. I asked the couple the usual questions, and invariably they would raise their eyebrows to which I would say, 'you have to speak so the witnesses can hear.' When the ceremony was finished, the groom left by the door that the men used and the bride by the women's door. The couple would not leave the church together.

After the war when I was stationed at Torokina, I was still getting to know everyone and understand the parish, so I walked into the mountains to visit a village. The catechist told me about a couple who wanted to marry the following morning, at Mass. I wrote down the names of the parents and the wedding couple in my book, said Mass and married the couple.

When I returned to the station and was updating parish records with the new marriage I noticed the bride was underage. You might wonder how I got it wrong. I did not take the parish book with me, and the other thing was the girl was wearing a blouse. *Mi no lukim susu bilong em. Sapos mi bin lukim mi i nap askim, haumas krismas bilong em* — If I had seen the bride's breasts, I would have queried her age.

When The Garamuts Beat

I called for the new husband to come and see me. We talked, and I suggested he take himself off to one of the plantations to work for a while, which he did. The catechist told me the reason for the rushed marriage was that there were very few girls in the area, and the boy's parents wanted to secure a wife for their son before it was too late.

§

Pigs are an introduced species in Bougainville. Locals called them 'Captain Cook' pigs because European mariners like Cook brought them to the island. Local pigs are small black and feral.

When Fr Fluet was at Piano he imported domestic boars from Australia, and like the villagers around him, he did not house them, so they roamed free in the bush, returning for a feed every afternoon. Domestic disputes about someone's pigs rummaging through another's garden were common. But nothing was ever said if Henry Fluet's pigs broke into someone's garden, as everyone hoped his pigs would mate with their smaller bush sows.

When I was settling into life at Piano and venturing out to the villages, I saw something I hadn't seen before. In the afternoons, women took food into their parts of the bush and banged tins or whatever was at hand to call their pigs. Sure enough, pigs emerged to eat before disappearing back into the bush. One Sunday, after hearing confession but during Mass, I noticed a woman being followed by small pig. It lay quietly nearby during Mass right up until it ended. Some women in New Guinea breastfeed their baby pigs.

White men, as with young missionaries, assumed bush pigs were wild, but most pigs have a mark on the ear or tail, perhaps an eye is taken out to indicate ownership. Most people will recognize a pig's owner by such marks. If a mission pig had a litter, everyone lined up to buy one. When I didn't receive financial assistance from friends in Germany, the money raised from piglets was a significant help.

Villagers had no way of keeping meat fresh, and pigs were only killed for special occasions such as when a male child was born. When a *haus garamut* was completed, the *luluai* put on a *singsing*. Meat was cut in long strips from head to tail, and distributed.

§

Today I cannot face eating chicken. You might think this is strange. Whenever a priest turned up at a village, people would offer cooked *kakaruk*. These birds were usually very *lapun*, and the meat was very tough. I have eaten enough chicken to last a lifetime.

This reminds me of a Piano story about *kakaruks*. One day I left the station for Patupatuai, and when I returned I found that all our eggs including some hens were gone. I spoke with Peter, our *boss boi* at the mission, who said, a *leguan* — large lizard, was coming out of the bush around midday looking for food.

At first I didn't believe him, but the next day I heard a commotion and went down to our *haus kakaruk*. There he was in one of the nesting boxes and no more eggs. Quietly I went back to fetch my bush knife. When the *leguan* saw me, he tried to run out, but I managed to strike a blow with my knife and kill him. As I held him up by the tail, several yellow yokes streamed out of his mouth. Peter was right.

After another visit to Patupatuai, Fr Dick O'Sullivan returned with me to Piano. Some school boys told me a dog had broken into our *haus kakaruk* and eaten the chickens and ducks. Dick offered to shoot the dog with his rifle, but I wasn't keen on the idea. He hadn't been at the mission long, and was not aware of *pasin bilong ples* — local customs and attitudes, whereas I knew how important dogs were to their owners.

That night as we were about to sleep, I heard the *kakaruks* making a lot of noise so I went down, and there was a dog. As I was blocking the hole in the fence, it ran passed me. Dick was a little annoyed that I let the dog escape.

I went back to bed but before long I heard the *kakaruks* again. This time I took my pillow down to the *haus kakaruk,* and quickly stuffed it in the escape hole so the dog *emi kalabus insait* — was trapped inside. I called out to Dick who immediately grabbed his gun and shot the dog. The poor thing was *bun nating* — skin and bone. It probably had pups in the bush waiting for food but nobody came forward to complain about a shot dog.

§

I thought readers might like to know about peoples' gardens, and the crops our farmers grew. Imagine two families; two brothers, married, and with their families they go into the bush that is part of their clan land, and select a piece of ground. Firstly, they must clear the undergrowth, cutting down the smaller trees and shrubs before ring-barking the larger trees.

Before I joined the missions and went to Bougainville, men used stone axes to remove the bark off trees, leaving them standing up until they died. Once they started using the white man's axe they cut the trees down, leaving them to die on the ground. It was a dangerous practice to let trees die standing up, especially when *gurias* shook the place. There were many instances of *gurias* causing a dead or dying tree to fall on people as they gardened nearby.

After the Second World War, when the missions first started using Dolmar saws, they targeted the older dead timbers, as they were fully seasoned and perfect for milling planks to build houses.

Back to the two brothers; after cutting down some of the smaller trees, they used branches and timbers to build a fence around the area they hard marked out to start a food garden. Once the bush was cleared and fences put up, the wives would plant enough food to last one month.

Kastom - Tradition

Villagers do not have the means to keep large quantities of produce fresh for months. The ground is rich enough to get three crops out of a garden before starting another. Once a garden is finished, the families will leave the ground lie fallow for eight to ten years before tilling the soil again. Grasses, small trees, and shrubs re-grow, but nothing like their original state.

Women are forbidden to go to their gardens alone. They can go with their husbands, other women, or their children. Little children are left to play nearby, whereas older girls are expected to help their mothers and learn how to grow food. They might also be expected to watch out for their younger brothers. If a woman went to the gardens on her own, it was assumed she was meeting her lover.

The children had school in the morning with the catechist, when they learned literacy, numeracy and the faith. If the priest had time, he would join the class. Everyone worked in the gardens during the afternoons, planting crops like sweet potato, bananas, peanuts, and other vegetables.

Another popular food is sago flour. After *saksak* — sago palm has fruited, the tree is cut down and its trunk split open. Men pound the flesh that is inside the trunk until it becomes a starchy pulp. A rinsing station is set up to rinse the pulp thoroughly in fresh running water. The pulp is wrapped in leaves and taken home for drying in a fire.

June and July are extremely wet months, making working in the food gardens impossible, but sago flour keeps well and lasts through these wetter months. If people are going on a prolonged *wokabaut*, a favoured food that is easy to carry and eat along the road is *manget*, made from sago flour, coconut, and galip nut, pounded into a paste and wrapped in banana leaf for roasting.

When I had time I also gardened. While I was still new to all this I was not pleased with the slow pace everyone worked. Thinking about how white people like to work fast to get their jobs done quickly, I showed them how to work more efficiently. I soon realized the villagers were much wiser than me. The heat of the tropical sun will always dictate the speed of work.

When The Garamuts Beat

6 Build up to war

Ren na klaud i paiarup long mipela

Stormy weather was coming. Josef Schlieker warned me that war in Europe was imminent and that I should get some *bulmakau* — cattle, so I could access fresh milk and meat. I heeded his advice and approached Pierre Schank at Muguai, a priest at Patupatuai, and Josef, who all promised me calves; this is how I came to be given two heifers and a male calf. As the heifers grew, the sisters milked the cows and made butter with help from young girls at Piano. The girls were not afraid of the cows as some of them had learned about dairying at Turiboiru.

Germany was at war with France and England, and later we learned that Japan had entered into a war with America. I asked myself, what would happen to us? Would the Australians *rausim mi* from Bougainville or let me stay? Would they bring me to a camp in Australia or allow us to remain and work as before? These were the concerns we German priests asked ourselves.

Once the war started, the Australian officers called us all together at Kangu, where a *kiap* told us we could continue with our work, but we had to remain in our parish and report to him once a month. At night we were to remain at our stations. My parish was Piano.

These were our rules:
1. No radios were permitted. That was easy because I didn't have one.
2. Anyone owning a shotgun had to bring it to the *kiap*. That was difficult because I shot pigeons for food.
3. Curfew was from 6 pm to 6 am. Wilhelm Weber called us

German priests 'The Sunset Boys'.

4. Report once a month to the *kiap* at Kangu.

We German priests were very happy that we could remain on our island and continue working with the people. Two priests felt differently however. Adam Müller's parish was Torokina: a great distance away. It was impossible for him to reach Kangu once a month, so Bishop Wade transferred him to Manetai and sent the Austrian priest, Fr Joseph Grisward, to Torokina.

Then there was Fr Bernard Tonjes at Sovele, who could have made it to Kangu every month, but the Methodist minister, Reverend Voyce, was not happy, as during The Great War, Bernard was a pilot in Germany. Voyce insisted to the *kiap* that he demand that Bernard be moved to Kieta, so Bishop Wade transferred Fr Tonjes to Kieta, and the French priest, Fr Gabriel Lebreton, went to Sovele.

Before the war, Bernard bought a fixed-wing plane up. He cut down a large area of coconut trees on the mission plantations at Tubiana and Tarlena to make airstrips, but the Australian administration told him to send the plane back. While Bernard was waiting for Burns Philp's ship, MV *Malaita* to arrive from Sydney, he and the pilot took the plane up for a spin at Tubiana. They mistimed the landing and crashed on the beach. Neither was hurt, but a large area was left in the plantation full of coconut roots.

6

Build up to war

We priests were of mixed nationalities, American, Australian, Austrian, French, German, New Zealand, etc. We got on well— *mipela i stap wan bel turu,* but for one incident. On one of my reporting trips to the *kiap* (a good man), he told me about the Germans moving into Paris, the capital of France. When I reached Patupatuai, I told Joseph Griswald, from Alsace, about it. On hearing this news he was a little angry with me. I was not happy about the German soldiers marching in either, but I wanted to tell him what I had heard.

From Piano station I could hear guns from the Battle of the Coral Sea. Later I heard that the American victory saved Australia from a Japanese invasion. Every day I saw planes flying over. While the Japanese had not yet landed on Bougainville, I gathered all the catechists together and told them about the coming war, and that they needed to prepare. I urged them to hide the parish books, and that the school children should hide their uniforms and personal items in the gardens. It was only a matter of time before the Japanese would turn up at Piano.

I gave most of my possessions to the catechists, but I still had an Australian flag, so I put it in a box and buried it in the *haus kakaruk*. Some months later I checked on the box—no flag. White ants had eaten the box and the flag. I fed my chickens white ants so they were well established in the dirt inside the haus kakaruk.

I gave Ekio our parish record books. He knew what termites could do so he hung them in a sack on a post, and returned them after the war, untouched. During the war people hid in the jungle to escape the American bombs, and most of the items I had given to the catechists for safe-keeping, did not survive. However, a chalice given to me by my family, was safely returned after the war.

Ekio saved the books, but during the war, he lost his whole family except for one young son. Moini, that son, grew up to become a doctor. He was working in the PNG Highlands where tragically, he was murdered in a revenge killing.

When The Garamuts Beat

Rumours of the Japanese advance grew stronger. They now occupied Rabaul, and there was an increased number of Japanese aircraft flying over from Rabaul to the Solomon Islands. The Australian government instructed all white people to evacuate. The District Officer, civil servants, and most of the white planters evacuated from Kieta on Friday 23 January 1942. Their sudden departure saw Kieta people looting the Chinese stores and Burns Philp's store. Dr Kroening and Fr Bernard Tonjes convinced them they were stealing and put a stop to it.

Dr Kroening, who had been in Bougainville since the German administration time, was married to Frances Kroening, a British Samoan, who owned Toboroi plantation. The Kroenings were eventually evacuated at gunpoint and interned in Australia for the duration of the war. After the war ended they returned to Bougainville, but Dr Kroening suffered from ill health and died at Sohano in December 1957.

Bishop Wade arranged for the white sisters and some elderly brothers and priests to be on standby for evacuation at mission stations near the coast. Some sisters refused to leave their people and ended up being imprisoned by the Japanese. They may have come to regret disobeying the bishop. Much later, Bishop organized for some of the older fathers, sisters, and brothers, to be evacuated off Bougainville in an American submarine.

7 Bougainville at war

Bel bilong mi krai

The Japanese invade—1942

Easter Sunday 1942 was a huge day for the church at Piano. After the service I rode my *wiliwil* to Patupatuai to visit Fr Dick O'Sullivan. On the way I met an Australian soldier near the mission, who everyone called 'Slim'. He gave me some cigarettes and chocolate, warning me not to throw the wrappers down in case it gave away their position to the Japanese. Slim told me the Japanese had landed at Kangu and it wouldn't be long before we were captured.

Before the Japanese landed, Dick took the precaution of hiding things from his house and the school in the big bush. He asked if I could bring some men to help carry everything else to Piano. On Monday, we left Patupatuai. Dick went to Laguai to look for men, while I returned to Piano in search of *Waitpus* Makis' assistance. The *waitpus* sent word out for men to come Tuesday to Patupatuai, to carry everything across to Piano.

I hadn't seen the ships coming from Shortland Island, but the Japs had burnt down the police station at Kangu, and all the houses on Kangu Hill where we used to stay. Not finding any Australian soldiers around, they turned up at Patupatuai as Dick O'Sullivan and his students were finishing Mass.

The Japanese did not burn the place but Dick was ordered to leave the mission and move into the interior. His students came to Piano and life went on as usual for a while as Dick trekked over the mountains to join the bishop.

Tome, the man from Nabaku village who I wrote about earlier, with a friend, stole clothing that the school children hid in the bush. I went to Nabaku and demanded that he and his friend return everything they stole. A crowd from the village surrounded us as I asked them why they would do such a thing. Tome denied the theft of course, but I insisted even though I had no authority from the Australian government. He became angry, accusing me of lying and threatened to kill me. I stood very close to him, but I knew that he would not kill me because I had the support of the village. Tome returned the students' clothes eventually, but he hated me after that.

When the Japanese were recruiting for *Kempeitai*—military police, Tome signed up, becoming an informer. He also forced one of the native sisters to become his second wife. Her bride price was already paid by the mission, which made it theft as well as marriage by coercion.

During the war, Tome told the Japanese that I was a spy for the Americans, producing a piece of paper that said 'made in Australia' as proof. I was tried by the Japanese, and thank God and His blessed Mother I was acquitted. One day a Japanese *Kempeitai* asked me what kind of man Tome was. I told him straight, that he was 'no good.' Tome was a traitor, and not long before the war ended the Japanese shot him.

Before the war, Kahili which was about six hours' walk from Piano, was the Protestants' headquarters. When the Japanese first came to Bougainville they built an airstrip there, and also one on Fauro Island in the Shortlands. Korean labourers and villagers were

forced to work on the construction of these airstrips. This was while the Australian forces and people like Paul Mason were active on Bougainville. They warned local people, 'If you help the Japanese we will kill you,' while the Japanese also told them, 'If you don't help us we will kill you.' Villagers were caught in the middle and confused about what the white man's war was about.

Pok Pok Islanders collaborated with the Japanese but as they were based close by in Kieta for a long time, there were reasons behind peoples' actions. It is said that Bishop Wade intervened to save Pok Pok from being bombed in retaliation.

When the Americans started bombing, people ran everywhere thinking they would be safe if they ran. We warned that pilots would not know if they were Japanese or islanders, so the best thing was, 'Don't run, drop flat on the ground, so your black skin can hide you on the ground.'

Brother Henry's dilemma

Br Henry Simmonds had come from Monoitu to Piano for a weekend. Sunday morning a catechist turned up with the news, 'Fifty Japanese are coming on bicycles!' Henry rushed into the bush to a house he had built for such an emergency, where he had hidden important papers and supplies, but he could not find it! On his return to Moinoitu, natives coming from Mass gave him directions as to where it was, so he ultimately found it. Amusing enough was his settling down. Matches—wet, no smokes, no food—except a few tins, but no tin-opener. And to complete his discomfit, down came a torrential tropical storm: Henry was marooned.

Meanwhile, I waited in Piano for the Japs to arrive, but the storm forced them back, apparently to have lunch at my sub-station, Morula. At about 5.30 pm Henry made his appearance—to be restored with nourishment and our company.

I continued with my work in Piano. In September 1942, word came through that the Japanese, led by the pagan Bau, went to the mission at Muguai. They took Fr Pierre Schank, Br Bruno Schilder, and three white sisters, back to Kahili. Bau thought that once the father and sisters were out of the way he could take everything left behind, and the Japanese would make him 'King of Buin'.

The Japanese did not believe everything Bau told them, using him as an informer when it suited. Not long after, Bau led the Japanese to Turiboiru mission, where Fr Poncelet, and most of the sisters, were taken to join the others held at Kahili. They allowed the elderly Sr Ignace, the first sister to come to

Bougainville, and the native sisters, to remain at Turiboiru. The missionaries at Kahili were later taken to a prisoner of war camp outside of Rabaul.

I went to Turiboiru to say Mass for Sr Ignace and everyone at the station. In his hurried departure, Fr Jean-Baptiste Poncelet had left a large ciborium with Sacred Host, that had to be consumed before I left.

About two weeks later, I returned to Turiboiru to bring Sr Ignace and the black sisters and orphans to Piano, as more and more Japanese soldiers were gathering at Turiboiru.

A *tultul* is a village leader, second-in-charge to the chief. He handles some of the colonial administrative tasks and acts as a translator when kiaps or foreigners come into a village. I overheard Bau telling someone, that Torokoi, a *tultul*, had a gun. I went to Torokoi and asked if it was true. 'Yes,' he had a gun, but it was old and did not work. I told him to be careful because he could find himself in trouble if the Japs discovered it. A short time later the Japanese raided Torokoi's house, found the gun and took him prisoner. Bau went to the prison to take Torokoi's *tultul* insignia. Later on a soldier handed Torokoi's scalp to Bau, announcing, 'The *tultul* is dead. Now you must give me his wife.'

A meticulous Jap

Towards the end of October 1942, I received a visit from a Japanese soldier. He searched my house at Piano completely, examining boxes, stores, the chapel, and the sisters' house, but kept clear of the native houses. He was looking for a radio transmitter because they used to hear Paul Mason's transmissions to Honiara and Henderson airfield.

The soldier knew some English words and showed his disgust through sign language, at seeing English books and games. He took a pair of trousers and a mosquito net, for which he paid in cigarettes, and then went to search the sisters' kitchen. He saw some eggs and cracked two, swallowing the yokes raw, then made signs to show he was after wireless sets.

The Jap told me to remain at Piano, but to get the sisters away into the bush as more soldiers were following. Sr Ignace and the black sisters took the orphans into the bush. Some boys came to my place, insisting on sleeping on my verandah to await the Japs, but they never came. Afraid of being ambushed on his return, the Jap demanded an escort of natives.

Two days later, Henry Fluet turned up in Piano with a message from the bishop. I was given the power to dispense the native sisters from their vows, to allow them to return to their families. One was the daughter of Mege, an elderly catechist. Mege's daughter was the first Bougainville girl to become a nun. Sadly, she did not survive the war.

Sr Ignace was instructed to go to Monoitu mission. On Sunday 1 November 1942, half of the native sisters remained at Buin with Mege, while the rest left the next day on Monday 2nd with Sr Ignace, for Monoitu. That Sunday I rode to Monoitu on my *wiliwil*. Later that night I was hit with a severe attack of malaria.

On Monday, the Feast of All Saints, Henry Fluet and I set out for Sovele mission which was about seven miles from Monoitu. Halfway there I started to urinate ink—Blackwater Fever. My medical training taught me that I would either die or go blind if I continued.

Henry called on some men from the nearest village for help. They made up a stretcher by cutting poles from the jungle, and six men carried me over the six-hour journey to Sovele. At Sovele we met Dick O'Sullivan, Br Henry Simmonds, and the four sisters, Blaise, Hortense, Gisèle, and Fabian. Dick gave me some Atebrine tablets which saved my life.

The following morning, Br Henry, Dick O'Sullivan, and the sisters, began their trek over the mountains to Tinputz, to meet up with Bishop and to await their evacuation. With the exception of Dick O'Sullivan, they all escaped in an American submarine to New Caledonia.

After a few days' rest at Sovele, I was able to walk again, but I was sick with fever for two weeks, when Wilhelm Weber arrived from Tunuru. Josef Schlieker then turned up and brought me back to Monoitu, and finally to Piano.

When The Garamuts Beat

A strange Christmas in 1942

While I was at Sovele, the catechists divided everything of value amongst themselves to keep safe from the Japs. On my return, I made my last wokabout through my district and that of Fr Poncelet's, at Turiboiru, as he was being held in Kahili. On the eve of Wednesday 23 December a young man came to tell me that Fr O'Sullivan was making his way towards us. He went to my sub-station, while I remained at Piano for what was my last Christmas in freedom.

Dick and I spent Christmas together quietly in the vegetable garden with one tin of preserves between us—expecting the Japs at any moment. We could not make a fire as Allied planes flew overhead, so there was nothing to do but sit in a little shed. What a dreary Christmas Day it was, waiting for nightfall to return to the house, secure in the knowledge that the Japs never ventured out at night in these parts.

The next day we walked to Monoitu, where Josef Schlieker was with three older sisters, Ignace, Martial, and Adalberta. I bade the group farewell, as they began their strenuous trip over the mountains to be evacuated. I returned to Piano to continue whatever parishioner work was possible, and wait for the Japs.

Paul Mason

Many planters on Bougainville enlisted during the Second World War. Before the war, Paul Mason was the manager of Inus plantation, but after the war, his was a name that everyone came to know well. I knew Paul, and had heard from many sources, about his work as a Coast Watcher fighting the Japanese. One day when Paul was not far from Piano, I showed him a good place to track Japanese ships and planes flying overhead between Rabaul and the South Solomons. He was able to transmit radio reports to the American Forces from this location.

When the Japanese were closing in on Paul, he had to leave his hiding place in a hurry, but he had run out of benzine—petrol to run the generator that charged his radio battery. I had a small supply so I told him to send a *polis boi* to our pre-arranged spot. I sent one of our bois with the benzine to the *haus pekpek bilong haus kiap*— the long drop toilet at the *kiap's* rest house. None of the locals would take it to Paul so he had to collect it himself, but after that, he was able to continue sending his reports of the South Solomons.

A local man came to tell me that the Japanese were searching for Paul with sniffer dogs, so I sent word to him. He sent me back a message, 'Be good.' I didn't see Paul again until I escaped from Buin for Torokina, when he was camped with soldiers in the mountain village of Sipuru.

New rules, more danger, bombing—1943. Enroute for Kieta

On the last day of January 1943, a message came from Josef Schlieker. He had received word from Tashiro that the Japanese army was coming, and if we wished to escape certain death we better get to Kieta. Before the war, Tashiro, a Japanese, was a resident in Bougainville. Josef wanted to leave as soon as possible; his note went on to say, that if I wanted to leave I must come quickly to Monoitu.

I put some things into a rucksack, and said my goodbyes to the bosboi and students who were looking after the station. *Bel bilong mi i krai taim mi mas lusim ol, na mi lusim stesin bilong mi.* I felt sick to the stomach having to leave everyone and our station, but off I went with two men and a few belongings to join Josef Schlieker. Fr Tonjes arrived at midday, and told us that Joe Grisward had escaped from Puruata Island off Cape Torokina, just as the Japs captured it.

The following morning, in came Fr Wilhelm Weber after escaping his Jap guards at Tunuru. What a grand reunion it was. Within a few days, on Tuesday 2 February 1943, all of us on bicycles, with several natives, set off for Sovele, enroute to Kieta and the prison camp waiting for us.

We slept the first night at Sovele before pushing on the next morning. Bernard Tonjes stayed back as he had some things he wanted to do before coming to Kieta. We crossed from one side of Bougainville to the other, sleeping in villages along the way. People were very kind, helping us in every way. At night we heard confessions and said Mass in the mornings, celebrating marriages, baptising children and stirring the peoples' already lively faith. As villagers heard we were passing through they flocked to us from near and far.

I really admire Wilhelm Weber; he was very brave and relaxed, knowing he would be in serious trouble when he arrived in Kieta, but he calmly continued his work. He was not at all afraid. Joe Schlieker was trying to rush us, he did not want to anger the Japanese by arriving late, but Wilhelm said, 'Joe, take it easy, you will be a long time in the prison camp. There is no need to hurry.'

After walking for four days or so, it must have been Wednesday 10 February, when we walked into Tunuru. At first there was no one about the mission, but we could see the station had already been pillaged by marauders. Within a short time a troop of Japanese soldiers appeared but they did not harm us.

Tubiana becomes an internment camp

We set off for Kieta the next morning. Walking down Kieta Hill towards the beach, we were stopped by a soldier; when he found Fr Weber with us, he flew into a rage. He wanted to lock Wilhelm up immediately, but said, 'You report to Mr Lebreton (meaning Fr Gabriel Lebreton) at Tubiana! We will see you later.' At Tubiana we found Frs Charles Seiller, Gabriel Lebreton, Adam Müller, Arthur Jünker, and Brs Karl, and Xaverius. They were so happy to see us. There were also three sisters from Koromira, and many Chinese residents.

The following day Fr Weber went to confession with Fr Seiller. Weber then said, 'Let them come. I am ready.' And come they did, shouting and carrying on—but they did not kill him, too many witnesses. On Friday 19 February Fr Tonjes turned up.

The Japanese put a guard on our house in case we decided to escape, but allowed villagers to bring us food and attend Mass. Following orders from the officers, we had to lose our beards. This made such a difference in the appearance of Wilhelm Weber, that when the Japanese were doing their rounds they did not recognize him. They were convinced he had absconded.

Very soon after, came the infamous Japanese system of questioning, 'What were our ages? Where were you born? Why were you born? Where did we come from? …' and so on. Officers who knew some English were too proud to speak to us inferior beings. On official occasions, privates were called like in school, to do the questioning.

It was comical to see one advance, draw himself up to attention, salute, and begin a few words in English before stuttering and nudging another to take his place. They started off in German, becoming nervous until someone more 'expert' from the volunteer ranks relieved the situation.

Food was scarce so we were always hungry. The younger priests decided to make a vegetable garden. At the beginning of our internment people were allowed to visit and bring us food, but we never knew if the Japs would forbid them. I worked on a piece of ground within the station boundary: it also gave us something to do.

Before the war, the mission ran a plantation, but when Tonjes bought the plane out from Germany, the mission cleared an area for the airstrip, as they did at Tarlena and Buka. How we sweated over that root-filled ground. I never got to eat any of the vegetables from our garden, as I was sent to Buin, never to return to Kieta. We had to work for the Japs, carrying food, making gardens, and building air-raid shelters: guards were everywhere, day and night.

A good conscript seminarian—Japanese Jesuit novice

Our religion was tolerated and the bishop's church at Tubiana was not touched. We were permitted to say Mass and our flock was allowed to assist and receive the Sacraments. Some of the villagers told us about one particular soldier who they felt close to. He reminded them to say their morning and evening prayers, and of their duty to keeping the faith. He would often join them in worship in their small village chapels.

It was a Sunday night when three soldiers came to our house. They could not speak English or Pidgin. One indicated that he wanted pencil and paper, the other one asked for a rosary and a bible, before writing out a message in Latin. His name was Matsumora; he was a Jesuit seminarian who had also served in Japan's war in China. From then on we conversed in Latin.

Before leaving and in spite of his companions, Matsumora knelt and asked for a blessing. Whenever he passed the church at Tubiana he always tried to visit. Matsumora often confessed and, whenever possible assisted at Mass and received Holy Communion. Later we learned that Matsumora was a Jesuit novice in Tokyo.

§

The locals were allowed to assist us on Sundays for Holy Mass, and as Easter was near, we invited everyone to Tubiana for Holy Week, to perform and celebrate with us, those beautiful Easter services of the Catholic Church. From far and near hundreds came, young and old, fathers, mothers with children on their backs, all speaking in different languages, so that on Holy Thursday, each priest assembled his flock for the Adoration of the Blessed Sacrament.

The number of newcomers grew each day. Kieta mission had never seen such a large gathering. At night you could find people sleeping everywhere. Some built small huts from coconut fronds, others slept on verandahs, some slept under the houses of the priests and the sisters, and even in the church.

On Easter morning, it was clear the bishop's cathedral was too small to hold everyone. Three times the church was filled to the last seat. We closed that beautiful day with a Solemn High Mass and Benediction with hundreds of people outside the church singing and praying. Matsumora, the Japanese Jesuit Novice acted as sub-deacon.

Towards the end of the war, Adam Müller was needed in Kieta to see some parishioners. The Japanese captain asked who he would like to accompany him, and Müller chose Matsumora.

This story has a sad ending. Müller was working in one of the Japs' food gardens and Matsumora was with him. Bougainvillean commandos working with the Australians turned up to rescue Fr Müller. Naturally they did not know about Matsumora. While Müller was resting under a tree, the commandos grabbed him and immediately shot and killed Matsumora.

After the war we buried Matsumora next to Wilhelm Weber at Tunuru. Fr Adam Müller wrote to the Jesuits in Tokyo, telling them about Matsumora and how he came to be killed. Fr Bitter S.J. replied to Fr Müller, telling him the letter was read to the seminarians who were all very proud. Many years later, Matsumora's bones were taken back to Japan.

Death from the sky

Easter Tuesday happened to be Japanese Empire Day—my first day to witness American bombs falling. Fortunately, it was not Easter Sunday when such a large population was in Kieta due to the church festivities. We were sitting on the verandah at about 5.30 pm when Bernard Tonjes thought he saw a flare drop over Kieta Harbour. A plane appeared and veered off into cloud.

Immediately four other planes appeared and dropped bombs over the spot. The Japanese boat and stores were bombarded. I ran like a madman to the priests' house and crawled under it. Many Japanese and some locals were killed or wounded that day. One poor man was killed by a splinter severing his neck. He should have been down on the ground, not upright like a good target. That evening officers came to inquire about our state, while soldiers went out onto the sea to collect large amounts of stunned fish.

We priests decided to build a shelter to hide in when the planes came. The fathers and brothers took turns doing night watch to raise the alarm if they saw airplanes approach, then we rushed for the shelters. The

Japanese wanted us to dig a shelter on the beach, but we knew it would fill with water. We dug ours in dry ground, covering it with coconut fronds on top of sand for camouflage. At first, I was claustrophobic and afraid I would suffocate inside, but my fear of death soon overcame the claustrophobia.

The new Order

From that first bombing raid, people were no longer allowed to visit us. They could bring provisions only to the Controller of Natives, and from then on we did not get the best food parcels. When we asked for provisions, the Japs always said, '*Assate*,' ('tomorrow' in Japanese). We later learned that *assate* was an idiom for 'NEVER.'

The Japanese took away our food gardens and we had to make new ones, which was strenuous work that fell heavily on our four younger priests. The strong roots of coconut trees had to be dug out and grass sods turned over. As we planted *kaukau* leaves, we all expressed the hope that we would not still be there when the sweet potatoes appeared.

The soldiers collected coconuts from surrounding plantations and brought them to Tubiana where natives were forced to scrape the meat. My job was to make soap for the soldiers. Fr Arthur Jünker's soap and oil factory, with ten local male workers scraping coconuts all day, produced about 120 cakes of soap daily.

Here is the recipe—nine cups of coconut milk, six cups of water, three cups of caustic soda. Mix it up and put in a small box; the next day you have soap. Sometimes we set coconut milk and skimmed the cream off the top to make margarine for ourselves. We also made coconut oil for cooking. The Japanese navy sold our soap to their army in Buin.

Bartering between guards and workers saw soap exchanged for cigarettes. I lent my watch to a Japanese officer only to learn later that 'lend' was equivalent to 'giving without hope of redemption.' After making a mild complaint, I caught the hint that I would have no difficulty finding trouble if I was looking for it.

Bougainville at war

The Japanese wanted to start an officers' *haus pamuk*— brothel, in Kieta, so they ordered people to bring some unmarried girls to staff the place. When Bishop Wade heard this, he told everyone to say, 'In Bougainville, it is custom to marry early, so there are no unmarried girls available.' That was the end of the officers' brothel in Kieta.

China remains placid

One night we woke to find Japs making an extensive search in every corner of our house, supposedly for a hidden radio transmitter. A submarine was seen near Numa Numa plantation, and they feared that we were in contact with a view to escape.

The episode had its humorous side. We were in the dark about the reason behind the search, as was a poor Chinese man who happened to call on us for a priest to go with him to baptise his dying wife. Circumstantial evidence seemed to involve both the Chinese man and us in some secret plot, him being a messenger from the sea. Our wonder increased when we saw them placing defence guns and guards along the beach, leaving them there for several days. It was only later that a Jap sergeant explained the whole story to us.

The subsequent fate of our Chinese friends is a kind of steadying relief from the hysteria of war. By the time Fr Müller obtained permission to visit the dying woman she had died, but Müller baptised her conditionally. The newly widowed husband attended to a Christian burial for his wife.

Mourners dressed in white, money was thrown into the grave, and sugar was given to each mourner at the end of the service. The grieving husband was about to complete a Chinese custom of burning bundles of his wife's clothing, but yielded to our caution when we reminded him of the scarcity of such material, for his growing children.

Prisoners of war

On Saturday 1 May 1943, the Japanese forced Frs Tonjes and Schlieker to travel with them from Kieta over the two old government roads to

When The Garamuts Beat

Nagovisi and Siwai. On Wednesday 12 May, we heard that Frs Florent Wache and John Conley were brought to Kieta from Nissan Island as prisoners. A Japanese officer told us the priests were sick and hungry, and we could if we wished provide a basket of food for them. They said that Fr Seiller could write to his friend Fr Wache, but of course not to the American, John Conley.

We sent bread and fruit which was carefully examined for hidden knives, razors, and other instruments of suicide. The following day Wache and Conley were sent to Buin headquarters, and we began a Novena to St Joseph, praying for their return to us.

One morning two truckloads of soldiers arrived. We were all lined up, including the sisters. All the houses were searched, and it was explained to us that surveillance was tightening up. We were told that we must all sleep and eat in the same house, and that any communication with villagers was now forbidden. The people who served our meals were to communicate only the essentials through guards as interpreters.

We explained to an officer that it was unheard of for priests and sisters to live in the same house. These rules eventually broke down, and they permitted the sisters to sleep in their own house.

Our first communal meal developed into a fiasco. The guards knew no Pidgin English so they could not understand the locals, nor could they understand us. Inevitably we spoke to selected individuals, four boys and three girls, who were summoned each morning and night to attend roll-call. They were carefully watched.

Twenty guards sat in the school behind our house, providing a changing of the six guards patrolling the houses in the vicinity. When an officer passed by it was amusing to watch the soldiers bobbing up and down making their military bows.

At about 4 pm a truck arrived with Frs Wache and Conley. Fr Conley was forbidden to speak of his interrogation at Buin, and any subsequent trips.

It was interesting to observe the professional jealousy between the Jap army and navy. The navy duly sent their troupe to guard our guards, professing fear that some harm would come to us from the army. The next day the military *Kempeitai* came to do further searches, for typewriters, pens, pencils, slates, etc., but left us carbon papers. We were subjected to constant questioning throughout our internment. Any sign of talent or skill on our part was turned into a useful advantage for our captors.

The mysterious wireless

One day a guard escorted me to an officer's house. The officer ceremoniously received me, plied me with cigarettes and sweets, and asked me to explain what a Tommy Gun was. He casually slipped in a question as to whether I could mend a radio, insinuating that I might be permitted to listen to it after fixing it. If I heedlessly admitted such a talent I would be marked as the likely organiser of a camp radio, and my friends would not see much more of me in this life.

Two motives were constantly evident in our captors' behaviour —fear of enemy communication and efforts to induce our cooperation. This is why the officer suggested that if I could repair the wireless I might go back to my station a free man, provided I could supply useful news from the wireless.

Searches alternated with questioning. My breviary was recognised as a book of prayer, but the printed psalm slips intrigued them, and probably suggested many a wild plot thanks to their active imaginations. As each new officer arrived, the whole rigmarole of questions and forms to be completed began afresh—filling in replies to, 'Where were you born? your age? what work can you do?' Etc., etc. We wrote up several copies so the next time it started, we would retire for a while and bring out our old copies. Each new officer had his unique whims, and if he was linguistically inclined, he would expect lessons in German, or perhaps French, or whatever else he could get.

Here are two examples of the odd bits of work extracted from us—one officer was very fond of brandishing his sword and slashing at an animal. One day he bent the sword, which sent him running to Gabriel Lebreton who was known to be something of a mechanic. He wanted Lebreton to make a new one. Another time, a Jap doctor brought along some French writing that he wanted translated into German. We were forbidden to use pencils so he procured one.

The navy supplied the necessary guard who installed us on the job in the morning, watching us all day and collecting the pencil at the end. With this set-up, the piece was translated by Arthur Jünker who like many great men was not a wonderful writer, so he dictated to me as his secretary. I further earned my 'living' by laboriously taking down word for word several old German folk songs from gramophone records.

Nerves and imagination produced another amusing incident; one night during an air-raid Br Xaverius and the sisters were in their shelter, when the guard outside thought he heard a wireless or radio transmitter in our shelter. So after the raid, everyone was searched and the shelter minutely examined. Officers came to investigate, as the guard was expected to substantiate his suspicions or justify them.

The next day everyone who was in the shelter was paraded and made to produce all the sounds they might have made, rattling rosary beads, repeating prayers, etc. As each sound was made the puzzled Jap sadly shook his head in growing confusion as none of these sounds corresponded with what he heard. The shelter was carefully photographed and a full report was sent to headquarters.

Peace in the midst of war

Before Pentecost, we retired spiritually into the desert for our annual retreat that was nine days. It was as if PEACE descended in the midst of WAR, as only the guards passed to and fro in their usual routine.

We depart for Buin

Ten cargo ships appeared in Kieta harbour on Monday 5 July 1943. Two Japanese officers turned up at our house asking for the two priests who had lived in Buin, as the natives were asking for us. So Adam Müller and I went. I was not to return or see anyone from Kieta again for the duration of the war. We left the next morning at 4 am and on the way, an American plane dropped bombs amidst the ships.

The Americans were now in the middle Solomons, and as we arrived at Buin we saw about 60 ships ready to reinforce the Jap forces in that theatre of war. To reach the shore we clambered from boat to boat, and then onto a truck that brought us near the old Muguai station, now a soldiers' barracks, where we found Bernard Tonjes. Josef Schlieker had already left for Monoitu.

Life in a Buin camp

We slept in the soldiers' quarters but ate with the officers. They gave us rice and rotting vegetables in a rusty tin, and we were introduced to the Japs' famous system of bathing, where everyone used the same water starting with the highest-ranking officer, running down in order of rank. Naturally, we demurred to bathe in the river. Bernard Tonjes, who became an excellent cook, contrived to fry us some potatoes from time to time in an old frying pan.

We were brought from Kieta with the promise of responding to parishioners' requests and to allow us to exercise our ministry, but the real motive was to make us a means of propaganda. Through our influence with the locals, we were expected to induce them to cooperate with and work for the Japs. They handed us a treatment plan for German missionaries.

German Missionaries

I Social status

1. The Japanese army will treat the German missionary as the status of a people of one of the THREE ALLIED POWERS.

2. The division will supervise and instruct all his conduct in the Bougainville Island in detail.

3. The divisional commander will give orders to the *Kensetubu*— the cultivating department established in the division, to supervise and instruct all his conduct.

II Points of supervision and instruction

4. The division will let him stay and get along in the barracks of the *Kensetubu* division.

5. The division will let him use his many years of lived experiences in the Island along the line of cooperating with the Imperial army administration, and admit him to promulgate Catholicism and educate natives as long as he does not violate the Imperial army administration.

6. The *Kensetubu's Somuka*, its general business section, is responsible for the direct supervision and instruction of his life in the *Kensetubu*. When the missionary wants to leave his house or do something beyond the instruction of the *Kensetubu*, he must notify beforehand, and get permission from, the general business section.

7. The conditions of Catholic promulgation and education for natives are as follows:

a. The division will admit him to promulgate Catholicism within the scope of not violating the sovereignty of Tenno Haika, His Majesty, for whose generosity he must be deeply grateful.

b. The missionary, under army administration, should in his preaching do his best to educate natives to recognize themselves as the cooperators of the New Order Constructing Movement in the Great East now being led by Japan, and to be favoured by the Imperial Family favours, the idea of which is to co-exist comfortably as if in one home, with every race co-operating with Nippon.

c. The missionary in his instructing of natives should try to let natives serve in the army work under the demand of the division, report news about enemy affairs voluntarily, and at the same time, to control rebellious natives by his own influence, to bear in common with the Imperial army's trouble and pleasure.

d. The division will dare to condemn him if he, contrary to the above articles, would not accept the instruction of the *Kensetubu* in preaching and educating.

e. Promulgation will usually be made at the preaching station at Komotaro plantation.

8. Men in charge of educating natives in Somuka should always be present at his preaching station, and report necessary affairs on every available occasion, and not so necessary affairs once every ten days through the medium of the head of *Kensetubu* to the divisional commander.

We had to go through the form and address the villagers, but the Japanese' ignorance of Telei meant they did not know what we were saying. We told them they were being forced to work, so they should offer their work up as a religious sacrifice and gain some spiritual merit. They understood that this cooperation was not our will but for fear of punishment.

The Japanese loved pork, butta, as they called it. Bau, the man from Buin, was keen to assist the Japanese whenever he could but not so keen to hand over his own pigs, so he took the Japanese to Mogoroi, and I was forced to travel with them. The villagers understandably were not happy about handing over their pigs, but they were well outnumbered by the Japanese. In any case the pigs were out in the bush foraging, which meant people would have to go and find them.

As it was getting dark and still no pigs, we stayed the night. The soldiers slept in the *haus garamut*. I did not want to sleep with them so I asked an officer if I could sleep in one of the village houses. He said it was alright, but Bau was not happy with this. I think Bau was afraid I would come with some men during the night and kill him. By morning people had caught their pigs and brought them to the Japanese.

I told the officer that it was customary to pay for them, but Bau said they could just take them. The soldiers and officer eventually paid a price for those pigs. Towards the end of the war, some men from Mogoroi threw a hand grenade into their quarters and killed quite a few.

When I returned to Buin after the war, people told me that towards the end of the war, villagers were running away from the Japanese and looking for

Australian soldiers. Bau also went to the Australian soldiers offering his support, by saying that he could show them where the Japs were hiding.

One of the Australian officers, who was a long-time planter on Bougainville before the war, was very happy to see Bau. He sent Bau to join his brother Kaibi on a bogus mission with some Bougainvillean commandos, who were instructed to kill them both. Bau must have sensed what was coming, because he pulled the pin on a hand grenade he had hidden in his bag, killing himself and injuring two of the commandos. The other commando killed Kaibi.

Crisis looming

Bernard Tonjes had not been able to say Mass since Saturday 1 May 1943. We brought a Mass kit and managed to say Mass in the house despite soldier movements. We urged them to keep their promise to us about exercising our ministry. One day, a Japanese soldier called Takista, wanted to visit Kikimogu, in Piano district, and took Bernard Tonjes and me with him. We asked if we could visit the mission while we were in the area and he agreed. When we arrived the people greeted me with '*Murugeinu!*'—loyal friend!

Adam Müller and I walked through the bush, visiting Yamaru, Momotoro on the coast, and Bogisago in the mountains. They allowed us to erect a chapel out of materials provided by villagers. The villagers however, did not come to Mass; they were exhausted from the forced work, and were in fear of bombing raids by the Americans.

In pressing too hotly for permission to complete the chapel, Adam Müller managed to offend an officer, so we began to receive rough treatment. The tone was hardly suggestive of 'friendly allies', but rather 'hated whites'. Work more than doubled, respect vanished, and it was explained to us that we were ungrateful persons unappreciative of His Majesty Hirohito's graciousness.

Fr Müller did not stay long with me. He was taken back to Kieta because he could speak Nasioi, the Kieta language. I was on my own at Buin.

Bogisago

There was a view that mountain people were a little bit 'behind' coastal people in the adoption of western ways, but living a more isolated existence meant they kept their culture and tradition strong. One day a *lapun* from Bogisago visited the Jap camp. He walked about in the state God gave him, except for a very old German army belt that he wore, bearing the words, 'God be with you' stamped on it. The soldiers did not like seeing the *lapun* in this state and gave him a *laplap*. The next day the *lapun* returned, no belt and no *laplap*.

The army put soldiers at Bogisago. Why? You might wonder, perhaps because the Australian administration neglected the mountain villages. I did not know the reason but I was happy to be there. The people fed me *kaukau* and banana and even *tabak*. Sometimes they even gave me a bit of pork. I asked the catechist, Kiau, to build a small bush chapel where we could all come to worship on Sundays.

The soldiers gave me some mushrooms one night, which I ate because I enjoy them. Within an hour I observed the soldiers falling ill so I quickly put my fingers down my throat, *autim kaikai*— forcing me to throw up.

I enjoyed eating possum and flying fox if it was cooked well. On another night I was given a plate of soup, kapul—possum, but the creature's eyes floated on top staring at me. I couldn't face kapul after that. Another time soldiers asked, 'Do you like horsemeat?'

'Yes,' I replied. 'I like horsemeat,' so they gave me a leg bone of a horse, but there was no meat whatsoever. They must have thought I was a dog.

When I came to Bougainville there were just walking tracks through the bush, no roads. The Japanese made roads good enough for cars and trucks by cutting down small trees and laying them across the ground with branches and covering them with sand. If the sand stayed in place on top of the timber and brush, the road stayed in good condition, but if the sand washed away, the trees rotted and the road became useless.

After the war, some of these roads were still in good condition. The Japanese did not build bridges because the Americans would bomb them, so they lined riverbeds with wire baskets filled with stones, making a causeway to drive across.

While I was in Bogisago, a Japanese soldier approached me for some tobacco. He had a camera that took good photos. I wanted the camera but not to take photos. I was more interested in the camera lens to start a fire, so I gave him some tobacco. The soldier was stationed at Yamaru, a long way from Bogisago. He promised to send me the camera and he kept his word. A local man looked after that camera for me, and after the war when I finally returned to Bougainville, he gave it to me. It still takes good photos.

The villain lays his charge

On Saturday 14 August 1943, I was allowed to travel with Bernard Tonjes to Piano, where the native sisters lived in the care of the catechist, Mege. It was a long and slow walk, painful for Bernard who was in the grip of rheumatism.

Walking into the station, I found the Japs in possession of Piano, now an observation station for aeroplanes. The place was looted, even the coconut trees were cut down. We arrived at the village as it was getting dark and the reception accorded us was tremendous.

The sisters had prepared a feast of pork, bananas, and other fruit. We took confessions that night, and 500 communicants attended Mass the following morning. Marriages were celebrated, and children from around the district were baptised. After Mass, I visited my old station at Piano. One old man rushed towards me shouting, *'Nkoma muruge! Nkoma muruge!'*—'My heart! My heart!' This show of devotion and respect greatly impressed our Japanese guard.

On our way to Piano, the villagers gave Bernard and me presents, but not the non-commissioned officer in charge of natives in Aku district. Having been rebuked by his superiors for consenting to the forced marriages of native sisters, he harboured a grudge against all us missionaries. He also said something against me to our Japanese guard.

After we left Piano, the non-commissioned officer had my catechist, Lauku, beaten. He was terrified enough to make a false confession that I was an American spy, and that I was speaking secretly to people against the Japanese.

We slept one night at Piano and the next day Bernard and I returned to the barracks. The poor sisters were inconsolable, imploring us to stay and protect them from bad men who were determined to marry them. We comforted them as best we could, encouraging them to keep their faith. It was good to know that throughout the war they remained faithful to their vocation.

Back at the barracks, my guard handed in his report about my alleged spying activities. The next day police turned up and told us not to leave the house again. An official car arrived to set up a court in the house, to try me under the charge of espionage. My catechist, Lauku, was questioned at the officers' headquarters, behaving as instructed by the non-commissioned officer who was present for the proceedings. It was clear Lauku was afraid of him. The officer-in- charge of our camp and the guards also faced trouble if I was found to be spying while under their control. One of the interpreters who was friendly toward us, took Lauku in hand on the way to court. He told Lauku not to be afraid but to tell the truth when questioned. The catechist was a good man, but he was nervous and nudged me as we sat at the table, wanting me to tell him what to say.

Encouraged by the friendly interpreter, Lauku told the complete story of his forced confession, and repeated it exactly when questioned again by the president. The interpreter's advocacy resulted in me being discharged.

I should add in fairness that there was a clear sense of justice in the conduct of the trial, and afterwards.

The commanders transferred the villain officer out so the frightened catechist was no longer in danger. Finally, comedy entered again as the officer-in-charge came to me that night with gifts of tinned fruit to celebrate my discharge. I believe that my discharge was effected under God's dispensation, by a private form of exorcism which was in my breviary, which I uttered in the chapel just before the trial.

The experience showed me how easy it was to fall out of Japanese favour and earn the death penalty. The consequence was that in spite of my discharge, we were no longer trusted, and visits to villages were banned for several months. Life grew harder than before which shows how little sincerity there was in the planned treatment of German missionaries.

In the middle of October 1943 the Japanese requisitioned Fr Tonjes to travel with them to Kieta, to find some goats and bring them back to headquarters. Tonjes found some goats and returned to Buin with them.

The Americans arrive

Leading up to Saturday 2 October, and Monday 1 November 1943, we experienced continuous heavy bombings. We managed to say Mass daily, but on the Feast day itself, I was just coming to the Consecration when the tactical bombardment of Choiseul by the American navy began. The intensive air bombardment on Bougainville was so severe I had to stop the Mass and head for shelter.

In the chapel, everything was blown to pieces, the altar, the communion rail taken from the new church at Turiboiru, and the vestments. Only one bottle of Mass wine which was in a trunk with the vestments, was saved. Miracle or not, it certainly demonstrated the divine protection because Mass wine was scarce, and we would have been unable to continue saying Mass without it.

A few days later, while we and some people were inland at our new vegetable garden, the chapel was destroyed by a direct hit. Villagers refused to work at the barracks, but they agreed to a compromise which was to establish gardens for the Japanese near their inland villages, and this is where we were sent to work.

We built a strong air-raid shelter, a new house, and attended to food gardens. The new officer-in-charge was friendlier than the last, allowing us, under guard, to visit surrounding villages on Sundays, to say Mass and administer the Sacraments.

Torokina Landing

The Americans landed at Torokina on the west coast of Bougainville on Monday 1 November 1943, but they wanted to fool the Japanese by creating a diversion at Choiseul from the sea and air. I was at Momotoro in Buin district at the time. The Americans lost many men and equipment in the landing because the Japanese had gun emplacements well-hidden.

One night Captain Uromoto told me the Japanese had inflicted a big naval defeat on the Americans, shooting down many planes and sinking some aircraft carriers. I listened, but when he came the following night with an even wilder story, I said that the Americans must not have any ships or planes left. He didn't talk about Japan's big wins after that. When I was in Australia, on reading some out-of-date newspapers, I learned that the opposite was true.

From late 1943 to the end of our war experience, that period of continuous bombings day and night was the worst of our trials. A bomb would explode not many yards away. If you were behind a tree, you would remain hidden until the plane came to your side, then you hid on the other side. Sometimes another person had also run to the same side. What to do then? Lie flat on the ground and hope for the best.

We could see the bombs dropping around us, and sometimes a little distance away we watched them falling through the air like eggs. Once, we rushed from the house to the shelter, and as I entered a bullet made two holes in my linen shirt. Afterwards I found the shell buried in the ground. A year or more of this kind of life without interval frayed our shattered nerves.

Keeping the faith

Amidst the noise from above we passed our second Christmas under fire. Despite the presence of Japanese soldiers, our people would begin to pray and continue praying in the shelters until the air raids were over, confessing their faith openly and without shame. Given the nature of the bombings, terrified villagers celebrated Christmas as if it were just an ordinary Sunday.

We were comforted to see people keeping the faith even when they had not seen a priest for many months. Naturally a few reverted to their old superstitions, but the great majority continued to say their rosary and morning and night prayers. The catechists had seen to baptisms, witnessed marriages, and kept their faith alive.

Once during a visit to a village, under the escort of two soldiers who watched my every movement, a young man came to me after Mass and said, 'Come Father and bless our shelters. If our shelters are blessed, God will protect us and we will be safe.'

Fear naturally would sometimes paralyse them, but they refused to take the charms or amulets from the Japanese. When I told them those things were superstitious and forbidden by God, they threw them away. I felt sure God was pleased with their simple faith.

New Year—1944

Fr Bernard Tonjes had to leave us for Numa Numa, and life continued with working in the gardens and the occasional visits to nearby mountain villages. But in early March 1944 when the Japanese were about to attack Torokina, we were brought back to headquarters and kept under close observation, in case we tried to communicate with the Americans.

We became real prisoners again. Food reduced to a vanishing point; we even tried eating grass to put some green vegetable content into our diet. During our famine, an unpleasant soldier offered us some meat which turned out to be a horse bone, completely bare of any meat. It had already been boiled in a soup.

The soldier's character progressively deteriorated from sanguine sociability to narrow and extreme egotism. He was cheerful while there was plenty of food, but shrank into a moroseness when forced to tighten his belt.

Fr Schlieker arrives at Easter

Josef Schlieker, whom we had not seen since May 1943, surprised us with a midnight visit on the Wednesday before Easter. He brought with him, biscuits, *saksak*, pineapples, and other food, which was truly appreciated. It was good to see a confrere again, and it was good for him to be able to at least perform his Easter duty. Josef remained with us until Good Friday morning.

Adam Müller was allowed to go out to say Mass in a village on Easter Sunday. I was not allowed to go, and as we had only one Mass kit, I was to experience a dreary Easter—no Mass—no confreres. The only relief was a chat with a man from Aku district.

Starvation spectre

With the Battle of Torokina lost, there was no special reason for the Japs to watch us. We were allowed to return to the villages, when we heard that the fathers and sisters from Kieta were in Buin.

We wanted to make contact with them, and on Saturday 20 May 1944, Adam Müller and I were allowed to visit them. Lieutenant General Kanda had visited us and distributed two packets of cigarettes to each of us. Armed with these and some rice, we made our way to Nakaro, to find the fathers and sisters in a terrible state.

They were in a hut in the swampy part of the bush, working with Formosan coolie labourers. Everyone—fathers, sisters, and coolies, were mere skeletons. They had been living on potato leaves and had to trudge knee-deep through mud all around the house in an extremely weak state. Poor Fr Karl Jaschke who, after more than 30 years in the islands, was so relieved to see a little rice.

We divided our cigarettes among the company and slept in their hut that night. As we left the next day our guard expressed his conviction that no one without spiritual help could continue living through privations such as these.

Fr Müller was summoned to Kieta, which meant that I was alone until Wednesday 28 June 1944, when I was sent on a trip to Nagovisi. Headquarters had given me some rice and other rations, and Fr Josef Schlieker, who I met up with in Siwai travelled with me. Villagers helped us along the road. On the way, we visited Nakaro and tended to Fr Karl's grave. When we reached Sovele we found it bombed out and everyone gone.

Japanese skeletons

We came across the skeleton of a speared Jap in a deserted food garden, and several more skeletons lay exposed along the road. At Nagavisi we reported to the Japanese officers, stories of cruelty to the locals. Women and children were often killed and this led to reprisals.

At first, locals appeared afraid even of us, especially when they saw our Japanese guard who was also afraid. Villagers were starting to side with the Americans, or rather fight against Jap marauders.

The Japs were aware of this but still hoped to win them over. The officer at Nagovisi appeared ashamed of his soldiers' conduct. We were amused when discussing the lack of food situation with a well-built Bougainville man. He showed us a brawny arm and declared that he was now, *'bun nating!'*

Our guard becomes a raving lunatic

After leaving Nagovisi, our guard quarrelled in violent tones with every soldier who did not salute him. He harangued a group of soldiers, forcing them to stand to attention until one fainted. Seeing us before he noticed the guard, another soldier took us for Americans and was poised to shoot. He received the full blast of our guard's fury. We missed the significance of these outbursts, until a friendly officer with whom our guard had argued all night, told us he was becoming strange.

I managed to persuade our guard to give his bayonet to a local man to carry, and his revolver to me. As we continued on, his demeanour worsened and he spoke of suicide but we urged him to keep going. People would not intervene or help us, as they felt it was none of their business.

Once he escaped into the bush, but with the help of villagers we eventually caught him. We had to hold him up when crossing creeks, otherwise he would try to drown himself. Finally, when he started raving, some soldiers bound him hand and foot. Other soldiers cudgelled him without mercy about the head, until we brought him to Buin but only after travelling through Siwai. Here the raving guard took a severe fit before seeming to recover his senses a little, but he died in Buin hospital after a few days, when a new guard was summoned.

In the meantime, we waited for soldiers to cut off the dead soldier's finger, after which his body was thrown with a jerk into a common grave, with several others similarly treated. The finger was covered with incense and placed in a little box before it was taken to headquarters, where it was saluted with honour and made ready to be sent to Japan. This was the way we returned at last to Buin.

A happy Christmas

After returning to Buin I had no settled abode, but I was allowed to visit villages and stay in different places. In the middle of October 1944 I was at Bogisago, where the Japs had a school teaching the Japanese language and Japanese culture. The children amused the soldiers with Japanese dance or a play. I was allowed to take them for religious instruction, preparing eight boys for baptism and some older boys for their first Holy Communion. This was how we passed the time until Christmas

1944. The planes gave us enough respite from bombings to allow us a little peace, so we could enjoy a happy Christmas.

The Bogisago people enlarged their little chapel in the jungle so that everyone in the surrounding districts could attend midnight Mass. Crowds came, and many Japanese officers and men respectfully assisted at the Mass. We had no candles so we gathered small sections of bamboo, filling them with sap from galip trees. The fragrance of the burning sap filled the church.

Buins used the same word '*moi*' for galip tree as they do for 'one year', because galip trees produce nuts only once a year. It was something novel for these Japs.

The *Missa cantata (De Angelas)* which everyone sang, was also novel for the Japs. People added their special hymns and we delivered a short Christmas sermon. After Mass, Benediction with the ciborium added to the solemnity.

People went to the barracks and held their own traditional *singsing*s, returning at 8 am for a third Mass, after which, at the barracks, we enjoyed a kaikai of pig, fish, potatoes, and coconuts. The Japs gave a few *laplap*s as presents to their favoured servants, but this was not the end of celebrations.

These Christmas celebrations were a three-cornered event. Bogisago invited Yamaru and Muguai for Christmas Day. After Christmas I travelled to Yamaru for the second celebration, when on New Year's Day, Yamaru entertained Bogisago and Muguai, offering gifts to the visitors. Muguai played host a few days later, completing the Christmas celebrations of 1944.

Devotion and escape—1945

At New Year in 1945, I wished to visit the fathers and sisters at Nakaro once again but I could not obtain permission. An officer was kind enough to send a soldier with some fowls, pork, opossums, pineapples, and local tobacco.

Last consolation before escape

After the New Year's feast at Yamaru, villagers from Koromira came. They searched for four days to find a priest who could come to their people. At first, headquarters granted permission for me to travel, but then the officer explained the danger of Americans who might attempt to rescue me.

The natives persisted in their plea for a priest, so at the Muguai celebrations, I told them an officer from headquarters was with us, and they should approach him for permission. They stood before him, waiting to have their say, 'We won't go home until we have a priest to go with us.' Finally, permission was granted for me to travel to Koromira. How proud they were, going home with a priest! News of a priest coming spread through like wildfire, or should I say native 'bush wireless'. As we approached the village, everyone was lined up by the catechists, and they all shouted, 'hip, hip hooray!' while shaking hands with us.

The Koromira women presented us with tasty dishes of taro, banana, opossum, fish, and more. The men offered us cool drinks of coconut milk and local tobacco. It was a great consolation to see the marvellous work done by the catechists during the two and a half years without a priest.

All the chapels were intact; catechists had performed baptisms for all the children and dying pagans. Marriages were performed, morning and night prayers were said in common, and daily, according to the instructions of the priest before he was interned.

All I had to do was to complete the ceremonies of baptism and matrimony. People came from far and near, so as not to miss the opportunity of assisting at Mass and receiving the Sacrament. I offered Holy Communion to hundreds and hundreds. One young man said to me: 'Father, I no longer fear to die because I have been to confession.'

Before we returned to Buin, we were given a great feast, a *singsing*, and farewelled with so many gifts that eight men were required to carry our cargo. People wept, saying, 'Father, don't go away. Stay with us. Stay with us. It is so hard to be without the Sacraments. Don't leave us alone.'

It may be interesting to liturgists that I came without my Mass kit, as the men said there was one at Koromira. On close examination, I found only a chalice, an altar stone, a missal, a corporal, and some vestments. As time went on, I found the other Sacred things, and a man brought me silken parachute material to fashion an alb. Finally, the Mass kit was complete.

Escape from the Japanese

Tuesday 17 April 1945 is a date I shall never forget. When we reached the last village in Kieta district on the border between Koromira and Buin, we heard that men from the mountains behind Buin had attacked and killed several Japanese. This action led to the Japs forcing villagers to drag a gun up the steep mountain, placing it in a position to shoot into the villages.

Surely it was divine providence that led me first to Mogoroi and later to Bogisago to where a friendly officer, Shimabukuru (Shima for short), obtained permission for me to return. Shima was a school friend of Matsumora; it was he who helped me at my trial. Shima had obtained permission for me to travel to Koromira and return to Bogisago. Fighting was getting closer to Buin and we overheard soldiers talking about battles in Siwai villages.

On our return to Bogisago we found houses surrounded by barricades of barbed wire and trenches, and several new soldiers installed. This meant we should not remain there.

On Saturday 14 April, Shima received a letter from headquarters. Returning from holding Mass at a bush chapel, I learned that he had gone to Buin for instructions.

On Tuesday 17th when he returned, Shima told me I was to go to Koromira again. Only later around dinner time, he visited me privately, telling me that I would not really go to Koromira. He began sympathetically by telling me to be firm as he had bad news.

Fr Jünker and the other fathers and sisters had escaped from Nakaro, but that was not all. Frs Schlieker, Tonjes, and Weber, had also made their escape. Consequently, headquarters had decided to kill me. I was to be beheaded the next day, he said. There was nothing to do but flee.

At his house, Shima asked me openly about my rice garden and casually suggested we go and see it. In the garden he proposed a plan for my escape. I was to show no signs of knowing anything and to join in the usual game of cards with the soldiers and himself after dinner. After the game when the moon was down, I should make my exit, find my catechist and he would hide me. I protested, 'I won't see the road in the dark! And what about the guards?' Trying to assure me, Shima replied that the guards would not be able to see much in the dark either, and likely to miss me anyway if they tried to shoot.

So, after dinner I publicly told the guard I was going across to the village for some things, having placed my breviary in my pocket and some Atabrine tablets. No sooner was I out of sight than I ran to the teacher's house: he was out. On being directed to another house, I was told he was away hunting. By this stage I was very frightened. Surely by now the soldiers would be out searching for me.

After much shouting, the faithful catechist, Kiau, was discovered a mile away down in a gully. We waited for an hour by the river when Kiau finally turned up. He was pleased to see me and told me that he already had a plan for my escape.

Kaiu also had a message for me from Paul Mason. I read Mr Mason's note: he was planning to send native commandos to come and snatch me. Kiau had planned that the friendly guard should get permission to bring me to a secret part of the jungle where there were two children, long overdue for baptism. The commandos could then capture us both and bring us to the Australians. He could not tell me all this before, as since the letter arrived I was always with the soldiers.

Kiau brought me barefoot over creeks and very rough country to a small hamlet, where at last I had the happiness of baptising the two young children. We then continued walking higher into the mountains until we reached Botulai. I sent Kiau back to Bogisago while I slept that night in Botulai. Early the next morning, I thought I heard guards coming for me, but it was Kiau with some of my things.

He returned the night before to the Jap camp to find them looking for me. They asked him, 'Where was the priest?' Kiau said he didn't know. 'Was he not in Bogisago?' Kiau responded. Shima asked him quietly if I was OK, to which Kiau assured him that I was safe and well-hidden.

The next day we walked to Kekemona, the home of Suavita, a man I had heard of, being a leader of local guerrilla fighters and a Protestant catechist in Siwai. Suavita sent a man off to bring me back some kaikai. The man went to a place used by Australian forces as a food depot for escapees. He carried 48 tins of bully beef on his shoulders for six hours up and down mountains back to Kekemona. I ate sparingly to avoid getting a stomach ache or diarrhea, and rested in Kekemona for a week.

Japanese soldiers were close by, but villagers kept watch, taking great care of me. They said if any soldiers turned up in the gardens or in the village, they would kill them with guns provided by Paul Mason. I wish to thank the people of Kekemona for their generosity and kindness, and the great risks they took on my behalf, and to the man who made that dangerous wokabout to bring me a carton of bully beef.

It was Sunday when we set off for the Australian base at Torokina. I left Kekemona with six of the bravest men who would not desert me in the jungle or run from the Japs. Their leader, Suavita, had impressed upon them their duty of guarding me to the end, with their own lives if necessary. I found the journey very severe with swamps and rain adding to the difficulties.

After one day, I rested at a Seventh Day Adventist village. On the Tuesday we went through the Jap lines following the same route that Br Xaverius walked some months before. We saw the spot where he was rescued. Two men walked 20 metres ahead, then another two, then me and one other, then two more, 20 metres behind all of us. This system was to protect me. The scouts up front would signal the two behind if they saw soldiers or anything suspicious. The next two could then signal us to take cover in the bush.

We used this system as we approached Liloki River. Sixty natives resting on the riverbank heard us coming. Thinking we were Japs, they were ready to shoot but they recognized their *wantoks* so we were safe. They were Buin and Koromira men, armed to the teeth. As I drew near, they recognized me and were delighted to see me. They said it was a good thing I wasn't up front or that we got passed, as from behind they would have shot us.

We came to a large lake, I forget its name, but one of the men said we were on top of a mountain. They said, *'mipela ol blak man, i go pas'*—'we black men will take the front'.

Mr Mason and some Australian soldiers were camped further along the mountain, with black scouts stationed as lookouts along the track. If they mistook us for the enemy they could easily have shot us.

Local militia, well-armed and cooperating with the Australians, were killing Japs. I did not see one sentry along that route but they were there. Before leaving Kekemona we heard from some Buin refugees that Japs were killing people due to the support from traitors.

By 6 pm we reached a barracks on top of the mountains. Paul Mason and his men were camped in the mountain village of Sipuru. The place was full of displaced Nasioi villagers, but the Australians were making food drops from the air. Paul and other soldiers were pleased to see me.

A story went around that Paul Mason painted his body and hair black as a disguise to check out the Japanese airfields. I never believed it because Paul was blind as a bat without his glasses.

While I was at Koromira, Paul was mistakenly told that Fr Junker was there, so he sent some of his commandos down to the coast to rescue him. But it was me, and I had already left by the time his men arrived. My mind was trying to take everything in, as I had not seen a white person for three years, just Japanese.

I rested in Sipuru for two days. Meanwhile, Paul sent word to Torokina that I was with him, but I would be heading for Mamaregu. He warned me that my first stop was a ten-hour walk. Paul gave me a guard of native soldiers, and we set off up and down mountains in the hot sun.

I drank from a river, giving myself diarrhea, a condition that lingered for a year. When I eventually saw a doctor from Vunapope, he diagnosed that I had amoebic dysentery.

We finally stopped for a rest, and a short while later it started raining. The guards made a fire, prepared some kaikai, and instructed me, *'Bai yu slip long dispela haus garamut.'*

The next morning we got up and walked, passing through Sovele mission station. But my energy was vanishing, and four miles from the Australian base I could not walk any further. We had reached a good road used by the army, where the native guards told me to rest. As there were no Japanese here, they would walk down to the coast to arrange for a truck to come and get me. An army vehicle turned up and brought me to an Australian soldiers' camp on the beach. I was a sorry sight with a long beard and unkempt hair.

The Australians were eager to hear the details of my escape and pressing all kinds of food on me, but all I could manage in my weak state was a cup of cocoa. On our way to Torokina we crossed a river where some Australian soldiers were bathing naked. On hearing our vehicle they took off into the bushes. Seeing my long hair, apparently they thought I was a woman, although I have never seen a woman with a bushy mausgras, not cut for three years.

We reached Torokina in three hours; it was Saturday 5 May. The place had good roads, lots of houses, and electricity: it was like a town. I was interviewed by an intelligence officer who asked for my estimation of Japanese numbers. I thought close to 20,000, but he was not inclined to believe me, thinking it was more like 9,000. After the war I read a newspaper dated Wednesday, 15 August 1945, it estimated there were 23,000 Japanese soldiers.

Following my interrogation, I was brought to Laruma, an Australian army camp that was like another small town. Laruma had a small *haus sik* for local people and another for service personnel which was called Angau. I was then taken to the priests' house where I found Frs Müller and Junker. Other priests were in the hospital, but I was not allowed to visit them; I never knew why.

There were many deaths in the hospital at Laruma. My belief was those people had been starving during their years in the bush, and when they finally arrived at a hospital where good food was laid on, they ate too much. This caused more illness that ultimately led to their deaths.

It was great to see my compatriots again. Müller and Junker gave me a set of clean clothes and some essentials as when I arrived I was wearing a shirt and trousers previously worn by a Japanese soldier.

I wasn't there too long before a New Zealand Marist priest came to see me. His name was Fr Feely. He was a chaplain with the New Zealand Forces. Fr Feely gave us some money in case we wanted to buy a few things. The first thing I did was to find a barber to cut off three years of hair. I felt like a newborn baby afterwards.

That night, Fr Jim Henessy's brother came to see me, promising to send me a new set of clothes and shoes. Sergeant Frank Hennessy obtained permission from the American Forces to search for his missing brother, who was captured by the Japanese.

7

When The Garamuts Beat

Fr Jim Hennessy died on the MV *Montevideo* Maru, when the Americans torpedoed the ship, sinking it with many lives on board.

As promised, Sgt Hennessy brought me some clothing, but Major Reed, the Australian Commanding Officer, was not pleased. 'I'm in charge of prisoners here,' he said, and asked us to provide an inventory of all of our personal items. I replied that I had only one shirt and one pair of trousers. For some reason, I was the only one placed under house arrest and forbidden to go anywhere. Frs Müller and Junker were free to go wherever they liked.

We left Torokina on Monday, 7 May 1945, on the MV *Katoomba*, a ship taking Australian soldiers home. Jünker, Müller and I were told we would also leave on that ship. I never got to see the other priests in the Laruma *haus sik*, but according to officers in the camp, they were not well enough to travel.

While on board I thought about Bougainville and its people. They were my life. Would I be able to return after the war? I did not know, so mentally, I said goodbye to my home and my people, and wept as we pulled out of Torokina.

After some days at sea, the commander of the Australian soldiers said they had to do air raid drills in case of an attack, and this included us. So we lined up with the rank and file. When the officer-in-charge saw us three in American uniforms, he assumed we were soldiers. After explaining that we were priests with nothing else to wear, he was not amused, but we promised our full cooperation.

8 Peace time

Olosem wanem baiembai mi i nap kam bek o nogat? Ailan bilong mi, mi laikim tumas wantaim ol pipol bilong em

We reached Sydney on Saturday 2 June 1945 and prepared for our arrival as the customs officer boarded. Fortunately I still had my passport so I was alright. When faced with Adam Müller and Arthur Junker, both without passports, the officer grew frustrated and annoyed. 'Why do you not have passports?' he demanded to know, not having any idea that we three had come out of the jungle after spending three years in *kalabus* by the Japanese.

No one came to meet us at the ship, but thankfully Red Cross took us in a car from their depot to Villa Maria at Hunters Hill. We knocked on the door and a brother opened it. No one had telephoned to say we were coming, and naturally he had no idea who we were. We asked to see the House Superior. We waited and waited.

Finally, I said to the other two, 'This is our house. I will find Fr Bergeron myself' (the Superior). Can you imagine Brother John's bewilderment when told the three khaki-clad strangers at the door were Marist priests? He ushered us in to see Fr Bergeron who was very happy to see us. At last, we felt we were in our rightful place, our Marist house. Fr Bergeron led us to rooms where we could stay.

On Sunday, we asked to visit the seminary at Toongabbie where Australian Marists were. This was a time when Australian girls fancied men in American uniforms, and as we were wearing the same, it was easy to be confused about who we were. Fr Croker, the Superior at Toongabbie, offered us some priest's black clothing. I spoke with Fr Croker about what work I could do. He said he would meet with the Australian Provincial, Fr Dan Hurley, at St Patrick's to discuss our future.

Some days later, we learned that Arthur Junker was appointed to St Patrick's, Adam Müller would work in the parish of Hunters Hill, and I was to teach scripture and Greek at Toongabbie. My English was not good, so Fr Dynan, a former lawyer, became my tutor.

Fr Albert de Theye, my old friend from St Olaf in Holland, and Fürstenzell in Bavaria, was allowed to return to his mission in the South Solomons. Albert had a motorbike, but there were no roads where he was going so he gave me the bike. I could now travel between Hunters Hill and Toongabbie, visiting our Sydney confreres whenever I wanted.

There was one student seminarian who thought he was very clever. He asked me if he could borrow my Greek textbook. We did not have enough books so two students shared a book between them. Because I was in and out of hospital with diarrhea, I prepared my lessons and exams well in advance, leaving my notes in the book. Later, I realised I had made a mistake with an answer to one of the exam questions, so when I found the seminarian had transcribed my incorrect answer word for word in his exam paper, I challenged him heatedly. He denied it just as vehemently.

We celebrated the ending of the war on 15 August 1945, by playing soccer with the seminarians, but after the game I could hardly walk. We German priests worried about what would happen to us. Would we be allowed to return to our missions? American nationals such as Bishop Wade, Fr Lepping, and Fr Lebel, were still in Torokina. I watched a newsreel, and there was my friend Takista on the Mivo River waving a white flag.

Fr Leon Chaize, who was a senior officer in the French navy, was very helpful to us German priests. He went to Canberra to negotiate with government officials for the German, French, and Luxembourg priests to return to Bougainville and other Pacific Islands. We waited for news.

Peace time

While he was gone, Fr Chaize offered me his room at a hospital where he was chaplain. One of the nurses said there was a private room in the ward I could use. I meant to say, 'I don't want to put you to any trouble,' but in my bad English I ended up saying, 'I don't want to molest you.'

The story spread like wildfire through the hospital, I was very embarrassed. Fr Chaize brought back good news. His trip was successful, as permission was granted in June, 1946, for the German priests to return to Bougainville.

Return to Bougainville

We left on our sea voyage for New Guinea in June 1946 with two nurses, and whilst on board, no news from the outside world reached us. Our first stop was Port Moresby. After we docked, white men called out from the shore, 'Have you got any beer on the ship? The town is dry—*nogat bia*!'

Much later, long after the war's end and services had started up, breweries were built in Port Moresby and Lae, but in those early years, locals were not allowed to drink alcohol.

The ship was only in Port Moresby a short time before it took another couple of days to reach Rabaul, the capital of New Britain. I was met by some priests who took me to Vunapope, the centre for the missionaries of the Sacred Heart. In the Tolai language, *vuna* means village, so Vunapope translates as village of the Pope. Before the war, it was a large establishment with all kinds of workshops. The brothers constructed prefabricated churches and houses to be re-assembled later on mission stations.

When we arrived we were given a drink of banana wine, when I remembered reading in the Sydney Catholic Weekly, that missionaries were using it for Mass. But this drink was very strong, more like whiskey. We stayed at Vunapope one night, and the following day we returned to Rabaul harbour to take a smaller ship to Buka. Before leaving Vunapope each of us priests were given a small bottle of banana wine.

When The Garamuts Beat

At first the sea was calm, but then it got very rough with waves breaking over the deck. We priests held on to whatever we could to avoid being washed overboard. The two nurses were lying in their tiny cabin suffering from sea sickness. Everyone was seasick except for Fr Boch, who sat smoking his pipe as though it was a calm sea.

When we reached Buka Passage we were so very happy to get ashore. Fr Albert Lebel met us in a Jeep and took us up to the parish house at Hahela. We were told not to worry about our luggage, that it would be transferred to another ship in the morning. The school children welcomed us by singing the Ave Maris Stella. We were given some dry clothes and a good meal, and found space to camp the night at Albert's house.

The next morning we went looking for the small hospital ship that was to take us to Torokina. We found it along with the soldiers who accompanied us from Rabaul. It seems they also 'found' my banana wine as I had none left. It seemed no time at all that we arrived at Torokina where Fr George Lepping greeted us.

George was a prisoner of the Japanese in Rabaul during the war. On his release at the end of the war, he travelled immediately to Torokina, to help the bishop procure housing, beds, and other essentials from the war surplus stores. An Australian kiap who was on Bougainville during the war told people that the Catholic faith was finished, and now it was time for the *Talatala*. He couldn't believe his eyes when he saw us priests returning, even us Germans!

Nearly all the Australian soldiers had now left Bougainville, but a few remained, as they were busy selling off surplus items from the war. With the Australian and American armies trying to get rid of things, our bishop was on a buying spree, such as his purchase of a large hospital with beds and equipment. At the time, there were numerous Jeeps and other vehicles at Torokina. The American army wanted the bishop to buy the lot at two pounds each. He bought some but not all. The bishop made ice cream which he gave to the Australian soldiers, and in return they provided him with fresh meat.

Peace time

A company bought the rest of the Jeeps, taking the engines out and leaving the bodies. Wong You, a Chinese trader, helped the company find workers for the job. He then drained all the petrol left in the vehicles into drums and later sold it.

Locals found abandoned rifles and ammunition and were itching for fun. One day Dick O'Sullivan heard lots of gunfire and went to investigate. He found several young boys shooting indiscriminately, so he fetched Mr Parer for assistance. Together with some local men they collected the firearms, put them in the back of his Jeep, drove straight down to the beach and dumped them in the sea.

Torokina parish had a coconut plantation near the beach, but during the war, the American Air Force bulldozed all the trees into the sea to lay down aero-matting (Marston matting) for the airstrip. Further inland, they made a longer airfield for the bigger planes. I learned to drive on that 'strip.

The soldiers had built a long-drop toilet, and every Saturday they put firewood and diesel into the hole, setting fire to it. One day, Sr Wendelina accidentally poured petrol down the hole and set fire to it. The explosion set her clothes on fire, almost blinding her.

Wong You opened a small store at Torokina, and the Methodist minister, Reverend A.H. Voyce, opened one at Kahili. Reverend Voyce asked Mr Parer for some saucepans left by the American Army, for which he was permitted to take some. Later that evening Mr Parer returned to find the storeroom empty of every saucepan. He asked the native storeman what had happened to all the saucepans. The storeman replied that the reverend's car was going back and forth, filling up until none were left. Mr Parer was furious and instructed Reverend Voyce to bring them all back. Later, Mr Parer gave all the kitchen equipment to the bishop.

When we returned after the war, we all wanted to return to our stations. The bishop told me I could return to Piano, but that all the other mission stations were flattened. Several Australian pre-war plantation owners who enlisted as Air Force pilots during the war made a point of bombing the missions rather than plantation buildings. Their thinking was that the Japs were more likely to occupy mission buildings than plantation buildings.

The two elderly priests, Frs Poncelet and Schank, were waiting for my return, so they could fill me in on what had happened since I'd been away. They were not ready to return to Buin. The bishop instructed me to go down to Buin for two months, to assess the situation and see if Frs Poncelet and Schank could realistically return.

There were a few Buin men at Torokina, and they travelled south with me. Fr Lebreton drove us as far as Koiare in South Bougainville where we spent a night. There is a small river at Koiare where one day villagers caught a crocodile. When they opened it up they found a Japanese ammunition belt inside its stomach.

American soldiers had built roads and bridges during the war but floods destroyed a lot, and rivers regularly changed course leaving bridges standing high and dry with no water under them. In Siwai, we found one bridge still standing and another standing all by itself on a small island. The river had long shifted its course and bypassed the bridge.

The next day we journeyed as far as Mamaregu where we spent one night. There was a wonderful Australian nurse, Miss Menzies, based there. She helped the mission look after patients in a small *haus sik*. One day nurse Menzies wanted to travel to Torokina on her own. Villagers warned it was a bad idea, that she should take some men with her when crossing the rivers, but Miss Menzies was determined to travel alone. She came to a small river not far from Mamaregu and started to cross, when a crocodile grabbed her. Later on people went looking for her; they found a few items but nothing of her body. *Pukpuk em i kaikaim pinis.*

Two brothers from Monoitu in Siwai rose early one morning to go to the beach. There were two sisters who wanted to come to Mamaregu, so the two young boys were to accompany them, but they needed to cross a river along the way. The younger brother was small, so the elder brother carried

Peace time

him on his back. Halfway across they were attacked by a crocodile. They made it to the other side, but the older boy was badly bitten on his stomach.

A ship arrived with Sr Martial on board. She had the injured youth carried to Mamaregu, where he was sewn up and nursed back to full health. When he grew up, that young man joined the Marist Brothers, becoming known as Br Bernard.

After making record time in a nine-hour walk, the following day we reached Monoitu, and Piano the day after. The bishop sent word to the Piano catechists that I was returning, and to have a house ready. A small *haus saksak* was ready with two rooms, but it was also occupied by Ekio and his young son Moini. This is the child who grew up to become a doctor, only to be murdered in the PNG Highlands. I took one room to sleep and say Mass.

I sent word to all the catechists to get started on a new church and that I would visit all the villages and hold Mass. I was so happy to find that Ekio had kept safe all the parish records, so it was not difficult to record all the wartime marriages and catch up on the backlog of baptisms. My records showed that two-thirds of the population died during the war.

American soldiers came looking for crashed planes, to take the names of the pilots and crew. I took them to Morula village, and asked Pokua, the catechist, to prepare a meal for everyone while we searched for crash sites. Pokua prepared sweet potato and chicken cooked in coconut milk. When the soldiers first saw the food they weren't too keen but I urged them to try it. They enjoyed the meal so much they ate everything. That evening when we returned to my house, the Americans were still talking about Pokua's beautiful chicken and coconut soup.

I promised Pierre Schank that I would visit Muguai after I had inspected my parish, Piano. It was the first week of August when I reached Muguai, and people showed me the place where I was to be beheaded. Revisiting these areas filled me with joy, to reunite with so many of my wartime friends. They too were happy to see me again. I was so happy to see that villagers had built a new church. It was only made from bush materials, but good enough to once again hold regular Sunday Mass. Also, now that I had shoes on my feet, it meant that I could walk well, but walking on a sandy beach was hard going.

Turiboiru lies between Piano and Muguai so we called in there too. Near the mission, the Japanese built an airstrip with large hangers close to the priest's house. The Americans sent a large spotter plane each day while the Japs were at work. They spotted the aircraft that the Japs had hidden in hangers on both sides of the airstrip, and bombed the hangers but not the strip because they wanted to use it. Turiboiru was littered with bomb holes.

The catechists built Fr Poncelet a new house amid the bomb holes. I asked why they hadn't built on the strip itself, where there were no bomb holes. They replied that with no bush for shade it would be too hot. I thought that made sense.

The bishop asked me to return to Torokina after two months, and having walked some days with my companions from Piano, we reached Torokina. The nearer we got to Torokina we came to rivers with bridges over them. Roads were well made, and Torokina, which had lots of houses with electric lighting, was like a big city for them! They were amazed.

The bishop was very happy to see me, and I was able to explain to Frs Poncelet and Schank, who despite being old, that it was safe to return to Turiboiru and Muguai. The road back to Torokina had changed a lot however since I was last on it. Big rains had washed away some of those bridges we saw, and the men who walked with me later, found bits of road gravel here and there. It seemed there was no longer any sign of roads or bridges. Realising that walking from Torokina would be too much for the two priests, they returned to Buin by boat.

Some of the Chinese community returned to Bougainville soon after the war and quickly set up businesses again. When I visited Piano, people asked, 'Can you go to Wong You's store and buy some white calico for us? The cost is ten shillings.' I agreed and took their money, as I wanted to help them. When I returned to Torokina, I turned up at Wong You's store saying that I wanted to buy a bolt of white cloth that cost ten shillings. As I handed over the money, he said: 'For you only, I sell it for five shillings.'

Another story about the Chinese—they can wait a long time for locals to have enough cash to purchase the items they really wanted. Plantation labourers were given a portion of their wages each month, until the end of their contract when they were paid out in full: the Chinese knew this.

A labourer might go into a trade store and buy one axe. Some months later he might return to buy another, then later, some *laplap*. At the end of their contract, when these labourers received their outstanding wages, they would go straight to the Chinese store and spend up until all their money was exhausted.

I wish to explain something to white people. Generally they think black people don't know how to say 'thank you,' when given a present. There isn't a word for 'thank you' in *Tok Ples*, but there are ways the person receiving a gift can show their appreciation, such as by saying 'what a generous or kind person the giver is'. Today people use the words 'thank you' more and more.

West coast

Bishop Wade was concerned about Protestant pastors and their catechists moving into the west coast of Bougainville, especially around Kunua and Kuraio. We didn't have any catechists in the area he could send to help with the situation, so I told the bishop I was willing to go if he agreed. Before the war, two Catholic priests worked in Sipai and Kuraio. The bishop gave me permission to visit the area and have a look around.

I chose some Buin men to travel with me, and we packed some American rations to take with us. Those rations boxes were popular as the food was good quality and they even provided tobacco. Dick O'Sullivan drove, dropping us at a beach site near Sipai, before returning to Torokina.

The first place I walked to was the *haus kiap*, where after some time a Buka man turned up. He said he was a catechist originally from Buka, but when the war started he was working as a catechist in Sipai, and had not returned to Buka due to the fighting. He took me to Adam Müller's old station where I met up with Fr Henry Hebert.

After a few days I came across Fr Jim McConville on the road. Jim was based at Hahela, and he had also come to check on the place. Once he saw what I was doing he returned to Hahela.

Before the war, the Australian administration encouraged the mountain people to settle on the coast, but malaria killed many, so during the war they returned to the mountains to live on a high plateau.

One morning we got up very early to walk up to to the mountains to find one of the villages. We must have walked about ten kilometres before we found the place. There was a haus kiap there also, and a little further along up the mountain on level ground, was a small hamlet.

I asked for the *luluai*, but people said he had gone a long way away and it would not be easy to find him. With the men travelling with me, I found a house for us to sleep in. Not long after, some of my team came to tell me that there were several *Talatala*—non- Catholics, around, and they too were asking for the *luluai*. I found them at the haus kiap. I asked them what were they doing here as this was a Catholic area. *'Mipela ol katolik i stap hia, na i nogat ples bilong ol Talatala.'* After our discussions the group left, returning to the coast.

It was near evening when some men came to see me. Their *luluai* had returned, and when he heard that I sent the *Talatala* away he was furious with me. The men added, 'The day before yesterday he killed a man, and now he would like to kill you.' I called for our catechist, giving him some rice, meat, and tobacco. I sent him to talk to the *luluai*, but the *luluai* would not see me. My students were afraid that someone would come for us during the night. Our house was built on the ground so I slept across the doorway.

I knew that in the past there were people here who had been baptised, so the next morning I decided to hold Mass. The *luluai* turned up but he didn't come alone. He didn't turn up with one child, he brought three,

Peace time

along with their three mothers. After Mass he asked me about my dog. I explained that it wasn't my dog to give; it belonged to a man from Torokina station. I spoke to our catechist, 'I am giving you ten shillings to buy the chief a dog.' I explained to the chief what I had done and he accepted it.

When it came time for us to leave the village, some of his men accompanied us down to the coast before returning back up the mountain. This was their *kastam—pasin bilong ol.* As we walked through the Sipai area people were very kind to us. They had also taken good care of the things belonging to Fr Hebert, who had to leave during the war.

Kuraio, on the west coast, was not like Sipai. Fr Leon Chaize started the Sipai-Kuairo mission in 1921, but a station was never established. Fr Roland Dionne took over many years later, but when the war started, he moved to another island. The people of Kuraio still lived in the old customary ways such as walking around naked.

That morning when we walked down to the beach, we had to find a track to other mountain villages. I thought these villagers still fought one another which is why they were in the mountains. Villages were sited so they could easily see people coming. If they were seen as enemies, then it was easier to kill them.

When we arrived at one particular village, we were given a house to sleep in. A *lapun* man brought us a bamboo basket of pork. He ate some first to show me it was not poisoned but I did not like the smell of it. I was afraid if I ate it and got *pekpek wara*—diarrhea, I would be unable to *wokabaut*, but the young men with me ate it and didn't get sick.

Over a period of two weeks we visited all the villages in the area. Sometimes people use the bush as a toilet, so it is easy to pick up hookworm if you walk in the wrong place. It is wise to keep to well trodden pathways. The medicine for hookworm tastes foul but it is better than the illness.

During our wokabaut some of our boys had caught a *liklik kapul*—baby possum, which they kept in a box. I was playing with it one day when it suddenly scratched me. I didn't take care of it and some days later I noticed a sore developing.

Dick O'Sullivan said he would arrive at Kuraio on 1 November and bring us back to Torokina. We returned to Kuraio on the appointed date but he was not there, so we decided to walk.

As we did not know the jungle track we thought it best to follow the beach. We had been walking for about three hours when one of the men saw a small ship. I tried signalling it with a mirror but it kept going. As I watched the boat travel northwards I thought it would anchor off Kuraio, so we decided to turn back for Kuraio, and hopefully catch up with Dick there.

By this time we were short on food. We had left Kuraio very early that morning and it was near nightfall. Our group started looking for turtle nests. Eventually they came across a nest with about 200 eggs. Turtle eggs have soft but tough skin and are slightly smaller than a tennis ball.

The next day we reached Kuraio and met up with Dick and 30 catechists from Buka. We caught the ship back to Torokina. When I arrived, Sr Martial took one look at my arm and told me to go with her quickly: I had blood poisoning. Sr Martial fixed me up but I remained at Torokina for some time.

Getting established in Piano again

The bishop allowed me to dismantle a building in Torokina that was used by the American officers; it was in very good condition. I numbered every plank and tied everything together. My plan for Piano was to build a new church. I returned to Piano, and not long before Christmas the mission ship brought all my cargo to Patupatuai, including a Jeep and a trailer that was loaded with my building materials. When I met the ship I could see the cargo was not how I left it in Torokina: pieces were missing, and I was unable to build my new church.

After getting everything off the ship and onto the shore, I tried driving the Jeep to Piano, but em i no isi. There were many creeks and rivers to cross and no bridges. In my cargo along with the building materials, there

Peace time

were sheets of Marston matting which I placed on the ground in front of the Jeep. After driving over it, I would take it up from behind and put it down in front again, but it was slow going. Night fell and I was still in the big bush, so there was nothing for it but to sleep in the Jeep. The mosquitoes made a meal of me.

The next morning I continued on until I came to another halt: a large river—the Porror. Not having ever driven a vehicle through a river before, and after saying a few prayers, I pushed on into the water. Some men from Piano had gathered on the other side.

They waded into the river and pushed the Jeep through. With the help of these men, we crossed several more creeks before reaching another big river like the Porror.

It was nearing dark again and I thought it best to leave the Jeep where it was and walk the rest of the way to Piano. My thinking was to return in the morning for the vehicle and cargo. But since the Porror, my helpers had grown to a large crowd, and everyone was keen to push the Jeep across. Once across, I thought we had a good road ahead of us to Piano.

But just ahead a huge tree had fallen across the road. It was now pitch dark. With the battery plugged in to give us light from the Jeep, *ol i katim diwai*—they cut the tree up. With the tree out of the way, I was able to drive the Jeep through to Nabaku village. There the motor stopped—no more benzine.

I would have left the Jeep on the road and walked the remaining four kilometres to Piano. There weren't any other vehicles in the area so we weren't blocking anyone, and no one would steal the car. 'No,' everyone said, 'Get in and steer, we will push.' When we finally limped into Piano, *batteri i dai pinis*—no more lights. My journey was over. I was completely exhausted but happy. Although I didn't have a battery or fuel, I still had a Jeep.

A few days later I sent some men with the battery to Kunka, a mechanic from Buin. Kunka charged the battery and found some fuel, so now my Jeep was alive. I could get around the station as long as I didn't go too far.

When The Garamuts Beat

Before the war, Kunka was a taxi driver and mechanic in Rabaul, but he returned to Buin after the war. Kunka found an abandoned Japanese car in the bush one day and got it going. With a piece of wire connected between his big toe and heel, as an accelerator pedal, Kunka could make the vehicle speed up or go slow.

Taro and sweet potato takes six months to ripen, so I had to get food for the school children from the villages until the school gardens started producing. Sago palm leaves for roofing and classrooms also needed to be transported. My little Jeep and trailer were very useful.

Kunka and I were talking in my house one day when a *lapun* turned up with a small bag of galip nuts. He offered them to Kunka, to which Kunka said he didn't like galip nuts. After the *lapun* left, Kunka explained that according to kastam, if he had accepted the nuts, it would have entitled the *lapun* to come to his store and take whatever he wanted without paying.

Another example of obligation was, when Peter a seminarian from Torokina, received a gift from some school children in Brisbane. He came to me asking to send a gift in return. Peter could not understand that the children would not have expected this.

Near the church at Piano, there was a bunker where the Japanese were supposed to have left a bomb. The head of it was visible and no one would go near it. When the bomb demolition squad came, I told them about it. They investigated and found that the 'bomb' was a small generator to power light on a pushbike.

I took them in the Jeep to Nabaku village where there was a large bomb. They said that they would detonate it and then I could drive them back to Piano. I preferred to walk home, offering them the Jeep to drive back later. They advised me to hide down a riverbank. I was afraid and with good reason, as shrapnel flew as far as Piano. They exploded another bomb near my house which blew my walls down.

The two Buin priests, Jean-Baptiste Poncelet, and Pierre Schank, returned to their parishes of Turiboiru, and Muguai, and while they didn't tell

Peace time

me directly, I heard that they were finding things very difficult. Fr Poncelet had spent more than 30 years at Turiboiru before the war. The people of his parish had by now, lived a long time with Japanese soldiers, and they could not go back to the way things were run before the war. No longer was the priest held up as before.

When Fr Poncelet went on leave, I think in 1952, he did not return to Bougainville. He opened a new Marist province in Belgium. A story I heard was that Fr Poncelet did not like the Buin language much. *Poncelt* in Telei means insane, and Jean-Baptiste felt it sounded too much like his own name.

Life in Bougainville changed after the war—people did not automatically obey white people, or their priests anymore. No more would they blindly accept and believe everything the priests told them. After spending such a long time with the Japanese, the Australians, and the Americans including African American soldiers, villagers were open to new ways.

After the war, some Australian priests travelled up to Bougainville to help us get the missions going again by re-starting a seminary. The most senior of the group was *Monseigneur* (Mgr) Hanan from Melbourne. Another priest travelling with him was Fr McGuire. Mgr Hanan brought his *monseigneur* robes which he wore during Mass. When the villagers saw how he dressed, they had a name for him, *'liklik bisop'*—little bishop. It was their way of saying they knew he wasn't a real bishop.

Torokina seminary

After the war, Bishop Wade and Fr George Lepping stayed in Torokina to organise the re-building of the missions. Bishop Wade bought a large hospital from the Australian army, equipped with beds and everything needed to treat the Australian soldiers during the war.

Before the Second World War, there was a small seminary in Rabaul. Fr Hohne tried to continue its education program during the war but it was impossible. After negotiating with Bishop Scharmack of Rabaul, and Bishop Sorin of Yule Island, Bishop Wade re-opened the seminary in Torokina.

Three students came from Yule Island, although the radio message said 300 were coming! Nine students came from Rabaul. There was also a real interest in the school from our own people of Bougainville. Mgr Hanan taught the major seminarians and Fr McGuire taught the minor seminarians.

A memory about the media beating up a story—when Mgr Hanan returned to Australia from Torokina, he was interviewed by the media who asked if there were food shortages on Bougainville. I know he didn't say this, but the newspapers ran a story about thousands of people on Bougainville facing starvation. The Australian government read the article and immediately got onto Port Moresby, which led to the Administrator flying to Bougainville to investigate the famine. Of course, it was all a media myth.

The Congregations of black sisters and brothers were reinstated at Torokina, and a married couple, the Fursts—both doctors, with their child, arrived from Vunapope. My old friend Xaverius was also there. He found all kinds of building materials, drums of fuel and oil, all of which he stored at the back of the mission. Near the seminarians' house was a water tank. We had to keep the lid shut on the inlet when Mount Bagana erupted, so volcanic ash would not foul the water.

§

I should tell you about Dr Karl Furst. Before the war, he married and went to Africa as a medical missionary, leaving his wife behind to finish her medical studies. During the war, the British and Australian governments rounded up all the foreign doctors and put them in a camp in Australia, where Dr Furst remained until the end of the war.

After the war, Australian missionaries heard about Dr Furst and invited him to work at Vunapope, which is where his wife later joined him. On a visit to Vunapope, Bishop Wade invited the Fursts to come and work in Torokina.

During the war, two villages at Torokina fought resulting in a woman being speared in the back. Part of the spear broke off inside the woman,

Peace time

leaving her in severe pain for the duration of the war. Dr Furst operated and removed the fragment. The woman was so grateful she remained with the Furst family for many years. Later, when Bishop Wade built a small hospital at Turiboiru, the Drs Fursts worked there for several years.

§

In July 1949, I rode my bike to Monoitu to visit Josef Schlieker, but I was greeted by an Australian diocesan priest, Fr Brady, who said, 'What are you doing here? You are an important man.' I asked what he meant. He said that I was to leave Piano and go to the seminary at Torokina.

It seems some toktok was picked up by some men who told Sr Martial, who then told Fr Charles Barrett, who was in Torokina celebrating American Independence Day on Monday, 4 July. Fr then told Fr Brady. The 'bush telegraph' was working. The next morning I rode back to Piano where someone brought me a letter from the bishop, who had since left for Australia. I was instructed to go to Torokina.

Jean-Baptiste Poncelet was in charge while the bishop was away, and he suggested I wait at Piano and let Charles Barrett go because he had been there before and liked it. But I felt it was more prudent to obey the bishop. George Lepping was replacing me at Piano. I was broken-hearted to leave Piano but I took the mission ship to Torokina. Now the hard work for me began.

I think this was the most difficult period of all my years of missionary work. I found only seven seminarians remaining, two had returned home. It is true to say I taught scripture and Greek for nine months at Toongabbie, but now I was expected to teach metaphysics, logic, church history, and Latin—with no textbooks.

I taught in the mornings and prepared classes in the afternoons and evenings. I tried giving the seminarians the same standard as in seminaries anywhere in the world. Bishop constantly warned me not to be too demanding, in case the seminarians could not understand the material and go crazy in the attempt.

One of our seminarians was Joseph, who we had to send home to Yule Island, as he seemed more interested in distilling alcohol than becoming a priest. Later, I was told that Joseph called me 'Hitler'. I think he found me too strict. Dr Furst gave us all some medicine, of which we were supposed to follow up with another dose, but Joseph wouldn't be in it, accusing Dr Furst of trying to poison him.

Another seminarian named Benjamin, the youngest of the seminarians, loved singing. One day when I walked into the classroom, Benjamin was directing a choir. I think he also found the study too difficult and could not focus. I soon realised we had to send him back to Port Moresby. He was accompanied by a Marist teaching brother, who told me later that Benjamin 'came good' in the end. This reminded me of when Bishop cautioned me about not making the course too difficult.

The seminarians were eating a lot of tinned food, so I suggested that when they didn't have class or had a free afternoon, they should make a vegetable garden, and plant bananas, sweet potatoes, and whatever else they liked to eat. I employed some boys to help them build a garden.

One of the workers, a Carteret Islander, had no idea about growing sweet potatoes and I got a bit frustrated with him, until a *wantok* explained that coming from a coral atoll, the man's diet was mainly fish. His atoll grew only coconuts and breadfruit trees.

I noticed the seminarians looked for dried coconut (copra), so I asked the bishop to bring some from the mission plantations whenever he visited.

One morning I woke to find the ground covered in grasshoppers. They stayed for two days. I don't know where they came from or where they went; I had never seen it before or since.

The burden of running the seminary by myself was too much, so I asked Bishop to find me another priest to assist. He tried Australia, New

Peace time

Zealand, and America, but no luck. Fr Cyr, the Marist Superior General, came to Bishop's aid by sending us Fr Leo Lemay, who had been teaching in the Boston seminary. Leo had long been wanting to join the missions.

Leo Lemay's arrival meant we could divide our workload, making it easier for me. Leo loved cakes and ice cream, and we had an army refrigerator from the Americans. So after finding some ice cream powder, we started making ice cream and baking cakes.

I should say something about ice. Bougainvilleans had never seen ice before, and when they first held a block of ice in their palm, they described it as *paia*!—fire! I guess the cold ice felt like it was burning.

On Ash Wednesday, I gave Leo a big juicy steak. He couldn't believe it. 'Ash Wednesday is a day of abstinence!' he protested. 'Not in New Guinea,' I replied, as meat was such a rare thing in the islands.

One day I felt a dreadful toothache and tried to kill the pain without result. There was no mission ship to take me to a doctor but Sr Hortense, who was not a dentist, gave me a pain-killing injection. George Lepping offered to pull the tooth, so with Leo Lemay advising, George pulled the tooth. When the injection wore off, the pain returned. He pulled the wrong tooth. Eventually, I was able to get to Turiboiru where Dr Furst took out four teeth.

§

Torokina had two airstrips, a long one for bombers, and one near the beach for everything else. Qantas flew from Sydney to Rabaul, and on to Honiara in the Solomon Islands, sometimes landing at Torokina on the way.

One time, a Qantas plane had engine trouble and could not take off from Torokina. One passenger gave the captain a hard time, saying: 'if you don't continue on to Rabaul, I will miss my connection to London.'

The pilot responded, 'Sir, I have but one life, and I am not planning on losing it just yet.' The following day an aircraft arrived from Rabaul with a mechanic. The other passengers were not pleased with the behavior of their London- bound companion.

§

I can't remember the year or month that polio came to Bougainville, but the government locked down parts of the region from Buin to Torokina. Fr Cyr, the world leader of Marists, and his deputy, Franz Wieschemeyer, came to visit, bringing a picture of Our Lady of Fatima with them. On the trip out from Germany to Buka, Fr Wieschemeyer taught himself English from zero to speaking fluently. Unbelievable!

Because of the epidemic, they could not disembark and returned to Buka, but they visited all the parishes from Buka down the east coast as far as Kieta. Later we met them at Mamaregu, once a mission station, and where the bishop offered the first sacraments to the Bougainvillean seminarians preparing for ordination.

§

The 50th Anniversary of Christianity coming to Bougainville occurred while I was at the seminary in Torokina. Bishop Wade invited Bishop Scharmack from Rabaul, Bishops Pelhans, and Bernaden, from New Guinea, Bishop Sorin from Yule Island, and Bishop Aubin from Honiara.

The two bishops from New Guinea tried to anchor off Patupatuai, but the sea was so rough they went to Moisurui, sheltering on the leeward side of sunken Japanese and American warships.

They tried driving an old car to Turiboiru but it broke down, forcing them to walk with copra bags over their heads to protect them from the rain.

The next day at Turiboiru, we planned a large outdoor Mass, but the rain was unrelenting so everyone crammed into the church.

Peace time

Bishop Scharmack arrived a couple of days later in his big ship St Paul, in the company of four of our small ships and many people from Buin; we all then travelled to Faisi in the Shortlands. The Shortlands were under British control at the time, but customs and health officers allowed us to enter. The weather was fine and the seas calm. Faisi was the starting point for the Bougainville mission but it is looked after by the Dominicans now.

The next day we held Mass on a mountaintop, as 50 seagulls circled the altar. It was as if they wanted to join the celebration of God's goodness. Fr Brosnahan, a New Zealand Marist, invited us to Choiseul for a big *singsing*.

When we returned to Buin, the health officers insisted on checking everyone on the boats. What a pain in the neck!

Mgr Clariziaro, the *nuncio* from Sydney, toured the Pacific, checking on the standards of the seminaries. He closed some because they had no capacity for teaching Latin, English, or French. The medium of instruction was in the local language, but the nuncio exclaimed: 'How are they ever going to read the Pope's instructions!'

When he came to Torokina I took him straight to our classroom, where he said, 'You ask the questions and I will listen.' I asked Peter Tatamas: 'How old does a priest have to be before he can hear womens' confessions?' Peter responded, 'In Italy it is 35.' Then Clarizio interjected: 'What's wrong with Italian women?' Peter rejoined: 'I don't know; I have never been there.' Clariziaro soon realized our seminarians were fluent in English, and he could question them himself. He did not close the seminary.

§

When the long holidays came, my plan was to visit the outlying islands with the seminarians, so I asked Dick O'Sullivan for the use of a ship. The morning we were due to leave, a sister showed up with an orphan in her arms. Sister wanted to take the orphan to Monoitu where she was stationed. I grumbled about the change of plans, when Sister quietly suggested, 'Father, if you had your breakfast you would not speak like that.' After that I shut my mouth.

As we drew close to Monoitu, I suggested a place where she and the child could go ashore, but the captain disagreed, saying it would be too far for Sister to walk to Monoitu. He knew of a better place further along; after that I shut my mouth again.

We slept the night at Patupatuai, travelling north the next day to Kieta where Charles Seiller welcomed us. The ship returned to Torokina, while we left for Tunuru the following morning to visit Adam Müller. We stayed at Tunuru for a week, while the seminarians helped Adam build his house.

We then went on to Manetai where the French priest Albert Binois was based. The bishop said we should not stay long with him and we were there but one night. On the evening of our arrival, Fr Binois said he would find some men to show us the way up to some mountain villages in the morning. This was our route to Torokina

We set out walking to Torokina thinking we would reach there by nightfall, as it was a fine day. We crossed rivers and climbed mountains. It was tough going, but villagers welcomed us with kaikai before we said Mass in their small chapels. Not long before dark, I knew I couldn't walk much further, so I sent a seminarian ahead with someone who knew the way, to let the Torokina station know we were coming.

Two men took off very quickly, while the rest of the seminarians and I followed slowly behind. After a while we walked into a giant spider's web stretched across the path. I knew this could not be the path followed by the first two; somewhere we had taken a different track. We were lost and without food. The seminarians built a shelter with wild banana leaves and we tried to sleep.

In the morning, from a long way off we heard voices and dogs. Retracing our steps we came to where we ran into the spider's web—it was gone. The sound of voices told us a search party was looking for us. They had slept beside a river with a thermal spring. Camping near hot water meant

Peace time

they enjoyed a warm night. People called this river 'Dirty Water' because it was milky with volcanic ash from Mt Bagana. We were exhausted but continued over the mountains to the seminary in Torokina.

Ordinations

Towards the end of 1953 Alois Tamuka was ordained at Turibouru. People from all over Buin attended; there was a huge crowd. Peter Tatamas was ordained in an outdoor ceremony at Hahela on Buka, another occasion that drew people from everywhere. Peter was appointed as my curate at Turiboiru, and Alois became curate to Willy Wöeste at Tunuru.

Bishop Sorin sent us an album of beautiful photos of Julian being ordained on Yule Island. Bishop Scharmach invited me to Rabaul for the ordinations of Herman To Paivu and George Bata. Herman was ordained in the large church at Vunapope. Bishop Scharmach hired a professional photographer to cover the event. He was a good man, but he forgot to remove the cover of his camera lens. George Bata was ordained at Vuvu in an outdoor ceremony by the retired bishop of Rabaul, Bishop Vesters. This time there were thousands of photos.

Herman To Paivu didn't start school until he was ten, so he would have been in his 20s by the time he finished high school. Then came the war, and then the seminary at Torokina. One day Herman came to me, feeling very despondent:,'I am getting old; I may die before I become a priest.' I explained that when I was teaching at Toongabbie, there were several Australians in the seminary as old as he. This seemed to encourage him: 'If they can do it so can I,' he thought. Herman said his first Mass to a full church in his home village of Paparatawava. The people were singing and all was ready to start, when Herman dissolved in a flood of tears. I calmed him down and everything proceeded well after that.

Herman's parents had died, but he came from a large family, so the blessings after Mass took a long time. At lunch he explained, 'When I was born, my parents brought me to this church. It is where I made my first confession and took my first communion and confirmation. When I entered the church I was overcome with memories and emotion.'

Herman and George were later made auxiliary bishops of Rabaul. Eventually, Herman was appointed Archbishop of Port Moresby. He returned to Bougainville on a sentimental visit, calling into all the places he spent time at as a young man, including Torokina. He came to Kieta and gave a retreat for the black priests and brothers. On Herman's return to Rabaul, he was found dead in his bed the following morning.

There was a vibrant Order of black nuns which included several girls from Torokina. With the help from some young men from Kuraio, Fr Roland Dionne took over the old seminary buildings at Torokina, and started the Brothers of St Joseph. After the ordinations, I was ready for a holiday—my first in 17 years.

First holiday

Bishop Wade and I left Torokina in 1954 by ship, sleeping overnight at Tearouki, our first stop. The next morning I returned to the ship, followed by the bishop, when he asked, 'Can you do me a favour?'

'Yes,' I replied.

'Give the Marist teaching brothers their retreat at Tsiroge. You start tomorrow.'

'But I have had no time to prepare!' I protested.

'You are a man of prayer, you will cope,' the bishop quipped. The lesson is, never agree to a favour without knowing all the details.

Leo Lemay, Kirk Clemens, and I, took the short boat trip from Tsiroge to Soraken on the Malaita as part of our journey to Sydney. Our first stop was Honiara where Bishop Aubin made us welcome. In the 17 years since I first visited Honiara I found many changes: Henderson airport was built, following the large American presence during the war.

We stayed in Honiara two or three days, but not before a brother asked Kirk Clemens if he could take a suitcase full of ammunition to another

Peace time

brother in Sydney. Kirk couldn't believe his ears, but Claud Palmer assured us the brother was joking.

After leaving port, we realised we had no hosts for Mass, so Kirk went down to the galley to make some, but they turned out more like pancakes. I tried, and they were good enough for Mass.

After about a week, we arrived in Sydney, but had to wait on board as it was a public holiday. I said to Kirk, 'I think we should look in that suitcase. We don't want any problems with Customs.' On opening the case, we discovered it was full of bullets. I threw them into the sea. Customs checked all our luggage. Fortunately, the ammunition was now on the ocean floor. Another lesson—never agree to carry someone else's luggage from one country to another.

We were met by Fr Jim McConville and Br Thomas who took us to Hunters Hill. I met Johannes Dieter, a German missionary, from Samoa who was later made bishop of Samoa. I also met Joe Schlieker on his way back to the Islands after holidaying in Germany. In the street one day, I saw Fr Herman Luecken. Bishop Wade asked Fr To Paivu to spend time in Australia to brush up on his English, but we did not get a chance to talk.

The *Viminale* 2 was the ship that brought me to Australia 17 years previously, and it was the same ship that took me back to Italy, along with a New Zealand priest, and Br Leonard Sydenham. Two days out from Sydney, the New Zealand priest told me one of the crew was selling exclusive rights to deck chairs for ten shillings each. 'It will have your name on it until we reached Naples,' he promised. The next morning the captain put up a notice, 'Deck chairs are for the use of ALL passengers.' I didn't get my money back.

At Bombay we picked up an Indian crew member from another ship who had been ill. He came to the passengers' dining room but some of the Australian passengers objected. A ship's officer said: 'You are a Muslim, you should not be eating this food.' He tried to assure the officer that he was a Christian. He was befriended by a black American woman who invited him to the evening dance, but when she tried to bring him into the dining room, the same protesting Australians walked out.

After a few weeks of calm sailing we arrived in Naples, where we were met by two German seminarians and taken by train to Rome. In Rome, I met Fr Franz Wiescheimeyer again, and I also got to see the Pope. After a few days in Rome, I travelled to München and eventually, just before midnight I arrived at Fürstenzell, where all the priests and brothers were waiting for me. I left Passau, changing trains at Cologne.

While I was waiting, a woman approached me. She was the mother of my sister's husband. When I reached Münster, my sister and her family were waiting. They joined me on the journey to our hometown of Osnabrück. It was April 1954 when we reached Osnabrück. My father, a local priest, and old friends, were waiting with a bus to take us to my home where my mother was waiting. I was so happy. I thought I would never see my family again, as my brother was killed in Latvia, Russia. His widow Angela was looking after my parents.

We had a solemn high Mass on Easter Sunday and I was the main celebrant. The curate, Hemesath, acted as sub-deacon, while the parish priest, Friesmann, acted as a deacon. Later the school students reported, 'We thought the three wise men had returned with the black man in the middle.' After 17 years in the tropics my skin had darkened. I then took my parents to visit the Marist houses in Meppen and Absean.

To raise money for the mission, I told stories of sleeping in a village. My mother was so sorry for me she brought me an air mattress which became very useful. I managed to keep it for many years. Germany had changed in 17 years. Many of my old friends had died or migrated out. I could not wait for the holiday to end to return to my beloved Bougainville.

9 Return to Bougainville
Kam bek long holide na tenpela krismas long Turiboiru

In December 1954, I took a job as chaplain to 1,480 Germans emigrating to Australia, on the Dutch ship Johan van Oldenbarnevelt. The Lutheran passengers had their own chaplain. I joined the ship at Bremerhaven and was given a private cabin.

Br Pius wanted to travel with me but as he had served in the German army, the Australian government had not yet cleared him of Nazi connections or war crimes, so he followed a few months later. My nephew Friedel, Angela's son, also wanted to come out to Australia, but my father said it was best he got a useful qualification first. The doctor gave my mother an injection to help her come to the train station to say goodbye. She wrote later saying she did not realise it would be goodbye forever. I never saw my parents again.

On board was a young girl from the town of Riesenbeck in Germany. Her parents asked me to keep an eye on her. At four thirty p.m. family and friends had to leave the ship, and at 5 pm the band played '*Nun ade, du mein lieb Heimatland*'—'Farewell, my dear homeland'. Plenty of tears flowed.

The following day an officer showed me to a salon where we could celebrate Mass. They provided everything we needed including holy oils—a change from the Australian and Italian ships which provided nothing. Officers and crew attended Mass with the passengers and everyone sang Gregorian chants. The Lutherans had their salon, but their pastor preferred to use ours, so their service followed.

When The Garamuts Beat

The ship was spotlessly clean, and from the captain down to economy class passengers, everyone ate the same food. Of course some passengers complained, but it was probably better than what they ate at home. The ship had its own currency but operated on credit, with everyone settling their accounts on arrival in Sydney. While we were on the high seas, cigarettes, alcohol, and shop goods, were cheap. They were even more cheaper for me; as chaplain I enjoyed the status of an officer. It was my most enjoyable boat trip.

Many of the young women on the voyage were emigrating to Australia to marry boyfriends, but fell in love with someone else on the ship. They would come to me for advice but I didn't know what to say. Regarding the girl from Riesenbeck, I wrote to Fr Herbert who found her a job in a hospital, so by the time she arrived she had both a job and accommodation lined up.

If any crew member deserted, the captain was liable for a hefty fine, so as the ship was entering Melbourne, he tried reverse psychology by putting up a notice in the dining room, 'Anyone wishing to desert, don't forget to pick up your sandwiches.' Everyone returned from shore leave, but in Freemantle some crew did not.

Most of the emigrants could not speak English despite having lessons on the ship, and by the time we reached Freemantle they still could not understand or speak English, so I acted as interpreter when they went through customs.

I was exploring Perth when I met some women from the ship. They were refused service in the public bar of a hotel. I explained that in Australia women had to be waited on in a private parlour. We found a parlour but there was a further problem: one woman was accompanied by her 15-year-old daughter. The waitress explained that the hotel would be in serious trouble with the police if the child was found there, so the mother and daughter had to leave. Australia has changed its laws since then.

One group went into a shop but didn't know how to ask for the items they wanted, but when the woman behind the counter heard them talking, she said, 'I understand German. Please speak in German.' If German emigrants did not have a sponsor, they were sent to a camp to learn English before they could find work.

Between Melbourne and Sydney we experienced huge seas, and during Mass I was thrown from one side of the saloon to the other. Most of the passengers were seasick and stayed in bed. You needed two hands to hold onto your food or drink. Fortunately, the bad weather only lasted a day or two. By the time we reached Sydney, the ship was almost empty. It then sailed to Indonesia with Dutch nationals returning from Holland.

I was scheduled to attend a six-month spirituality course in Sydney called the Second Novitiate, led by Fr Oreves from Fiji, but I arrived six weeks late. Leo Lemay, now the provincial, ordered that I, and another latecomer, make up the six weeks after the course finished. We cleaned house and wasted time until our six weeks were up, before I returned to my work in Bougainville with a young Australian priest, Vince Mills.

The day before our departure, Vince and I were crossing a street when I was hit by a car. I was taken to a hospital, but there was no serious damage so we boarded the MV *Malaita* for Bougainville as planned. Vince did not realise guns had to be handed in when boarding the ship, and that passengers could reclaim their firearms at disembarkation. The captain was very angry with Vince when he found out he had a gun in his luggage.

Our first stop was Espiritu Santo in what was then the New Hebrides (now Vanuatu). We went looking for the local priest when I noticed that local women were all wearing bras. The custom in Bougainville was for women to go topless, except for when Sr Ignace told the Buin women that it was a sin to come topless when attending Mass. Some little girls who came to Mass were upset because they had forgotten their blouses. I explained things a little better.

We found the mission station and visited a classroom, but because we were not wearing cassocks, it had to be explained that we were priests. The priest had an old Jeep, but his driving was so bad I offered to drive for him. I heard later he had an accident and almost killed himself. He did not invite us to stay the night so we walked back to the ship. The next day we returned to the mission where a young priest was very kind to us.

At the end of the war, the American army could not take all its equipment back to the U.S. The French did not want to buy it so they dumped it in the sea. This is how that area came to be called 'Million Dollar Point.' We wanted to find the place and knocked on the door of a house asking for directions, but the women inside refused to speak to us.

We eventually found the place. The water was so clear we could see Jeeps, cars, and all kinds of war equipment, on the sea floor. When we returned to the station, the young priest who was with us told the old priest about the women who refused to speak to us. The old priest asked, 'Were you wearing cassocks?'

'No,' we said.

'Well that is why they would not talk to you,' the priest explained.

The *Malaita* stayed two days at 'Santo before sailing to Port Vila. Once docked, Vince and I went looking for Marist priests. The parish priest made us welcome, but he could not believe we were priests because we were not wearing cassocks. I suggested: 'Ask Bishop Julliard—he is a friend of mine.' The next day we were invited to inspect a plantation that the bishop was thinking of buying. The young French priest took off his cassock, but put it back on again when he returned to the mission at Montmatre.

When Leo Lemay did provincial visitations, he did not wear a cassock, so the young French priest followed his example. The Vanuatu approach was to bring the people in close to the mission, whereas the Bougainville approach was for priests to go out to people in their villages.

After leaving Port Vila our next stop was Kieta, where we were welcomed back by Fr Paul Caffiaux. The school children had caught a crocodile, and being new, Vince wanted to see it. I wanted to sleep the night in the priests' house, but a child turned up with a piece of 'croc' meat. I was not so keen on the idea of *pukpuk* for dinner, so I found an excuse to return to the *Malaita*.

After Kieta, we called at Numa Numa, a large plantation further north where several Europeans visited the ship. One of the sailors caught the same shark three times; the shark somehow unhooked itself each time he landed it. The next stop was to be Soraken on the west coast, but because the currents through Buka Passage are so treacherous, we travelled right around Buka Island to reach it. The priests from Tsiroge came to pick us up, and so ended our journey.

While I was in Sydney, Bishop Wade gave me a 'flash' Hawaiian shirt. I think he forgot that it was he who gave it to me, because when he saw it, he told me not to wear it around the place. I ended up giving it to one of his staff.

§

Frs Pierre Schank and Leon Dowden travelled from Turiboiru to Tsiroge for a retreat, so Bishop Wade sent me down to Turiboiru, but no one there knew I was coming. I found a bed and slept the night, and the next day Sr Sevarina found me a room. When Pierre and Leon returned, they told me they had to leave immediately for the parishes—Pierre Schank to Tunuru, and Leon Dowden to Faisi, in the Shortlands. However, Fr Schank did not stay long at Tunuru, as he was sent to Sydney to take charge of the Second Novitiates. He was later killed when he was hit by a tram.

Fr Peter Tatamas was sent to assist me at Turiboiru. Fr Alois Tamuka went to Tunuru to assist Fr Willy Wöeste. Alois and I wanted to visit Pisinau, but I was exhausted when I reached Bolcoku. Alois went ahead and I followed the next day. Alois and Willy had gone on to Deomori, but I collapsed on the bed at Pisinau, where the two priests found me sound asleep when they returned.

When The Garamuts Beat

10 Turiboiru mission

Ten years at Turiboiru from February 1955

Turuboiru is a large parish next to Piano and Muguai. It stretches from the coast up into the mountains. In front of the priest's house was a disused airstrip built by the Japanese during the war. The only aircraft servicing the area was a seaplane that sometimes landed in Tonelei harbour. To reach it, passengers travelled by small boat from Kangu near Buin. People often made the journey only to find the seaplane hadn't turned up, so they turned around and motored back to Kangu.

The parish had a bull and some cows, so we built a sturdy fence to keep them in, feeding them on rice husks and tapioca leaves that grew near the airstrip. The cows loved it and became very easy to handle. They waited by the fence for the school children returning from their gardens, hoping they would feed them. We had plenty of fresh milk and butter.

I did not own a gun, so I asked the kiap to send a policeman with a shotgun if we ever wanted fresh meat. One time a policeman turned up, but he didn't know how to use the gun. Fortunately, a man at the station brought his gun, and shot the animal for me.

Mr King, a representative for the Australian government, was sent to assess whether the old war strip could be extended and widened for use. He concluded it could be done, but the mission hospital, church, and part of our coconut plantation, had to go. There was no hotel in Buin or accommodation anywhere for Mr King, so he stayed with us as we negotiated our compensation.

The heart of a coconut tree is white, soft, and delicious, and the only way you can get to it is by chopping the palm down and cutting it out, which is why it is called 'Millionaire's Salad'. Several trees growing alongside the 'strip had to come down, and one night Sr Wendelina surprised us with a dish of the famous salad. Mr King and I feasted like millionaires.

When the airstrip was finished, a DC-3 flew from Australia to Port Moresby, then to Rabaul, Buka, finally landing at Turiboiru. The kiap asked if I would do the weather reports. A police runner would leave Buin at daybreak, run to Turiboiru to pick up my report, and run back to Buin. The kiap would then radio my weather report through to Rabaul. The trouble was the weather on Bougainville changed very quickly, so by the time a plane landed the weather might be completely different.

Fr Bob Fahey was staying with me one time, and he wanted to return to Buka on the plane, but it was raining heavily. The airstrip flooded and I thought there was no way the plane would come, but then we heard the noise of a plane, and sure enough it landed. Water lay everywhere and I asked the pilot: 'How come you flew through this rain?' He said he had a plane load of passengers and had to land. With Bob Fahey on board, the airstrip was still covered in water as he took off.

Some aircrew were very good to us. They asked us for hot water for the crew and passengers, and sometimes they brought us goods from Australia such as fresh meat.

I had an old Jeep, and Katsia was my driver. This was useful if I, or the sisters, wanted to go to Patupatuai.

When I came to Turiboiru, the hospital was falling down. I got men from the village to level a building site. I filled in numerous forms and eventually got a grant from Miserior in Germany. Katsia and his team of builders soon had us a new *haus sik*.

Turiboiru mission

Sr Sevarina was a skillful midwife. Sr Wendelina, who was fluent in Telei, joined her, assisted by local sisters. Katsia and Kabui built a new house for the sisters. Katsia could build houses and repair cars, but he had never been to school. I asked him where he got his knowledge; he said he observed what other tradesmen did and copied them.

The schooling custom for children was to attend a small school in the village for the first two years, then the last four years of primary school at a large parish school, but not every village had a school. I called a meeting with all the luluais and landowners and explained that if their children did not receive a good education, people from the PNG mainland would come in and take the jobs that might otherwise go to their children. Eventually, I approached the German government for financial assistance to build some village schools.

When the funding came through I approached the chiefs again. I would supply a concrete floor and corrugated iron roof for their school if they supplied the land, labour, and other required building materials. I then drew up written contracts with ol papa bilong graun so that no one could reclaim the land back once the buildings were finished. Once the luluais i.e. chiefs were of wanbel —all agreed, I prepared agreements for them to sign. I knew then we would have no further issues.

Sometimes, *lapuns* came to me asking to be taught to read and write. Why? I wondered. When they went to Tong Lep's store at Patupatuai, they saw white people buying goods with paper (cheques), not real money, and they wanted to do the same. For this reason, I always paid for goods with cash.

§

During the war, I contracted amoebic dysentery, which I suffered from for years. Bishop Wade visited me one day, I forget the year, but he was shocked at my condition and said, 'After Easter, you are coming with me to Vunapope to the hospital.'

When The Garamuts Beat

We travelled by mission ship calling first to Nissan, a small island part of Bougainville diocese, where Fr Henry Fluet met us. Nissan was not bombed by the Americans nor by the Australians during the war. The bishop wanted to spend one night at a really beautiful spot, so we didn't leave straight away. The ship's cook prepared a wonderful meal of fish caught that day.

The next morning we left for Vunapope, where we were met by the elderly missionary, Fr Paul Montauban, and two recent arrivals, the Australians, Frs Walter Fingleton, and Tom L'Estrange.

Wally Fingleton was appointed to Faisi in the Solomons, and Tom L'Estrange was to be the business manager at Tsiroge. The bishop was sending Paul Montauban to Nissan to help Henry Fluet, who was on his own. I found a very good doctor at Vunapope who diagnosed my illness and gave me some injections and medication. His treatment got me well again in no time.

Another time I was very sick, George Lepping sent his old car with a mattress in the back to bring me to Patupatuai. Once there, the St Joseph sisters took me to Sr Mary Leo, an American doctor based at Tearouki. She soon brought me back to health.

I received a letter from my father saying my mother was very ill and may well have died by the time his letter reached me. Some time later, Henry Fluet brought me another letter, telling me my father had died. He fell sick on the morning he was taken to hospital and died that evening.

§

Each year, delegates from the United Nations Organization came to check on people's welfare. One Russian asked me about the number of girls in school. Sr Foott, an Australian, was investigating the right to drink alcohol. Some people were drinking poisonous home brew and going blind as a result. Once Papua New Guineans were allowed to drink beer, and later spirits, there was a lot of drunkenness. The attitude was—drink until there was none left.

Turiboiru mission

An Australian government officer came around checking for war damages with a view to compensation, but not everyone told the truth. Some reported big losses of pigs, coconut trees, cats, and shell money, even when they didn't have any. The local *kiap*, Tony Redwood, was the nephew of Archbishop Redwood, of Wellington in New Zealand. The archbishop was an accomplished violinist who took his instrument all over the world. He lived into his 90s.

§

I organized the children to help me plant up a coffee and cocoa plantation. We worked on Saturdays for which I paid them. After four years the coffee trees bore fruit like cherries. They had three skins to be removed before roasting. Wally Fingleton, a great tea drinker, loved our Turiboiru coffee. The cocoa was not as hardy as the coffee trees. If cocoa seedlings are not planted in good soil, they wither and die. Coco pods, which can have up to 40 beans inside, grow directly on the tree trunks.

Cocoa beans are fermented in a series of wooden boxes. They spend two days in the first box where they get quite hot. Then they are shovelled into a second box for another two days and so on until the fermentation process is complete. The beans are then dried. I didn't have a dryer, so I sold our wet bean to a man who did. He then sold his dry beans all over the world.

It is interesting to note that fermentation boxes must have no metal nails or bolts, because metal somehow contaminates the cocoa beans. I also planted orange and mandarin trees, but in the tropics the fruit remains green even when ripe.

The chief from Okoiragi, whose name I have forgotten, put on a big feast for his successor, Paul Nerau. They built a tower stacked with food and a long table with lots of shell money, Australian money, and pig meat. The chief climbed the tower and made a long speech, praising his successor. Paul finished his primary schooling at Turiboiru, before going to high school at

Rigu near Kieta. He went to the University of PNG in Port Moresby and graduated with a law degree.

At Kukumaru village, there lived an old man called Moatsi, who had a swollen stomach. Every day he came to the hospital and talked to Sr Sevarina. He was still a pagan but also a true believer. Sr would say: 'Moatsi, isn't it about time you were baptised?'

'When I feel death approaching, I will let Father know,' he would reply. One day Moatsi called for me and I baptised him, but later on he said he felt much better. Some women in the village chimed in: 'Moatsi, you told Father you were dying, and now you say you feel better. You should be a man of your word and die.' The next morning I set out to visit Moatsi, and on the way, I heard the *garamut*s announcing Moatsi's death. I was so angry with those stupid women I refused to attend his funeral feast.

Motorbikes

We were all invited to a catechist graduation ceremony at Patupatuai. I set off on my motorbike but halfway there, I crashed, breaking my nose and glasses. Every time I stood up, blood poured out of my nose. I was in serious trouble as very few people used that track. God must have sent Martin Baubake, as he found me and reported back to Sr Sevarina, who came in a vehicle and took me home.

Bob Fahey who was at Monoitu, came to visit me one day. We went double on my motorbike to Tabago to visit Henry Fluet. During our visit the rain started and the rivers flooded. Bob did not want to stay the night, so some young strong men on bicycles travelled with us to help us across the rivers. We carried the motorbike across all the rivers except the last one. It was too deep and running too fast, so we left it and crossed the swollen river by walking over a fallen log. We continued walking the rest of the way home, returning the next day for the motorbike.

Good Friday 1958, Henry Fluet who was still at Tabago, had an accident on his motorbike, but he still struggled through the Easter ceremonies. Sr Sevarina was given a motor scooter by an Australian friend and she tried it out around the station. After Easter, I said to her, 'Let's go together to visit Henry Fluet. I can help you across the rivers.' She said she was not feeling well so I went alone intending to stay the night, when I heard the news that Sr Sevarina had an accident on her scooter. She ruptured her spleen and died. The doctor from Kangu came but he couldn't save her.

I sent a telegram to the bishop. He thought it was a mistake, 'Surely it was old Sr Ignace, not young Sr Sevarina?' The sisters from near and far came, along with great crowds of people. Everyone loved Sr Sevarina.

Mr Wearne, the kiap, was helpful when she died, using his vehicle to pick up sisters from other parishes. The fact that his wife was a nurse and a close friend of Sr Sevarina may have had something to do with his generosity.

Wearne was obsessed with rules and regulations, however. Fr Nick Kutlas received a food parcel from his parents in America and *kiap* George Wearne confiscated it because the cake contained animal fat, even wanting ten shillings for duty on the sweets. Nick told him to eat them himself.

On my 50th birthday in June 1959, I flew to Kieta to celebrate with my old friend and compatriot from Osnabrück, Xaverius Koch. It rained all the time I was there.

On the flight back, we flew over the Laluai River which was in flood and inundating the surrounding jungle. I went on my motorbike to Kangu, but there was still water everywhere, so I pushed the bike to Kunka's place at Patupatuai, and rode home the next day.

§

Bishop Wade retired in 1959, and there was much talk about who the new bishop might be. Rome took its time making a decision, and it was some months before we received any news.

Eventually, word came through that the newly appointed bishop was to be Leo Lemay. Bishop Wade was a man of the people. He would meet and greet everyone he met. If the crowds were large and he had to leave, he would ask them all to kneel so he could bless them.

Bishop Lemay did not have that gift. On his first visit to Turiboiru, the sisters prepared the school children for singing and dancing to entertain the bishop, but when he arrived, he said, 'Let's go inside and drink coffee,' leaving the children and assembled crowd very disappointed.

I flew to Kieta for business one time, but when I was due to return, the captain of the St Joseph fell sick, so I was told to captain the ship. On leaving Kieta the sea was calm, but as we arrived at Patupatuai it got very rough.

There was no wharf at Patupatuai, so we always had to climb down into a dingy and row ashore. The crew wanted to assist the now very old Sr Ignace down the ladder, but she would have none of it. Then bang! Down she went like a bag of cement into the bottom of the boat. Thank goodness she didn't fall into the sea.

8

Near Patupatuai, there was a government hospital made from bush materials. They had a doctor and two nurses, one male and one female. During the war, many women died in childbirth, so the government bribed them to come to hospital by giving away free dresses. If a mother had twins they gave her money to buy milk powder. For some reason, one day the government changed its tune, becoming big advocates of vasectomies, contraceptive pills, and injections.

Fr Emery de Klerk was conducting a catechist school at Patupatuai, when he found some abandoned Japanese buildings near a small river in the jungle and moved into them. Locals told him that the river was flood-prone.

Turiboiru mission

'No problem,' said Emery. 'I built a levy bank around it.' The rains came, and of course Emery was flooded out and had to return to Patupatuai.

Remember Friedel, the son of my brother who was killed on the Russian Front in Latvia? He wanted to come with me to Bougainville, but my father, Friedel's grandfather, suggested he get a qualification first. He did, after which he emigrated to Australia in September 1958. Friedel got a job at the Government Printing Office in Sydney, and saved enough money to fly up and visit me.

He travelled with Fr Franz Elixmann and Br Herbert, (later known as Fr Heinrich Kasselmann), in June 1960. Friedel stayed with me at Turiboiru for two weeks, before we travelled to Koromira for a few days, to visit Brs Xaverius and Herbert. We then decided to walk to Kieta.

The road was long and hot, and halfway there a white man and his wife came by in a Jeep and offered us a lift. We chatted away in English. When we reached Kieta, we noticed Fr Tom Hogan calling him Fritz. It turned out our Good Samaritan was Fritz Hockenbrink, a German, who worked on the Malaria Control Program. We ended up becoming good friends.

The theory behind malaria control was this: the anopheles mosquito sucks the blood of someone with malaria, and then the mosquito catches malaria. It then sucks the blood of someone else who does not have malaria. When its proboscis sinks into a healthy person, it injects them with anticoagulant saliva loaded with the malaria virus, infecting the healthy person. The mosquito fills up with blood and then lands on a wall to rest.

Fritz and his team used to spray the walls of people's houses with Dichloro-diphenyl-trichloroethane (DDT) so the little 'super spreader' (vector) died if it landed on a sprayed wall, breaking the cycle. He also sprayed areas that held water where mosquitos like to breed, such as coconut shells, banana trees, puddles, old tin cans, etc., We noticed anything that came in contact with DDT also died, e.g., cockroaches, cats, some humans. DDT is now banned.

I had to conduct a retreat for the sisters in Buka, and Friedel came with me. This meant he visited all the parishes on Buka and met all the priests—Hermann Luecken at Gagan, Franz Elixmann at Lemanmanu, and Joe Lamarre at Hanahan. He also visited Tsiroge, Tarlena, and Chabai, before we returned to Turiboiru. Friedel also accompanied me when I made my parish rounds of the villages.

He was lucky to witness a Corpus Christi procession with the little black angels strewing flower petals before the Blessed Sacrament, and no rain to spoil things.

On Wednesday, 29 June 1960, I was 25 years a priest, and Joe Schlieker, Franz Elixmann, Herman Luecken, other priests and sisters, and many villagers, came to celebrate with me. It was a happy day. Mid-August however, Friedel returned to Australia, and I missed him greatly.

Leaving Turiboiru

The Marists brought in a new law: missionaries were allowed home leave once every ten years. I had spent ten hard but happy years at Turiboiru, and now Fr Pat Mallinson was to replace me.

People brought me gifts of all kinds of food such as taro and pork. The Luguai villagers brought me a turtle. I had eaten turtle meat and enjoyed it, but that was before I realised that turtles kept moving long after they were killed. Everyone sang and danced all night, and when the plane arrived the next morning, they danced me to the plane. Martin Baubake asked me to bless everyone before I left.

I went first to Sydney and stayed some days with Friedel. After some difficulty finding the departure gate for Dusseldorf, I landed in Frankfurt and waited an hour because of engine trouble.

My sister-in-law, Angela, and some friends, were waiting for me at Dusseldorf. When I didn't arrive at the expected time, they thought I wasn't coming and were on the point of going home. I realised the importance of giving people a flight number if they are coming to the airport, as it makes it much easier to find out what's happening.

Angela and I boarded a train for Osnabrück. At Recklinghausen, a friend wanted to take me to their place, but I really wanted to get home. My sister and her family had boarded our train at Münster, searching until they found me, so we could all travel together to Osnabrück. I stayed with Angela, and Ingrid her daughter, at Steinbeck. The local priest, August Brüser, was always kind to me.

Germany had changed; there was more money about and many new houses. I received news that two of my seminarians, Peter Tatamas and Alois Tamuka, had arrived in Koln, so I had to meet them. The American Cardinal Cushing, was a good friend of Bishop Wade, and he paid for the newly ordained Bougainvillean priests to have a world trip, visiting America, France, and Germany.

At Meppen, I stayed with my brother-in-law, Fritz Stuer, in Recklenghausen, while the Marists looked after the Bougainvillean priests. The Marist Superior told me to buy them new shoes and clothes.

Fr Hanneken took Peter to one parish, while I took Alois to Steinbeck parish to talk with people. Peter then joined us at Steinbeck along with Ingrid and Willi and their children, Petra and Wilfrid. Petra was calm, but Wilfrid was terrified of the black priests, hiding until we left for Fürstenzell.

When they were seminarians, I told them how German people ploughed fields using oxen, and I wanted to show them an example, but when we got to Bavaria, everyone was using tractors.

I put Peter and Alois on a plane at München for Rome, and was to join them later. While we were in Rome, Bishop Lemay told me he intended to appoint me to Piano mission station, Alois would go to Tsiroge and Peter to Torokina. We travelled together from Rome to Beirut, where we slept in a hotel before continuing to Jerusalem. Alois was used to the green tropical jungle, and couldn't understand why Jerusalem was so dry and rocky and without grass.

When The Garamuts Beat

When we arrived at our accommodation, a swarm of beggars pestered us. I asked the doorman to get rid of them. Later I asked the doorman to recommend a taxi to Bethlehem, and then he started pestering me for money. At that time Jerusalem was full of goats eating bits of paper along the road.

While we were in Jerusalem, Alois, Peter, and I, discussed where we hoped to go. Peter preferred Torokina, and Alois wanted to return to Piano. I then told them what the bishop said, and there the conversation ended.

I flew to Cairo, then to Sydney, and on to Buka where I met with George Lepping. George told me Alois had sent an angry letter to Bishop Lemay, so plans had changed. Alois returned to Piano as he had wished. Peter went to Monoitu for a short time, while I went to Tabago to fill in for Wally Fingleton who was on holidays.

Tabago had three lay missionaries, a man and two women, who Wally Fingleton put in charge of the station. I would say that before he left, Wally was not aware another priest would come to replace him during his absence. So when I arrived, there was some ill-feeling between us.

Before I went to Tabago, I would hear Wally complain about the lack of land to feed the school children, which meant they carried all their food with them from the village. One day when I was riding my bicycle to Patupatuai, I noticed a man near the station planting coconuts. I asked him if the students from Tabago could plant a food garden between his trees. He said it was fine, but offered better land for a garden on the other side of the road. I was so happy to think we could start a large food garden for the school. By the time Wally returned, the students were enjoying a large productive food garden.

11 Tubiana mission

1964 to 1972

One of the female lay missionaries working at Tabago visited Kieta, and returned with the news that I was appointed to Kieta. Sometime later, I received a letter from the bishop confirming my appointment, and when Wally returned I packed my bags for Tubiana.

Fr Franz Geers was at Tubiana when I arrived, he was Fr Thomas Hogan's assistant. Tom had fallen ill: heart I think, and returned home to America. Two brothers were also at Tubiana, Xaverius Koch, and Don Bosco, who managed the mission's plantation. I had known Xaverius, my *wantok*, since our student days in Meppen.

Xaverius was building a church at Tubiana that ended up looking like St Peter's in Rome, without any mechanical help such as a crane, etc,. Many people warned him he had taken on too much, but he finished it.

When The Garamuts Beat

Included in Tubiana parish was Marai station, although it was in the mountains and a long way from Tubiana. Fr Geers took Mass there on Sundays while I remained at Tubiana.

Kieta at this time was the main centre for Bougainville, with business houses, stores, even a China Town. Kieta also had a small *haus sik*, one doctor, and one cemetery dating from the German times. The earliest headstones bore the names of Germans who died in Kieta.

The original Kieta road built by the Germans, followed the beach as far as Aropa *ples balus*. The government built a bridge near the airport across the Aropa River. Locals told them that floods would carry the bridge away if they built it where they proposed, but officials knew better. When the rains fell and the flooding started, the bridge was carried out to sea.

The airstrip at Aropa was too short for large planes, and Mr King, who stayed with me at Turiboiru while building the Buin airstrip, wanted to lengthen it. One *lapun* woman refused to give permission to allow her coconut trees to be cut down, so Mr King had to find another solution to the problem.

Leaving Tubiana heading north towards Kieta was China Town. Not far passed China Town, was a turn-off which wound up and over some hills around Kobuan Bay, to a very large cocoa and coconut plantation—Arawa.

Where the road turned off from Kieta up over the hills, there was a memorial put there by the Australians, for a paramount chief who refused to collaborate with the Japanese and give away Paul Mason's hiding place. The Japs forced all the surrounding chiefs and luluais to witness his execution, to show what would happen to them if they helped the Allies. Charles Seiller stood with Chief Barosi *taim ol Japan i katim nek bilong em*.

Every six weeks the Malaita arrived from Sydney, bringing store goods and news of the outside world, before uploading copra and cocoa grown on the plantations for export. When Bishop Wade retired to America, he raised enough money to buy the mission a ship that Bishop Lemay renamed St Thomas. Most people referred to it as Tom in recognition of Bishop Wade's efforts to buy it.

Tubiana mission

We had many visiting priests, but our house was old, and we did not have enough accommodation for outside visitors. St Thomas was big enough to sail to Rabaul and bring back building materials, so that Xaverius could build a priests' house large enough for visitors, as well as a large storehouse.

After completing these buildings, Xaverius built eight classrooms for Tubiana's expanding primary school. Students went home on Fridays, returning on Sundays after church with a week's supply of food. I wanted to clad the new priests' house in aluminum, so I wrote to Friedel to arrange for some to be sent up from Sydney. The firm somehow got my order mixed up with another order from New Guinea, so we had to ask kiap William (Bill) Thomas Brown, to sort things out.

The innovation was a success. And the new priests' house was wonderful. I had a bedroom and a separate office where I could meet with people privately. To raise funds to run the house, I rented an empty classroom to a company that stored cocoa beans waiting for shipment overseas.

The brothers at Rigu stayed with us while their new house was built. When it came time to put the roof on, they asked Xaverius if they could make a very early start before sunrise. Xaverius was very sceptical but sure enough, at dawn the next day when he walked over to Rigu, he was greeted by one brother already climbing a ladder, ready to work. They were all up early and keen to start.

While we were still in the old house, we would get Xaverius to tell us stories about the old days, hiding a microphone to record them. We encouraged him to continue another night, but he would not say a word. Franz Geers, God bless him, told Xaverius what we were up to.

Tubiana station had a high school that came to be known as Rigu. It was started by three brothers who had originally started at Torokina. The brothers were killed during the war by the Japanese but nobody knows how or where. Some say they went down with the Montevideo Maru; others say the Japanese killed them in Bougainville.

When The Garamuts Beat

When I arrived, Rigu had three teaching brothers and a female Irish lay missionary teacher who liked to drink and smoke large cigars. Kieta held choir eisteddfods every year, and Reverend Taufa, the Methodist minister from Tonga, entered the Roreinang choir. They always won, until Br Julian joined the staff, and then it was Rigu's turn to win.

I was not long at Tubiana before I received a letter from Elizabeth Ntuga, who grew up at Turibioru under the watchful eye of Sr Wendelina. Elizabeth was a very good cook so I was very happy that she wanted to work at Tubiana. It wasn't long before she arrived, to be followed by the man she was 'marked' to marry, Itanu. I married them in the haus lotu at Tubiana. The Irish woman left for home, so Elizabeth and Itanu occupied her house.

Itanu milked the cows and made butter, while Elizabeth cooked and did housekeeping for the priests. She was absolutely honest, a statement I can't say about everyone I have employed. If a visiting priest had to leave early in the morning, Elizabeth sent him off with freshly laundered clothes and a packed lunch. She later went to keep house for Herman Wöeste at Tabago for many years.

During the war, Franz Geers had to run from the Russians, an experience that had a lasting effect on his mental health. He was always having accidents in the car, and the repair bills kept me poor. In the end I had to ask him not to drive the parish car.

One Sunday, Franz came back from Marai feeling quite disturbed, and he would not eat. We eventually learned there was a fight, and Franz took a badly injured man to hospital. The violence had upset him. Xaverius reassured him, 'Franz, in the old days there were fights every day. Get used to it.' Franz was called to give evidence in court, and he seemed better after that. He loved classical music, especially Handel's Alleluia. He would play it over and over from morning till night.

After about a year at Tubiana, he was appointed parish priest for Nissan Island. When Franz went to Nissan, I added Marai to my duties. I really liked the Marai people. Normally people asked for last rites only if they thought they were dying, but at Marai, for the first time in my ministry, a man who was sick but not dying, asked for an Anointing of the Sick.

§

We all have car stories we would rather forget. I loaned my Land Rover to Sr Juliana one day as she wanted to pick up some students from Asitavi. On the route, she opened up the side of the vehicle on the guard rail of a bridge. Fortunately, two German friends knew where there was a wrecked Land Rover, so we could replace the wrecked panels.

The road to Koromira that passed Aropa plantation was narrow and rough, so the government hired a surveyor to survey a new road. An old planter said that if the Germans were still in charge, the money spent on the survey would have had the road built.

I visited Fr Edmund Duffy, an Irish Marist, stationed at Koromira. He asked if I would mind giving a schoolboy a lift back to town. This was fine with me. On the journey back to Tubiana, when I tried taking a corner, my Land Rover hit a coconut tree. The student thought it best to walk the rest of the way.

I used to drive the Land Rover into Kieta to collect the mail, one day as I reached China Town, I stopped to fill up with petrol at Wong You's. The next day, driving passed Wong You's store, I noticed the fuel gauge showed empty again—*nogat* benzine. This time I watched the man operating the hand pump. He was letting the petrol run back into the holding tank before it could flow into the vehicle. They didn't charge me a second time.

§

There was a technical school in Arawa, whose headmaster was no friend of the Catholics. When I turned up to instruct the Catholic students, he stuck us in a room next to a loud generator. The students walked out and found another classroom. The headmaster did not stay long, and fortunately for us, the new man was much more helpful.

As I mentioned earlier, Tubiana primary had eight good classrooms. Marai didn't have any, nor did they have enough teachers, so students ready to enter classes six to eight, boarded at Tubiana. There were a few village schools in the parish where their upper primary students attended at Tubiana.

Two such schools were in the villages of Ankanai and Pidia. Sometimes I found teachers did not show up for work. I approached the community leaders, asking them to look for a place where we could build a combined school to cater also for both Ankanai and Pidia. After consulting with various communities, we came up with Kerei as a possible site. Most were in agreement, except for Ankanai village.

Kiap Bill Brown wanted to build a good road between Kieta and Arawa, but this meant crossing Kerei land. He made an offer to the landowners, 'If you let the government have some land for a new road, I will build you a new school at Kerei.' Everyone was in favour except for Ankanai village. They became very angry with me, but it remains a good school and is still going strong today.

§

I've talked about Pok Pok Island before, in Kieta Harbour straight across from Tubiana, silhouetted in the shape of a crocodile. The Nasio Tok Ples name for the island is Bakawari, but perhaps the name Pok Pok was well-known because of the island's shape.

I might have mentioned that Tubiana had some cattle. They were not fenced and often wandered along the beach at night. Sitting in my office one Sunday afternoon, I heard two women chatting as they walked passed my office. They were talking about some people from Pok Pok who had taken one of our cows, '*Ol Pok Pok man ol i kisim bulmakau bilong patere. Em i stap long ples bilong ol.*' I immediately went outside and caught up with the women, to confirm if what I thought they said was true. *'Tok i stret,'* they said. I went looking for Br Don Bosco, to ask him to get a canoe and investigate.

Sure enough, our cow was lying on the ground in the main village covered with roofing iron. The villagers claimed they found it on the reef, and if I wanted it back, I had to pay. Cows do not wander into the sea and swim to offshore islands.

I waited until morning and drove to Mr Brown's office to report the theft. He responded, 'First a dinghy, now a cow...' The MV *Malaita*, which was anchored in the harbour, had a dinghy tied up to the ship, but during the night some people from Pok Pok cut the rope and took it back to the island. Their story was they found the dinghy adrift and wanted a reward for returning it to the ship. Now it seems they were asking for another reward, this time for a cow.

Bill Brown sent a policeman to fetch Pok Pok's *luluai*: a man called Stima. As I drove away from Bill's office, Stima arrived. Mr Brown directed Stima to bring the cow back to the mission, but Stima turned up later at the mission and said, if I wanted the cow back I could come to Pok Pok and get it. I refused, telling him he needed to bring it back to us. They picked this particular cow as it was old and quiet to handle being half-blind. They wanted to make a *singsing*, but needed money for beer. They never forgave me for reporting them.

§

John Momis graduated from the government high school at Kangu near Buin, and was awarded a scholarship to attend university in Port Moresby. He went to Mr Clancy, Bougainville's DC at the time, telling him he wanted to go to the seminary in Madang, to which Mr Clancy said to me, 'Our loss is your gain.' Mr Clancy was a Catholic and knew the church needed quality priests.

While John was attending the seminary in Madang, he wanted to further his studies and become a priest. On one of my trips to Germany, I flew to Madang via Goroka from Port Moresby. Leaving Goroka meant flying through a small passage between two mountains. I was terrified, but the pilot was very skillful.

Fr Pat Murphy was in charge of the seminary where the Bougainville seminarians, John Momis and Leo Hannett attended. I employed John to teach religion at Rigu High School. Later, Bishop Lemay arranged for John to continue his seminary studies in Brisbane, Australia. John was ordained in 1970 at Turiboiru, and Pat Murphy was there.

§

Many years ago, there was talk of a gold nugget as big as a matchbox, found at Moroni. Before the war, Archbishop Duhig had shares in a gold mining company, but they did it all by hand and the company soon folded.

Conzinc Rio Tinto Australia (CRA) arrived in Bougainville in the 1960s, to mine for copper, silver, and gold. The United Nations Organisation was happy about this because they wanted independence for PNG, and this looked like a means to pay for it.

One day near midday, I noticed some men outside my office. I asked what they were doing, wondering if they were looking for the gold mine. 'No,' they were going to the airport to speed-test some cars. They told me one reached 200 mph.

Itanu, Elizabeth's husband, went to the movies at Kobuan to see 'The Sound of Music' one night. When he returned, he found two white men lurking around the girls' dormitory. He threw them out and took the number of their car. I reported them to the police, who explained that Queensland law applied in Bougainville. If a property is unfenced, trespass does not apply.

Tubiana mission

Two weeks later, they came again. This time, Itanu kept them talking while I phoned the police. They were arrested and locked up. Two days later, they were fined and released.

§

From 1968 to 1969, Bill Brown looked after the government and Bougainville Copper Limited (BCL) matters, and Des Ashton looked after the Nasioi people.

CRA built a large base at Kobuan. Wanting to do things properly, and to avoid creating bad relations with local communities, they took advice from anthropologists and the missions.

While I was at Tubiana, we met Dr Eugene Ogan, an American anthropologist who lived with the Nasioi people in Daratui for some years. Dr Ogan often stayed with me at Tubiana while sorting through his research papers. I found him to be a good man who was also well-liked by the Marai people.

Kip McKillop owned the large Arawa plantation, and coconut trees were an important source of his income. I knew he was not happy about the government cutting down his trees for new roads. The government approached me, asking if they could cut down trees on mission land, but there would be no compensation. I responded, 'Sure! If Mr McKillop agrees, then I agree.' I never heard another word.

The Australian government wanted to buy some of our Tubiana plantation land to build a radio station. Joe Tack Long also wanted to buy some land. Bill Brown, now the District Commissioner, said to the bishop, 'Don't sell the land piecemeal. Sell the whole plantation to the government, and we will sub-divide it for a neat town.'

I knew there could be criticism about this down the years, so I made copies of every letter between myself and the bishop, to keep the record straight.

CRA was often helpful in its dealings with priests. Franz Elixmann was based in Sovele, and Willy Wöeste lived in Deomori. If they needed to travel to Kieta, it was not unusual for CRA to pick them up in a helicopter. Bishop Lemay and I have also been taken up in a helicopter. One time, we flew to Deomori, where New Zealander, Fr Denis Mahoney, was stationed. One day, Denis showed me a little bottle of what he thought was gold, but it was fool's gold.

Once CRA was better established in Panguna, Br Finan, from Rigu College, asked the mine's general manager, Mr Colin Bishop, for a helicopter ride to Panguna. Xaverius and I were also invited. At first, Xaverius refused, until he was told the tour would include a visit to a tunnel. He worked in an underground coal mine in Germany before the First World War, and this made him interested. The helicopter later took us to visit Deomori and back to Kieta.

Soon, there was a good road from Kieta to Panguna. When the mine was up and running the name changed to Bougainville Copper Limited. Gold paid for the running of the mine, while the revenue from silver and copper was pure profit.

On Thursday of Holy Week in 1969 at four pm Xaverius and I were having a cup of coffee when we heard a commotion outside. The church was on fire. People were running with buckets to put it out. A sister was cleaning the church and thought she had extinguished a candle when she put it in a box full of candles. The altar and the tabernacle were destroyed.

Br Xaverius had a persistent ulcer on his leg, so I sent him to Rabaul for treatment at Vunapope Hospital, and while there, to purchase materials to repair the church. Xaverius stayed with his friends Fritz and Elizabeth Hockenbrink, who noticed he was drinking a large quantity of sugary drinks. They wanted to take him back to the hospital. At first, Xaverius refused, but eventually he agreed, only later that night he died. The cause of death was sugar diabetes. On 24 May 1969, Herman Luecken, Franz Elixmann, and I flew to Rabaul and buried Br Xaverius in Vunapope cemetery.

Joe Tack Long and his wife Pauline were well-known Chinese store owners in Kieta. They were also Catholic. They started raising funds for a new church. Bishop Lemay wanted a steel structure spanning the whole area without supporting pillars. The structure was fabricated in Brisbane and shipped on the Malaita. The Dutch lay missionary, Peter Kuijpers, worked on the foundations.

We had some good fortune. When the steel arrived BCL workers were on strike, so they transported and erected our structure with a BCL crane, free of charge. However, the manufacturers had made a mistake. One beam would not fit, so they sent a new beam, erecting it at their expense.

Two new German priests arrived, Willy Tangen and Gunther Köller. Gunther was appointed to Gagan in Buka, and Willy was with me at Kieta. They swapped over after a short time, Gunther to Kieta and Willy to Gagan.

The mine needed a harbour and a power plant, and both were built at Loloho. The Rorovana people were against it, and in August 1969, their women were throwing themselves in front of bulldozers in protest. The police came, put them on trucks, and took them back to their village. The power station at Loloho eventually supplied all of Panguna's electricity. The Port had large storage sheds for concentrating copper, silver, and gold, before being shipped to Japan, Germany, and elsewhere. They also had a cinema. BCL had a rule, any racist talk from blacks or whites would lead to immediate dismissal.

When Prince Phillip, the Duke of Edinburgh, made a royal visit to PNG in March 1971 on the Britannia, he also visited Kieta. The Duke was driven up to the Panguna mine by Bill Brown in an almost brand new black Ford Fairlane that was sent across from Port Moresby, especially for the royal visit.

When I was to return home to Germany in early April 1971 for my leave, I phoned Bill Brown to say goodbye. He offered to drive me to the airport, and showed up the next morning in the 'royal car'.

My first trip home in 1954 took more than five months by ship. One of the reasons for such a long time between breaks in those early years was the length of time it took to travel took to the missions. After 17 years we could cross the world in 30 hours, so it became possible to take holidays every five years. I can't count the hours I have spent on a plane.

Edmund Duffy replaced me in Kieta, and he finished building the church with the help of Peter Kuijpers. Fr Herman Wöeste, who worked at Marai, built a beautiful altar for the new church.

12 Arawa parish

Arawa was a large copra plantation once owned by Mr Ellis. When he was leaving Bougainville, he offered it to his good friend Bishop Wade, who decided not to buy it. Kip McKillop subsequently purchased it, planting cocoa under the coconut palms.

The plantation grew into a very large and profitable enterprise, but Mr McKillop did not enjoy a reputation for generosity to his workers. Their living conditions were primitive, but maybe no different to some other plantations.

CRA needed land to build a town for its workers so, in 1969, the government purchased Arawa for a rumoured half million pounds. The McKillops had a large orchid collection, most of which went to the botanical gardens in Lae. Kip and his family moved to South America in 1974, where he bought land in Brazil to start another agricultural project. He died there a few year later. CRA also wanted to buy Toboroi plantation, but the widowed Mrs Frances Kroening would not sell.

Before leaving for holidays in Germany, I told Bishop Lemay that I didn't want to be in charge of anything when I returned. 'Could I go to Turiboiru as an assistant to Franz Elixmann and teach religion in Buin High School?' I asked. The bishop had me in mind for the new parish of Arawa.

I found out years later that some of his advisers said I was too old to relate to high school students and that I had a drinking problem. They also thought I was unsuitable for Arawa. None of it was true.

When The Garamuts Beat

During my leave while at home in Germany, I stayed with my sister-in-law Angela, and the Schneider family in Steinbeck.

I visited the Marist house in Meppen, and my old teacher Franz Wieschemeyer at Fürstenzell, who visited Bougainville with Fr Cyr. I also called on the Marists at Koln.

When I left for my leave in April 1971, they started cutting down the coconut trees on Arawa. By the time I returned to Bougainville, Arawa had paved streets and houses, large and small.

Arawa wasn't simply a mining town for BCL. The government-built houses for civil servants as well. It was a planned town, for example, police housing was in one section. BCL houses were always of better quality than government houses. They came fully furnished, with electricity, even washing machines, and built to a style according to ranks in the company. A large hospital was built in a short time, supposedly for one million dollars.

On my return I had nowhere to live, and we didn't have a church in Arawa, so I lived at Tubiana for a while. I heard that European Catholics were attending Mass at Tunuru, so I decided to hold an early morning Mass at Tunuru one Sunday. After Mass I invited the congregation to catch up at the priest's house.

Tunuru parish was in the care of a diocesan priest from Nasioi, Fr Edmund Tsivara. I met with the Arawa Catholics, explaining that the bishop had sent me to the new parish of Arawa, and that I wanted to know when it suited people to hold Mass. Nearly everyone preferred the afternoon, because earlier in the day they wanted to visit the beach and have a swim, or spend time looking around. Finding a place large enough in Arawa for the black and white congregation wasn't easy.

I found an empty shed that was once the plantation's cocoa fermentary and drier. I used an old door and two drums for the altar and we had bags to sit on. John Mirinu and his PNG wife Ribe, a nurse, were married in that old shed. After a while, the townspeople started showing movies in our shed, then they started having drunken parties on Saturday

Arawa parish

nights and left the place like a pigsty. The president of the drinking 'club' wanted me to pay twenty kina (K) every time I used the shed for Mass.

After a few months, I moved to Tunuru as it was closer to Arawa. Br Lawrence, a New Zealander, was building a new house for the sisters. Sr Margarete Wöeste, who ran a dental practice at Tunuru, was always urging me to visit the sick in Arawa Hospital.

Br Michael, the business manager, bought a piece of land in Arawa for a priest's house, and Bishop Lemay granted approval for me to find a builder. I had plans drawn up and presented them to the Housing Commission. Bill Brown was on leave, so our application sat on his desk until his return.

When he returned, he suggested some alterations to make it more earthquake-proof, and in no time at all the house was built. It was highset with a laundry, car park and a small chapel underneath. BCL donated a washing machine. Upstairs were the usual kitchen, bathroom, and four bedrooms. This was my first time living in such a house on Bougainville.

We started a parish council, for which the Australian, Pat Gilles, was chair, and Chris Molas from Lemanmanu on Buka, was vice-chair. Many BCL workers from mainland New Guinea wanted to become Catholics. Joseph, who used to be known as Br Kevin, helped me instruct them. One Easter, 40 men and women were baptised and made their first communion.

When I started working in Arawa, there were five religions, Catholics being the largest in number. The others were Uniting Church, Lutherans, Seventh Day Adventists and Anglicans. There were no Lutherans or Anglicans on Bougainville before the war; they arrived with the mine. The Lutheran pastor offered me his house when he went on holidays, as my house was not yet built.

While I lived at Tunuru, we found that money was being stolen from the priest's house. Fr Tsivara had given me the Sunday collection to bank in Arawa on Monday, but when I went to leave for Arawa the next morning, I discovered the money was gone. I could only think the thief must have come into Edmund's house and my room while I was at Mass in Arawa on Sunday afternoon.

I alerted the police, who watched for anyone who went to my house while I celebrated Mass the following Sunday, but they must have spotted the police as the stealing stopped.

One day, while Fr Tsivara was away, someone came to Tunuru asking for a priest to visit a sick man in the mountains. We drove to Arawa and up a steep road, leaving the car where the road ended. The climb was steep and the sun was hot. I was dripping with sweat. As we drew closer to the village I took my shirt off and wrung it out to dry in the sun. I drank some coconut water and freshened up before visiting the sick man.

On entering the house I found a *yangpela manki*—a youth, with a sore on his head the size of a foot. I offered him the Sacrament of the Sick. On the way home it poured rain, causing me to fall many times along that slippery track. I was very dehydrated so I asked my companion, Michael Mirintoro, to buy us a cool drink from a local store. I was exhausted, but content that I was able to anoint the sick boy, as he died very soon after.

§

The government reserved some land in Arawa for a church. The four churches agreed to build one church that we could all share. The Anglicans pulled out because they had fewer numbers, and the priest had a small chapel under his house, so then there were three.

The Lutheran pastor, Dean Zweck, said the Lutherans had an architect and a building team in Lae who could do the job for K40,000. The cost was split, K20,000 from the Catholics, K13,000 from the Uniting Church, and K7,000 from the Lutherans. We talked about a name. Some suggested St Paul, but Tunuru already had that name, so we called it *Marimari Haus Lotu*—Church of Mercy.

Arawa parish

The building had two rooms, for Sunday School and meetings. We divided up the times to use the church. The Catholics had Tuesdays and Fridays, and Sundays from 8 to 9 am. Uniting Church had Mondays and Wednesdays, and Sundays 9 to 10 am. The Lutherans had Thursdays and Saturdays, and Sundays at 10 am. I felt sorry for the Lutherans because the Uniting Church service always went over their allotted time, keeping the Lutherans waiting outside. I made sure we always finished Mass on time.

All the schools allocated time for all the religions to teach students of their faith. The sisters and I were regular, but sometimes the local-born pastors failed to show up, throwing the school's schedule into chaos. The high school's headmaster wanted to cancel the whole thing but I appealed on account of our regularity. I was later appointed school counselor and also to the boards of all the schools in the area.

I used to also celebrate Mass in peoples' homes. One day when preparing for Mass, I noticed a letter with a German stamp. I asked the householder if he received mail from Germany, 'No,' he said: 'That's for you. It was in my post box, and I forgot to give it to you.'

One day I went to baptise a child, and the child's father said that there were two more children for baptism. Three families were living in one tiny house. Families came to Arawa looking for work, finding none, they ended up imposing on friends. Squatter slums sprang up on the edge of town, bringing all kinds of crime with them.

A policeman from the New Guinea mainland wanted to marry a nurse, who was also from the mainland. I explained that they had to contact their respective parishes to establish that they had not been previously married. The man said he had contacted their home parishes and that everything was OK. I was doubtful, so I asked an Australian police officer who claimed he had known the man since he was a boy. He assured me the man was never married before. The police formed a guard of honour at the wedding, and I attended the party afterward.

Some weeks later I was called to the police station. 'Why did you marry this man? He already has a wife,' the officer said. I explained the situation and then went to the hospital to break the news to his 'wife'. The policeman went to prison.

A young couple from Buka came to be married. They already had children, but it was one of my most memorable marriages. Bringing with them clothes for the wedding, it looked like any European wedding. The groom was dressed in a suit, white shirt, tie, and all the somethings, and the bride wore a white bridal gown with a long white veil. In the middle of the ceremony, their baby, who was being held by the bridesmaid, started crying. The bridesmaid helped the bride out of her gown to breastfeed the baby. She then climbed back into her bridal dress and the ceremony continued.

Another time I went to baptise a child, the parents told me about their friends, a couple who lived together and wanted to marry. I went to their house and took their details, parents' names etc so I could write to their home parishes on the PNG mainland. I received a reply from a priest who knew the woman. He said she already had a husband in her village. The priest who also knew the man, confirmed he was free to marry.

I conveyed the information to the couple. The woman said: 'Not true, that is my sister. We both have the same name.' I checked again with her home parish. 'Not true,' assured the priest, 'She is definitely married.' I returned to the couple's house only to find they had moved.

Pastor Jack Sharp of the Uniting Church rang me one day. There was a woman in Arawa hospital who wanted to see me urgently. I went straight away. She was from the Gilbert Islands but had been living in the Shortland Islands. The woman was in a large ward full of other women. I advised her to make her confession so I could give her absolution.

She had a lot to say, but it wasn't easy to hear her as she spoke so softly. I gave her the Sacrament for the Sick and as I was finishing my prayers, the woman said, 'I am not married yet but I am living with a man who is of the Anglican faith.' I asked her if the man lived nearby, to which

Arawa parish

she said: 'Yes.' I asked him to come and see me. I wanted to check if he wanted to marry this woman, and he also said, 'Yes.' So I made the necessary arrangements and they married, with one of the sisters as a witness. A few days later, I went to offer her morning communion, but she had died.

As the town grew so did the number of religions. The Jehovas visited me while I was out and left me their magazine, Watchtower. A policeman put a sign on his house: 'Please do not visit again.' I went to visit some friends, knocking on their door, no answer. I knocked again. This time the wife came out and apologized: 'We thought it was the Jehovas.'

The Uniting Church pastor asked us to join his Carols by Candlelight celebration at Christmas. It poured rain so we took refuge in a classroom where I gave a small talk on the meaning of Christmas.

I was asked to organize the next carol evening, so Sr Michaeline and I printed out a list of carols. The wife of the Uniting Church pastor objected, saying the songs were too Catholic. I was annoyed, as was the pastor. It was then that I realized they only wanted to swell their numbers. From then on we held our own carols at 11 pm followed by Midnight Mass.

When the government put telephones in the houses, I kept getting nuisance calls with people phoning and then hanging up. One time the man did not hang up. I was just about to blast him when he said, 'Happy Christmas Father.' My anger dissolved.

Another night my ringing telephone woke me. Someone in Panguna was badly injured in a work accident: 'Could I come, please?' I explained that I didn't know exactly where the accident site was, but was assured a car would wait for me on the road up on the mountain. I rushed to get ready.

Driving up the mountain I was surrounded by thick fog and could hardly see a thing. All I could do was slowly follow the white line in the middle of the road. When I reached the mountain top, I spotted a white car signalling me to follow. A man had fallen into the mine Concentrator plant. People were trying to revive him without success, but I anointed him and left to drive back down to Arawa. As I reached the mountain top before descending, the fog lifted.

I took the news to his wife. She asked if her husband had said anything before he passed, but I couldn't say, as he was dead by the time I reached him. They had only been married two months.

On one of my visits to Arawa hospital, I came upon George Fahey, Panguna's first parish priest. As I was about to leave, the doctor, also a Catholic, called me over. He explained Fr Fahey was very ill and that I should give him the Sacrament for the Sick and arrange his travel to Sydney. I discussed this with George, who agreed. He flew to Australia with Sr Augusta as his carer.

That same doctor told me about a Buin man who had cancer in his leg, and unless it was amputated he would die. The man was afraid of amputation, and the doctor asked me to talk with him. He agreed to the operation only if I was with him as they cut off his leg.

I dressed in a white gown and then the man said he wanted to be awake while it happened, and he would only consent to local anaesthetic. The doctor gave him an injection which put him to sleep. After the operation the man was given an artificial leg. He was pleased with his decision.

Keeping with memories of the hospital, a nursing sister called me to the birthing room one day. A woman had given birth to twins, but the second infant had not made a sound. I quickly baptised the child and left the room. I was standing outside, not far away, when another nurse approached: 'You helped that child. He is bellowing and looks good now.' I don't know how many infants I baptised in humidicribs who hadn't cried or didn't appear strong enough to live.

An Indian doctor worked at the hospital for a time. Some of the parents came to me saying the doctor was asking women how many children they had, and if they had several, he encouraged them during the birth to be sterilized—*katim rop*. Some said: 'yes,' but came to regret their decision

Arawa parish

after the birth. I advised them to keep me informed, and if necessary, we would report him to the police.

Between 1972 and 1982, I held classes each year underneath our house to prepare people for baptism. I recall a man from Mount Hagen who trained at the university in Port Moresby to become a geologist. He was baptised and then married straight after; his wife was also a Catholic. After some months, he came to see me. 'Father, I need you or a sister to help me. My wife and I cannot have children.' Could I help them adopt a child, he asked.

Sister wrote to Port Moresby and Vunapope. A reply came back from Port Moresby, '*nogat*,' but Vunapope had a little boy. A mother had given birth to triplets and could not care for all three. She was willing to give one up for adoption. The child had a European name given by its mother.

The man and his wife were on the next plane to Rabaul, and returned with the little boy. They were overjoyed. The husband told me that in his people's custom, he was obligated to produce children. If he couldn't, the *lapuns* from his village would apply pressure and find him a second wife, and this was not what he wanted.

We German missionaries received a visit from Fr Rudolf Bleischwitz, the German Provincial. He went first to Suva in Fiji, then to Samoa to visit old Fr Albert Merten. He then visited Fr Everwin in the Solomon Islands.

When he arrived at Aropa airstrip on Bougainville, most of the German priests went to meet him. A young Customs officer asked him to open his bag but then a senior official stepped in and waved him through. On Bougainville, Fr Bleischwitz visited Herman Luecken at Hanahan, Br Pius, and Bishop Lemay at Tsiroge. He went for a swim in the sea, but something bit his foot so he returned to Kieta to recover. While he was recuperating, he received news that his mother had died. When his foot healed he returned to Germany.

German ZDF Television came to Arawa and interviewed Franz Elixmann, Willi Wöeste, and myself. Franz Herkenhoff was in Germany when it was broadcast and sent us a tape. We were quite upset when we saw it as it was full of untruths about the mine and the mission. They said that the missionaries came in canoes, saw good land and then stole it from the people.

Arawa town was expanding. It had a new supermarket, more banks were opening, and there were more venues to show movies. A new Anglican minister arrived and soon found that having a chapel under his house was limiting. He was interested in joining our group if we could add another room to *Haus Marimari*. The other religions were also keen for *Haus Marimari* to expand as their congregations were growing. They all wanted another room for Sunday School.

I could see the need for a larger church, but I also felt we needed a small chapel as another option to a large church. We held a meeting, but it wasn't easy as 'sparks' flew. The others were thinking only of their immediate needs, not the bigger picture.

Pastor Sharp argued strongly for two additional rooms, but Chris Molas said that we would move out and build our own if we could not have a small chapel within the church. The others wanted two rooms just for Sunday School, but Pastor Sharp did not want us to leave, as the Catholics made the largest contribution to the communal church's upkeep. In the end, we all got what we wanted.

The protestants imported a Billy Graham-type evangelist. He worked up the crowd, telling everyone to come back in four days. Very few did. It was like a fire that lights quickly but goes out quickly.

I was so happy so see our little chapel built. The Haus Marimari was wonderful. It was open on the sides which made for good airflow and kept the heat down when the church was full of worshippers. The Lutherans and Anglicans had their own new space. The Lutherans were very happy, as previously they were third in line on Sundays before their service started. Now they could start at their own time and not wait for anyone. The *Talatala* were notorious for not finishing on time.

Arawa parish

Sr Immacula decorated our small chapel beautifully. Jesus came to Bougainville by sea, so she had a small canoe carried in, placing the tabernacle in it.

A friend of mine from Germany, Pastor Angrest Bruder, donated a beautiful crucifix. Franz Herkenhoff put it in his suitcase to bring back from Germany but his case was stolen.

One day I went to the church to pray and found two small girls also praying. They said their teacher told them to pray in the church before and after school. I showed them into the little prayer chapel and said, 'This can be your special place when you want to pray. God is in the tabernacle.' Later I would see many children, girls and boys, praying in the chapel. What a wonderful teacher Helen Mamats was; she was from Taiof Island.

§

In 1974, Bishop Lemay communicated with the Pope, giving notice that he did not wish to continue in the role as Bishop of Bougainville. The Pope heard his wish and Rome put its mind to a replacement. The person chosen was Fr Gregory Singkai of Koromira.

Prior to the Consecration, I went to Rabaul and Vunapope, the centre for priests of the Sacred Heart mission. I knew Tubiana did not have enough space to accommodate all the visiting priests and dignitaries, so I invited Archbishop Hohne to stay at my house in Arawa. He agreed. Fr Willi Wöeste also stayed with me.

I wondered how Willi and I should address the archbishop. It was appropriate to use '*sei*', but '*du*' is customary when speaking German. The archbishop permitted Willi and I to use '*du*' when no one else was present. We smiled at each other, as we knew Bishop was conscious of his importance.

The new bishop's Consecration on Sunday, 24 November 1974, was a large outdoor ceremony held at Tubiana, with all the priests from around Bougainville dressed in white cassocks. The one exception was the Anglican minister who wore black.

§

With the approach of independence for PNG, men from Port Moresby came to Bougainville to conduct surveys about the people's attitude to BCL. A reporter came to my house with a list of questions. He turned up to interview me the next day, but I was unwilling. He returned some months later, giving me an hour-long interview about when I escaped from the Japanese.

About a week later, the interview was aired on the radio. I received two phone calls from Port Moresby, one from Paul Nerau thanking me, and one from the priest in charge of the seminary, saying that seminarians enjoyed the interview.

I was constantly called out at night to anoint sick patients in Arawa hospital, where we held Mass every Monday evening. Two sisters were doing nurse training at the hospital. As the Arawa church grew, we held Mass in the small chapel. Sr Noreen and Sr Bernadette helped me with the running of the parish from 1976.

There were two government primary schools, a high school, and a technical school. At first, all the teachers were white, but then there was a mix of black and white, as were the students. Later BCL paid for the white students of their employees to attend schools in Australia. To be honest, I was happy when that started.

After 40 years of peaceful living on Bougainville, the PNG mainland squatters, with no home and no work, were turning Bougainville into a place of violent crime.

One evening I heard a noise. A man had crept up my steps, removed the fly wire, and was trying to remove the window. When he saw me he ran away. I called the police, who took fingerprints but they did not catch the thief.

Arawa parish

My car was broken into and things I took when visiting the sick were stolen. They were given to me by a Dutch family. Another day I was in my office when I heard a noise downstairs, and as I looked out the window I saw a PNG mainland man walk under the house.

I couldn't remember if I had locked my car, so I went quietly down the stairs to investigate. The man did not see me, but as he was walking away I could see he had taken my car and house keys out of the vehicle. Before he got too far, I confronted him. 'Give me my keys please,' I said. He turned, replying, 'I don't have your keys,' lying. I slapped him on the face.

'Give me the keys or I call the police.' He put his hand in his pocket, took out my keys and gave them to me before running away.

I learned another lesson, to make sure I always kept the car locked and to keep the keys in my pocket. I think he planned to watch the house and if I went somewhere, he could let himself in to help himself.

§

I think it was 1977, a letter came from Fr Willy Weemaes, saying that I was not doing a good job and could not work effectively with young people. I was shocked and devastated. I was to learn soon after that three priests were behind a move to push me out—Frs George Fahey, Henk Kronenberg, and Weemaes. They wanted to work as a team to run the parish, and felt they would be more effective with young people.

That night I drove out to see Franz Elixmann at Tunuru, and showed him the letter. I wanted to know what he thought. The letter left me heartbroken—*em letta em i mekim hat bilong mi i krai*. When I sat down to reply to Willy's letter, I outlined what I had been doing in Arawa over the five years and that there was never a complaint from any young person. I never heard any more from them.

When The Garamuts Beat

They also wanted to remove Franz Elixmann from Tunuru, but I never knew the reason for this. Franz Elixmann returned to Germany in 1977, and it wasn't too long before he passed away.

The Provincial (based in Fiji) at the time was an American, Fr Frank Lambert, who was hearing *planti tumas toktok* from Frs Fahey, Kronenberg, and Weemaes. He did not approach Franz, me, or anyone else about the situation.

I received a letter from him saying that after my holiday, I would no longer work in Arawa. I was being replaced by George Fahey. I had my doubts about George because he never seemed to stay in one place for very long. When he came to Bougainville from Fji, George worked at Sovele, managing the diocese, then later he was appointed Regional Superior before ending up in Panguna.

While I was in Fürstenzell, Mr Faulhaber took me to München, where I met his daughter, Birgitte, and her family; I also visited my niece in Nuremberg. I caught up with Franz Elixmann, who was the hospital chaplain and parish priest in the small parish of Lathen-Wahn. Unfortunately, he wasn't there long, as he died the following year from a brain tumour.

When Fr Elixmann was on Bougainville, he told me that he collapsed at the station one afternoon, but he didn't want me telling anyone about it. I wondered if that was the tumour. When I returned to Bougainville, George Fahey was on holiday in America, so Bishop sent me back to Arawa.

§

On the eve of Holy Saturday, 18 April 1981, we had so many adults and infants presenting for baptism. Among them was a New Zealander who received four sacraments, baptism, confirmation, holy communion, and marriage. His Fijian wife, Laisiana, would visit me later in Germany.

One day when I left the hospital, I noticed a police car following me. Have I done something wrong? I asked myself. When they saw me turn into my house, they drove off. All the police in Arawa knew me by sight.

Arawa parish

An Australian nurse working at the hospital had an accident in her car and did quite a bit of damage. Later I brushed her car in the supermarket car park, and she reported me to the police for causing serious damage. The police examined my car but found no damage. I wanted to avoid possible litigation, so I offered to pay for her costs. When the rest of the hospital staff found out what she had done, she was not the most popular person in the hospital.

On Tuesday evenings we held Mass. I liked to cook a meal beforehand so I wouldn't have to cook when I got home. One evening, when I arrived home, my dinner was gone, eaten by ants. After one of our Tuesday evening masses, I went out to my car and as I sat behind the wheel I realised it was Sister Michaeline's vehicle not mine. Where was my car? Word was quickly sent to the Arawa police who found it smashed up against a tree.

During Mass, some Seventh Day Adventists had stolen and wrecked it. I knew that if left overnight where it was found, it would be stripped of its wheels, battery, seats, etc. The police caught the culprits and put them in the watch house. Meanwhile some of my parishioners kindly organised a tow truck to bring the vehicle to the workshop where it was repaired.

The following Sunday I drove up to Panguna to hold Mass, and after church I met up with Henry Moses, a successful businessman and union boss for BCL employees. On hearing what happened to my vehicle, he donated K100 towards the cost of repairs. Other parishioners also helped out. I was very grateful for their generosity.

Everyone was talking about emancipation. Sister Michaeline who helped me with our work in Arawa, gave a talk to a group of Catholic white women on female emancipation. The next day she was driving from Tunuru to Arawa when she got a flat tyre. Not knowing how to change it, Sister waited for someone to stop.

An Australian man stopped and asked if she needed help. Sister explained her tyre was flat and she needed assistance to change it. He changed her tyre but as he drove off, he said, 'Sister, next time you give a talk, don't talk about emancipation unless you can change your own tyre. My wife came home last night talking non-stop about emancipation.'

Before taking leave in 1982, I approached the bishop during a retreat to consider looking for a new site to build our own church. Arawa was growing into a large town, and the current church was too small. I knew the bishop was reluctant, but several priests supported me, so he agreed.

With Chris Molas and others, we searched for a suitable piece of land. We found a block on the other side of town, large enough for a church, that could in the future, cater for a school, youth centre, a priests' house, and a sisters' house.

We went to see the town planning officer, who told us to draw up plans and he would look at it. Many times I called on the department before we eventually received a negative response.

While I was on leave in Germany, Fr John Begg continued following up on our behalf. He finally received word to see the *kiap*; we were granted a block, but it was much smaller than what we applied for. The other issue was we could not have another building on the block.

We started fundraising in Germany and other places for the new church in Arawa. Sr Michaeline showed films after Mass as a way to raise funds locally. She was given the movies for nothing. I was in Germany by this time.

The Apostolic Nuncio visited me at Arawa. He told me to write to him, co-signed by Bishop Gregory, and he would ask Rome to help fund our church. However, it took some years for any funds to come through. It was 1985 when Rome sent the bishop some thousands of kina for the church that was eventually completed in 1987. Fr Gerard Pelletier was the parish priest.

In March 1982, I went home to spend time with my family in Steinbeck, and visit Marists in Meppen and Fürstenzell. I flew to Perth to see my nephew Friedel, and on the way, I stopped in Sydney, to visit Joe Tack Long and his wife Pauline. Then I visited Anna Clark and her family in Adelaide. The Clarks used to live in Arawa.

Arawa parish

Friedel travelled with me to Germany as he wanted to see his mother, Angela, again in Steinbeck. We had good flights to Germany, but when we arrived at Ingrid (Friedel's sister) and Willi's place, I found money missing from my luggage. It was PNG kina, but perhaps airport staff in Australia knew how and where to change it.

My Golden Jubilee for belonging to my home parish of Steinbeck was on 13 April 1982. The parish priest, Fr Brüser, and my niece hosted a party with all kinds of people attending. In Meppen, Frs Willy Kayser and Otto Goldhagen organized another celebration with Marists. Everything went off so well. I wish to thank Ingrid, Willi, Fr Brüser and Rudi Bleischwitz for organizing things.

One morning I looked out the window, and everything was white. I woke Friedel and asked him to take a photo so I could show it to people in Bougainville.

During that holiday I fell ill, and Dr Schedding of Ibbenburen thought I might have gallstones, so he sent me to the local hospital where it was confirmed. I needed an operation. I asked Dr Schedding if I could have a private room, but the only one available was in the women's ward. When the cleaner came into my room the next morning, she nearly hit the floor in shock. The nurses later told me that I was listed as Mrs Miltrup.

After the operation, which was not a total success, I was transferred to a larger hospital in Münster, where I needed an endoscopy and the remaining gallstones removed. I recovered and went home.

When my holiday was over, Annie Wessel and Fr Hubert Gelholt drove Br Pius, Fr Herman Luecken, and me, to the airport at Dusseldorf. On reaching Australia, we visited Friedel and his family in Perth. Cyril Butler met us at Sydney airport and took us to Hunters Hill. On our return to Bougainville, Herman went to Hanahan, and I was to return to my new station at Panguna.

When The Garamuts Beat

13 Panguna—my last parish

Fr George Fahey left Panguna in 1982 to work in a hospital in Sydney, and I was to replace him. Panguna was a small but growing town built by BCL, and situated next to the mine site. It had a church with a small Catholic chapel, two small hospitals, one owned by BCL, the other by the government, with only one doctor. Separate buildings housed the unmarried men and women, and all employees were provided three meals a day in the company canteen.

The mine dump trucks had wheels that were about four metres in diameter and could carry 200 tons. Drivers were trained but their line of vision was limited. One day a truck ran over a small car; the driver was not even aware that it had happened.

Before Fr Fahey left Panguna, he drove me around, including a visit to Dapera, a new village built by the company for the villagers displaced by the mine. Their houses were made of permanent materials and they had a small church. Once a week, Chris Molas picked me up and took me to Dapera to hold Mass although few people attended. They were often drunk, children were neglected, and the walls of the houses were smashed. It was sad.

The parish council was excellent. They arranged for me to have a fully furnished two-room apartment in Panguna, rent-free. They looked after the collection and bought all the candles and Mass wine, etc., and even gave me an allowance for food. The parish treasurer was company-trained and presented a financial report in company-style, which nobody could understand. Fortunately, he was sent down to Australia for advanced training, after which Regina from Manus took over the books, and reported in a way we could all follow.

We Catholics held our service in the Panguna church first. Following us, the Anglicans used the small chapel as there weren't so many of them. The Uniting Church used the main church after that, then the Lutherans after them. In the evenings, I took a service where everyone was welcome, and it was well attended.

During Lent, when we carried a bare wooden cross, so many people attended. I think back to one night, it was Good Friday, as we walked the Stations of the Cross, with people from all religions attending. Bikpela guria i kamap. I was looking for a place to shelter, but as not one of the congregation moved, we continued our service without damage or commotion.

Children took bible class on Saturdays, but I thought what they were learning wasn't enough. That is how I found Balbina, a school teacher, who was excellent in preparing the children for their first communion. Balbina's father, Michael Kereari, looked after the Sacristy. The first communion was followed by a feast for children and their parents. I was reminded of the early church's practice and hoped that day stayed in those children's memories for a long time.

I wanted to see Buin again, so I asked Herman Wöeste if he could take me one day, which he did. The road was so much easier to travel on now that there were good bridges crossing the wider rivers. Taim bipo, it took a ship seven hours from Koromira to Turiboiru. On the way back, we stopped at Koromira and had a cup of coffee before Herman brought me back to Tubiana.

As I was preparing to leave for Panguna, I realized that I had left my cigarettes at Koromira. By the time I reached Panguna, I decided to give up smoking. I found some packets in my house and gave them to friends who smoked. I was very glad that I did it.

Panguna - my last parish

In Panguna, I noticed that peoples' lives and customs bilong bipo were almost gone. Education was one example. Before the mine, Catholics had separate high schools for boys and girls, but co-education was now the fashion.

In Bougainville, babies were given an individual name, not their mother's, not their father's, their own. Now, as students enrolled in high school, they were called by their father's name, like the white custom.

People dressed more like white people too. Girls were wearing bras, blouses and skirts etc. Students were studying for all kinds of professions at university. Young people were picking up *kastam bilong waitman* that were not so good, and forgetting their own valued customs. As Bougainville women took jobs in town as secretaries, nurses, and teachers, newfound freedoms drew them away from village life forever. Misuse of alcohol became a social problem for men and women.

Some girls started taking their husband's name, and instead of parents selecting a partner for their child, young people were choosing their partners, often with disastrous results. Domestic abuse was on the rise.

Some women thought that marrying a white man would lead to good times and wealth, without considering or understanding the man's culture. The mine brought men who thought it was a great idea to have a woman while they worked out their contract, but not to take her back home. I must be honest that there were white men who married local women and cared for them, and educated their children.

Suicide was another issue on the rise. In times past the common method was hanging, but in recent times people were overdosing on anti-malarial tablets or drinking some sort of herbicide. Chris Molas took me to a man who died after falling from a window. In this case, it was an accident, but unfortunately, he hit the cement. Deaths by accident were surprisingly uncommon.

§

When The Garamuts Beat

Since returning from my last holiday, I knew my health was not good. One evening, I was unwell so I phoned the doctor in Arawa, a lady from Poland, who ordered an ambulance to bring me down the mountain to Arawa hospital. I waited for the ambulance, only to see it scream passed my house. They eventually found me and took me to the hospital.

When the doctor saw me, she knew straight away what was wrong. She gave me two glasses of water to drink and a couple of sugar pills. It seems I was diabetic. I checked out the next day returning to Panguna, but when I saw the cost of my hospital visit, it almost put me into a state of shock.

I really enjoyed my time in Panguna. The people were kind, there wasn't too much trouble, and attendance for Sunday Mass was always good. The one issue that concerned me was how much alcohol people in Dapera drank. The men were usually too drunk or hungover for Mass, so it was mostly women and children on Sundays.

I did not stay the full five years at Panguna before taking leave. I approached the bishop for permission to take holidays a bit earlier, to celebrate my Golden Jubilee being 50 years in the priesthood (from 29 June 1935), with my family in Germany. It was similar to how we celebrated my Golden Jubilee of being Professed in Meppen a couple of years earlier. We had a wonderful time in Steinbeck. And for the gatherings in Meppen, again, I wish to thank Ingrid and Willi, and my good friend Fr Brüser and Fr Rudi Bleischwitz.

On this holiday I fell ill again, this time it was Angina pectoris. The gallstones were also giving me trouble, causing me to spend a few days in hospital. When I was discharged I returned to Bougainville with Br Pius.

When the parish council heard I recently celebrated 50 years as a Marist priest, they organized a celebration in Panguna. Bishop Gregory Singkai, all the priests nearby, and local ministers joined in. There were many speeches, feasting, and dancing. My gifts included a small canoe because I came to Bougainville by sea, a small map of Bougainville made of stones on a plank, and a small *garamut*.

Panguna - my last parish

Christmas services in 1985 drew in very large crowds, but my heart was giving me trouble again. I looked for John Davimaku who usually stayed with me, to bring me to Tubiana. John Begg drove up that night, and with John Davimaku, they brought me down to Tubiana. I was so happy not to end up in Arawa hospital. I felt that I wasn't as strong as I used to be, and that it was time to give up my work in Panguna.

Fr Willi Wöeste had recently returned from his holiday in Germany, and I asked him whether he would consider taking on Panguna parish. He said he would like that, so I went to see the bishop. The bishop agreed that I should step down from Panguna, but he wanted to discuss the matter first with Willi. They talked it over and it was agreed, that Willi Wöeste would replace me in Panguna. I loved my time at Panguna, except for those poor people in Dapera village.

Koromira 1986

Herman Wöeste ran the station at Koromira mission which was started by Fr Rausch from Luxembourg. Fr Goldert followed, along with Srs Lidwina and Ludovica, all from Luxembourg. Before the war, Fr Junker, also from Luxembourg, was stationed there, so the station was known as Parish Luxembourg.

I asked Herman whether I could come and assist him, and he agreed. He made me welcome by giving up his bedroom and moving into a smaller room in the house.

Herman helped rehabilitate young people who had committed crimes. He would do the weekend Masses at Marai, and I would do Koromira. During the week, I worked on the 'family book' which was not easy, as several people often had the same name, and people moved to another village once they married.

I had a little money put away, so I gave it to Herman to buy a new water tank and solar hot water unit. From then on, it was clean drinking water and hot showers for us.

When The Garamuts Beat

While I was at Koromira I was getting malaria all the time, and the medication was not working. I was also losing a lot of weight. In October 1986, Herman drove into Kieta and returned with the Regional Superior.

I didn't hear them come back except when they came into my room. 'We have bad news for you,' Herman said. I thought he was going to tell me a family member had died, but he said, 'Dr Charles Loubai thinks you have cancer, and he can't take care of you here. You need to go down to Australia or back to Germany.'

And so my life's work on Bougainville ended after so many years. That afternoon Fr Willi Tangan came to see me. He got in touch with Meppen and they were sending my air ticket.

14 Leaving my home Bougainville
Bel bilong mi i hevi tumas

I sorted and packed what to take with me, and said goodbye to the priests and sisters who were on retreat at the time. Herman brought me to Laisiana and Ron Redman's house in Arawa, where I stayed until my flight left Bougainville. When people heard that I was returning to Germany and the hospital, they came to shake my hand and say goodbye, many bringing gifts. Laisiana, a lady from Fiji, travelled with me as far as Port Moresby, where I caught another plane to Australia.

I landed first in Brisbane and cleared Customs. Malaria hit me on the flight to Brisbane and the air steward arranged for a customs officer to see me on the plane. I was met at Sydney airport by Srs Noreen and Bernadette, and Joe Tack Long. Joe took me home for the night, and the next morning I flew to Perth.

I landed in Adelaide but only for a short while, not long enough to see Anna Clark. In Perth, I reunited with Friedel and Jean, staying with them two days before flying to Germany. It was a Wednesday when I arrived in Greven. I arrived at Ingrid's place on Friday and went to see the lung doctor, who could find no evidence of cancer. I was so happy. But on Saturday, I collapsed.

The family took me to the hospital where the doctors confirmed it was a severe bout of malaria. I finally recovered, but bel bilong mi i hevi tumas—I was very sad because I knew I could never return to the land that I loved—my beloved Bougainville.

Two lines in the poem '*Dreizehnlinden*' by Friedrich Wilhelm Weber summed up my feelings:

Unter den plamen, da mochte ich einst wohnen

Unter den palmen da mochte ich einst er uhen

Under the palm trees, where I would like to live

Under the palm trees, there I would like to lay to rest

LATHEN
Saturday, 11 November 1989, the Day of St Martin
FRANZ MILTRUP SM

10

Leaving my home Bougainville

" I know that my saviour lives, therefor I will raise again on the last day. I will see God in my body."

Today God the Lord called, after an industrious and life of service, our Brother

Marist Pater

Franz Miltrup

To his eternal peace. The deceased was in his 88th year. In his 65th year since his profession and in his 62nd year of his work as a Priest.

We lost a Brother in Pater Miltrup who with exemplary enthusiasm and work as Missionary in the service of the proclamation of the Gospel in the South Seas and in later years worked as Pastor in the Hospital in Lathan.

The Padres and Brothers   ***The Relatives***
Of the Marist Monastery   *Willi and Ingrid Schneider*
In Meppen   *and Family*

49716 Meppen, the 3rd November 1996
Herzog-Arenberg-Strasse 65

The Requiem Mass will be celebrated on Friday the 8th November 96 in the Chapel of the Marist Monastery Meppen. Afterwards the funeral will be held at the cemetery on the Markstiege in Meppen.

For the drive from the Marist Monastery to the cemetery and back
A bus will be provided

When The Garamuts Beat

Marist confrères

This section contains biographies of selected clerics mentioned in Fr Miltrup's memoir; most of the information on the following individuals was obtained from two editions of In Memoriam, published by The Society of Mary (SM), Oceania Province, dated 1990 and 2021. Whilst not conclusive, they were a key source of reference.

Photographs in this section from sources other than The Society of Mary in Rome, Italy, are numbered and listed at the back.

Fr Francois Allotte SM b: 26 Oct 1866 Belley France d: 23 May 1948 Torokina Bougainville

Fr Allotte was professed as a Marist in 1898 and left for the new mission in the Solomons in 1903, at 37 years of age. After being based at headquarters on Poporang Island in the Shortland Islands group, he moved to Buin in south Bougainville in 1905, before founding the Marist's first mission at Patupatuai. With great courage, he helped to bring peace between warring villagers in the area.

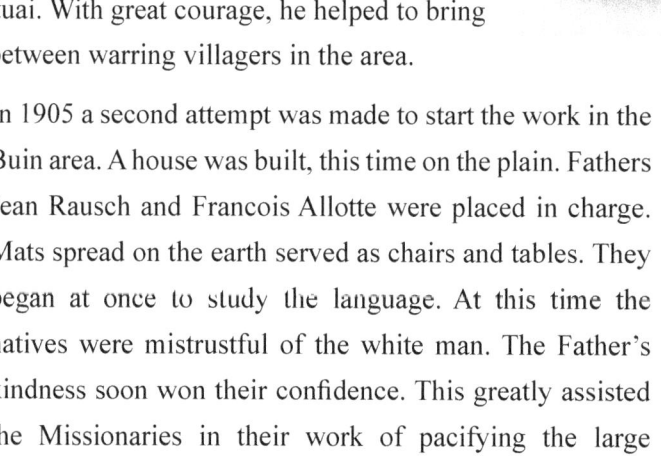

> In 1905 a second attempt was made to start the work in the Buin area. A house was built, this time on the plain. Fathers Jean Rausch and Francois Allotte were placed in charge. Mats spread on the earth served as chairs and tables. They began at once to study the language. At this time the natives were mistrustful of the white man. The Father's kindness soon won their confidence. This greatly assisted the Missionaries in their work of pacifying the large district in their care, where some fifty villages were continually at war with their neighbors [sic] (Kronenberg, H. Saris, H. year unknown, p. 92).

For some years during the First World War, Fr Allotte was Pro-Prefect of the mission. In 1918, he founded the mission at Tinputz, remaining there until 1940. During the Second World War, he was evacuated from Bougainville to Australia. Immediately after the war, Fr Allotte insisted on returning to Bougainville, spending the last two years of his life at Torokina, where he died aged 82.

Fr Albert Binois SM b: 16 Jul 1880 Tournay France d: 6 Aug 1950 Manetai Bougainville.

Albert Binois was professed in the Society on Wednesday 27 December 1905, and ordained the following day. Two years later, aged 27, he arrived at Poporang Island in the Shortlands. Fr Binois stayed at the headquarters of the Bougainville mission for three years, after which, in 1910, he founded the first mission on Buka, at Burunotui, with Fr Karl Flaus. This mission was opposite Pororan Island, and where he worked for ten years.

After a short time in Buin, Fr Binois founded the first mission in Choiseul, where he spent 25 years isolated from other Marists.

> He often went many months without seeing a confrère, living on local food and occasionally something else. His home in Sirovana was the nest of an eagle and difficult to access. He made voyages along the coast to visit his people and to be in touch with those who were not Catholics. In spite of the efforts of the Methodists he cornered about 20 per cent of the population. A missionary who followed said, 'P. Binois was not a missionary; he was five missionaries' (Saris: 2008, p. 5).

In 1948, Fr Binois was sent to the mountainous parish of Manetai, north of Kieta, learning to speak Nasioi so he could minister to the people. Villages in his parish ranged in distance from four to nine hours' walk from the mission. The following is an extract from Fr Saris' contribution to information on Marists who served on Bougainville:

> On 16 July he went to Tunuru to be with P. Müller to celebrate his 70th birthday He was in good health and always happy. On Sunday 30th he blessed a new chapel at Atamo and on the 1st August he went to Tarara to celebrate the mass on the next day. He passed the night at the home

of a Chinese Catholic. He was sick and on the 5th he sent word to P. Mueller [sic] to come. The latter left the same day with a doctor; but when they arrived P. Binois had died about an hour earlier. The diagnosis was cerebral malaria and haemorrhaging of the brain. The body was taken to Kieta and he was buried there. [Acta SM Sept 1950, p. 96] (Saris: 2008, p. 5).

Fr Binois was aged 70 when he died.

Fr Maurice Boch SM b: 14 Sep 1875 Reims France d: 25 Jul 1953 Hantoa Bougainville

Maurice Boch was a young cavalry officer when, following a chance meeting with Marist Bishop Broyer of Samoa, who was in France at the time, he decided to live as a religious.

In 1907, Fr Boch left Europe for the Pacific missions with seven other Marists. He was appointed to Poporang Island in the Shortlands in 1908, for eight years. Fr Boch was at Burunotui on the west coast of Buka Island from 1916 to 1918. In 1920, he was made Prefect Apostolic of the North Solomons, holding that position for ten years.

When Bishop Wade was named the Vicar Apostolic, Fr Boch became Pro-Vicar. In 1938, he was transferred to Sydney, following his appointment as superior and master of the second Novitiate for two years, before returning to Bougainville.

Captured by the Japanese in 1942, Fr Boch spent three years as a prisoner of war in Rabaul on New Britain. After the war and following six months of convalescence in Sydney, Fr Boch returned to Poporang for four years, after which he went to Hantoa in north Bougainville, where he remained until his death aged 78.

While Fr Moore was at Hantoa, he laid a slab on Boch's unmarked grave, scratching his personal details into the still wet cement. A subsequent priest put a proper memorial on it.

> He was especially good in the language of Alu, which he knew perfectly. There are many manuscripts, many

polycopied texts and some printed works. A Manual of Prayer and canticles was printed at Visale; the history of the Bible was published by Vitte, Lyon. The Culture in the mission, the Alu catechism, Manual of prayers;
Grammar of Alu etc. etc. all flowed from his pen. He has rendered a great service to the local people and to the young missionaries. [Acts SM, 1 November 1953, p. 65-66] (Saris: 2008, p.7)

The following extract provides additional insight into the man.

Boch was the most colourful of the Marists to work in the North Solomons. Born in Alsace, he had been a subaltern in a French cavalry regiment when a sermon preached by Bishop Broyer at Sedan in 1897 aroused his interest in the Pacific missions and inspired him to join the Society of Mary. The decision was bitterly opposed both by his allegedly bigoted German Protestant father and by his French Catholic mother, who was counting on his military career to boost the family fortunes. But to no avail.

Boch reached the Solomons in 1908, where he soon became a popular figure. Among the islanders he had a reputation for openhandedness, while in 1916 the European residents of the Shortland Islands district petitioned Forestier not to transfer him to Buka. Among his colleagues he was known for his fondness of classical music, for his carefully waxed moustaches and for his urbanity.

Boch was also a man of combative dislikes and possessed a strong detestation of Germany, exceeded only by his obsessive horror of Protestants (Laracy: 1969, pp. 114-115).

One of the SMSM sisters heard classical music coming from Fr Boch's house one day. The sister thought he must have been playing old 78 speed records but when she went inside, it was Fr Boch playing his violin (pers. comm. Moore: 2022).

**Fr Leon Chaize SM b: 26 Feb 1885 Loire France
d: 18 Jul 1964 Sydney Australia**

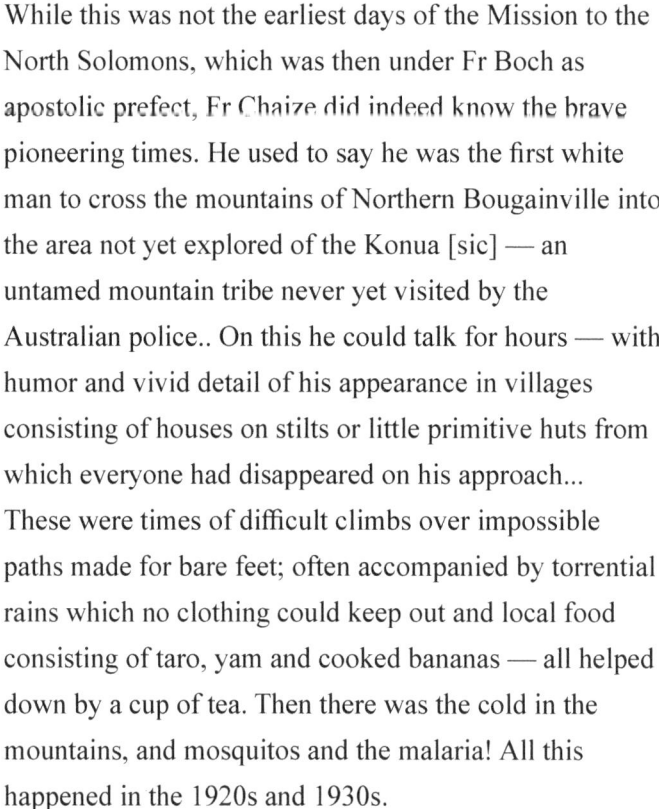

After his novitiate in Italy, and seminary studies in France and Belgium, aged 26 years, Leon Chaize was ordained in 1911. He began his missionary life that same year, at the foundation of Torokina mission station.

Fr Chaize was appointed to Sipai on the north-west coast of Bougainville, in 1921, an area that was at the time still uncontrolled territory (Laracy: 1976, p. 59).

The following extract is from Fr Hendry Saris' document:

> While this was not the earliest days of the Mission to the North Solomons, which was then under Fr Boch as apostolic prefect, Fr Chaize did indeed know the brave pioneering times. He used to say he was the first white man to cross the mountains of Northern Bougainville into the area not yet explored of the Konua [sic] — an untamed mountain tribe never yet visited by the Australian police.. On this he could talk for hours — with humor and vivid detail of his appearance in villages consisting of houses on stilts or little primitive huts from which everyone had disappeared on his approach...
> These were times of difficult climbs over impossible paths made for bare feet; often accompanied by torrential rains which no clothing could keep out and local food consisting of taro, yam and cooked bananas — all helped down by a cup of tea. Then there was the cold in the mountains, and mosquitos and the malaria! All this happened in the 1920s and 1930s.
> Due to security concerns Fr Chaize left Torokina district,

transferring to Buka for the next 12 years. There, the original station, Burunotui, was re-structured into three stations in 1922, Gagan in the centre of Buka, and Lemanmanu and Hanahan, on the cliff tops of the north west and east coasts, respectively.

Fr Chaize spent a year in France from 1929 before returned to Buka. He returned to Australia in 1938. During the Second World War, Fr Chaize worked with the Intelligence services for the Allies. Due to his deep knowledge of the Torokina area, Fr Chaize assisted the American forces to draw up maps in preparation for their landing. He was chaplain for the marines, appointed first captain and then commander, and was awarded the Legion of Honour for his services (Saris: 2008, p. 13).

Fr Chaize returned to PNG from 1955 to 1963, before going back to Sydney where he worked as a hospital chaplain. He died aged 79.

Fr John Conley SM b: 2 Jul 1898 Philadelphia USA d: 10 Dec 1943 Kieta Bougainville

Following the future Bishop Thomas Wade, Fr Conley, aged 28, was the second American to arrive in the Bougainville mission, in 1926. After three years at Turiboiru in Buin district Fr Conley spent the next 11 years on Buka, first at Burunotui and then Lemanmanu.

In 1939, he began the first mission on Nissan. In 1943, Fr Conley was suspected by the Japanese of communicating with the American forces. He was taken to Kieta and beheaded. He was 45. The following article describes Fr Conley's fate.

In 1939 Father John Conley took charge of the mission on Nissan or Green Island, forty-two miles north-west of Buka, and when war spread to the South Pacific he remained at his post. He could have escaped from the Japanese had he so wished, but he wanted to stay with his people, to minister to their spiritual needs, and to try to talk the invaders into giving the natives a better deal than they themselves might obtain.

> While on his way to visit members of his flock in high, wooded Pinipil, a little island to the north, with a population of some 1500 Melanesians, he was captured, and transported by warship to Kieta, around whose harbor [sic] the Japanese had built a powerful base. There, according to persistent reports from the natives, he was beheaded on December 10, 1943. His body has been discovered and buried. The grave is marked (Decker: 1948, p. 97).

Fr Edmund Duffy SM b: 29 Mar 1930, Ireland
These reminisces come from Peter Fenton, lay missionary who worked in Bougainville for some years.

Bishop Leo Lemay was at Buka airstrip to meet Peter Fenton, a new volunteer from Sydney, arriving on the weekly flight from Rabaul. It was June 1962. The American bishop took his new charge in the mission workboat across Buka Passage and down the west coast of Bougainville to Tsiroge Mission, where Peter was to work with the station procurator, Queensland-born Brother Phillip. In 1980, Br Phillip was ordained a priest, after which he took his Baptismal name, Kevin Kerley. Along with then Br Phillip was a young Irish priest, Edmund (Ed) Duffy.

Peter remembers Tsiroge as a good mission to meet people. It was the central hub for the Bougainville Diocese. It included a Technical School, sawmill, large workshop, a seminary for the Brothers of St Joseph, a chapel and a ship's slipway. Missionaries and staff from parishes around Bougainville frequently called in to pick up supplies or bring in boats for repair. Tsiroge also had a store that kept inventory for the all the Marist missions around the island.

Whilst Peter remembers Fr Duffy being easy to get along with, the new volunteer soon ran into difficulties. Being a keen gardener, Peter decided one Sunday to plant some runner beans near the store. Fr Duffy was not impressed to see someone busy working on the Sabbath. His Irish sensibilities were that it was 'not the done thing.' This didn't preclude the priest's weekend ministry trips to Taiof, an island community within view of Tsiroge.

The following year, Peter left Tsiroge to complete a six-month teacher training course in Rabaul in East New Britain, during which time Fr Duffy was transferred to run his own mission station—Koromira, on the east coast of Bougainville, south of Kieta. Despite those cross-cultural differences in the early weeks of Peter's tenure, the two men kept in touch, maintaining a friendship to this day which sees Peter and Ed Duffy having regular phone catch-ups; Peter in Parramatta, NSW, and Ed in Coolock, Dublin, Ireland.

Note: The editor thanks Peter for these reminisces. Fr Duffy served in missions in Nissan and Fiji.

Fr Franz Elixmann SM b: 15 Oct 1917 Osnabrück, Germany d: 11 Sep 1978 Germany

Fr Elixmann was professed on Sunday 30 October 1938, after completing his novitiate in the Netherlands. He served in the German army during the Second World War, before completing his seminary studies and teaching in Meppen for two years.

Fr Elixmann arrived in Bougainville in 1951, aged 34. He spent 12 months at the Chabai seminary, followed by 25 years at Lemanmanu, Sovele, Turiboiru, and Tunuru missions.

While Fr Elixmann was teaching young Bougainvillean seminarians at Chabai, he was reputed to have said: "Today we practice the letter double-u (w). Repeat after me, ve vill vork vit Villy" (pers. comm. Moore: 2022).

Ill health led to Fr Elixmann returning to Germany, where he died shortly after, aged 60.

Fr Joseph Grisward SM b: 13 May 1878 Luxembourg d: 18 Apr 1946 Australia

Joseph Grisward was the youngest in a family of 14 children. After preparatory studies in Differt, Belgium, he entered the Marist Novitiate at La Bousselet.

An anti-clerical regime in France at the time led to

12

many religious houses closing, and so Joseph Grisward went to the Marist College in Washington DC, USA, in 1901. He was professed two years later.

In 1905, aged 28, Fr Grisward, described as an "ascetic looking but sturdy missionary from Alsace Lorraine," went to Bougainville (Decker: 1948, pp. 101). Nearly all of Grisward's missionary life was spent in the Buin area, where as a pioneer missionary, he endured great hardships and privation. He founded the mission at Monoitu in Siwai in 1922, where he remained until 1938.

Over a period of 40 years, Fr Grisward only left Bougainville twice, once for a second Novitiate, and the other occasion was to take a holiday.

Fr Grisward was detained by the Japanese in 1942, but he escaped after three years, and was evacuated from Bougainville by Allied troops. Those war-time years caused considerable suffering and ill-health in the longer term. He was brought to Australia, but he never regained good health. He died in Sydney at the age of 68.

Fr James (Jim) Gerald Hennessy b: 24 Sep 1905 North Cambridge Massachusetts USA d: 1942

13

Jim Hennesy studied at St John's Seminary and North American College in Rome, where he was ordained on Saturday 20 December 1930.

Prior to his missionary work, Fr Hennessy was an associate pastor at Immaculate Conception Parish in Malden, Massachusetts, in 1931, after which he served for almost five years as an associate pastor at the Cathedral of the Holy Cross.

Fr Hennessy applied to the Boston diocese to serve as a missionary abroad and was finally granted a five-year term, becoming the first Boston diocesan priest to serve in a foreign mission. His first appointment was to the Solomon Islands, where he founded the first seminary in the Pacific islands. Fr Hennessy was transferred to Bougainville in 1936, taking charge of the catechist school at Chabai at the request of Bishop Wade (Laracy: 1976, p. 107).

He was captured by the Japanese in March 1942 while stationed at Lemanmanu on Buka (Lockwood: 2009). Fr Hennesey's name appears amongst the list of prisoners loaded onto the MV *Montevideo Maru*, in Rabaul. More on Fr Jim's story is in the Appendix.

Marist confrères

Fr Emery de Klerk SM b: 31 Dec 1907 Kruispolder Lamswaarde Netherlands d: 9 Mar 1985 Port Elizabeth South Africa

Fr de Klerk was ordained in 1933, and left for the Solomon Islands the following year. He was assigned to Tangarare, on the Weathercoast of Guadalcanal, in the Solomon Islands.

> Tangarare was considered a difficult, even dangerous, place where, under the influence of Father Rinaldo Pavese, a considerable part of the Catholics had separated into a sort of schismatic grouping. Emery brought them back into the fold, through manly leadership, intensive pastoral work, concern for people and a phenomenal knowledge of the local language.
>
> During the war he refused to be evacuated to Australia, by withdrawing into the bush when the navy sent a ship to pick him up. He acted as a coast watcher, and organized armed patrols to keep the bush behind Tangarare free of straying Japanese soldiers. He received a high honor from the American government and was an honorary member of the 1st marine division (Saris: 2008. p. 40).

After 30 years in the Solomon Islands, in 1962, Fr de Klerk was transferred to Bougainville. A seminary professor, he taught at the catechetical schools in Patupatuai and Tarlena before TB forced him to seek treatment in Australia. After his recovery, Fr de Klerk volunteered to work in South Africa. He taught at the Marist Brothers' School in Port Elizabeth, where he died at 77.

Br Xaverius Koch SM b: 18 Jul 1901 Osnabrück Germany d: 24 May 1969 Vunapope East New Britain PNG

Br Xaverius was professed in the Marist Society in 1926. He arrived in Bougainville four years later, aged 29, accompanied by the newly ordained Bishop Wade.

Br Xaverius served in the mission for 40 years, primarily as a carpenter and builder, before and after the Second World War.

Before the war, he worked in Patupatuai and Tunuru with Fr Wilhelm Weber. They were both interned by the Japanese. Br Xaverius was permitted to work in the mountainous interior of Bougainville, until local commandos took him through to the Americans at Torokina. After the war, Xaverius was based at Torokina, Tsiroge, Koromira, and finally, Tubiana missions.

Br Xaverius built an enormous wooden church at Tubiana, a feat evidenced by the master-builder he was. Aircraft pilots used Tubiana's church tower, with its cross on top, to line up for landing at Aropa airport. Br Xaverius was not only a master builder, he was a teacher of master builders.

One of his students, Ntompo of Koromira, could build a European style house from start to finish. Xaverius was a hard task-master though, and when Ntompo was helping Xaverius build the church at Koromira, he complained about Xaverius' strict German discipline. Xaverius responded, 'Don't be foolish boy. When you are old you will point to this church and tell your grandchildren—I built that.' (pers. comm. Moore: 2022). Without wishing to inconvenience anyone, Br Xaverius would make a coffin for his funeral.

> Always a practical man, he stood it on its end and used it as a cupboard for the few clothes he had. The sisters must have thought they were immortal because they never had a coffin on hand when one of their elders died. They knew Xaverius would have one, which he always gave them. Then he would 'get to' and make himself another (pers. comm. Moore: 2022).

Br Xaverius died after travelling to Vunapope mission hospital for a medical check-up. He was diagnosed with diabetes but it was too late to rectify. Br Xaverius never got to use one of the coffins he made.

Bishop Henk Kronenberg SM b: 29 Sep 1934 Enschede Netherlands d: 25 Mar 2020 Enschede Netherlands

Henk Kronenberg was professed a Marist on Friday 12 September 1958, and ordained a priest on Wednesday 18 October 1961, when he worked as a teacher in Hulst, Netherlands, until 1964.

Fr Kronenberg served as a priest in Bougainville from 1965 to 1990, in various mission stations. In 1982, Bishop Gregory Singkai appointed him as director of the Mabiri Ministry School that was established after the Second World War. Fr Kronenberg held this position for nine years.

Following the outbreak of the Bougainville Crisis, Fr Kronenberg relocated to Port Moresby in 1991, teaching catechetics at the Bomana seminary until 1995.

He was appointed as Bishop of Bougainville on Monday 19 April 1999 and ordained at Tsiroge by the Archbishop of Rabaul, Karl Hesse MSC, on Wednesday 14 July 1999. Bishop Henk headed a diocese that was striving to recover in the aftermath of the ten-year civil war.

In 2009, Bishop Henk was awarded the highest honour on PNG's Independence Day, with the title of Chief, and the Order of Logohu, the principal order of the Order of PNG.

Logohu is a Motuan word for the bird-of-paradise, the official national symbol of PNG since its independence (Begg, J. Duffy, E. O'Connor, M. and Weemaes, W. 2020).

In December 2009, Bishop Henk retired to his hometown and Marist community of Enschede, in the Netherlands.

Fr Joseph (Joe) Lamarre SM b: 20 Jan 1909 Portland USA d: 9 Sept 1979 Vunapope New Britain PNG

Fr Joe Lamarre was a missionary in Bougainville for 43 years. He arrived in 1936 to work in the Shortland Islands, having been professed a Marist in 1930.

During the Second World War, Fr Lamarre was taken prisoner by the Japanese at Hanahan. He spent one year interned on Sohano Island and in August 1943, he was sent to a prisoner of war camp in Rabaul for five months, doing hard labour whilst trying to survive the American bombing raids. 'Bombs by the thousands and bullets by the millions. Dozens of warships were sunk, scores of other ships were sent to the bottom,' Fr Lamarre SM wrote in the Hartford Courant, Sunday, July 10 1994.

After the war, Fr Lamarre was sent to Australia to recuperate, before returning to Bougainville. Most of Fr Lamarre's missionary life was spent on Buka—18 years in the parish of Hanahan.

He died at Vunapope on New Britain at the age of 70 after 43 years as a Marist. Fr Joe Lamarre was buried at Hanahan, where his requiem and burial was attended by thousands of people.

Fr Albert Lebel SM b: 1904 Maine USA d: 1975 Bougainville

After studying in Washington DC in the US, and Differt, in Belgium, Albert Lebel was ordained in 1930, aged 26. He left the following year for Oceania.

Fr Lebel's first two years were spent at Visale in the Solomon Islands. In 1933, he transferred to Tinputz on Bougainville, before going to Tunuru. Fr Lebel left Tunuru in January 1937, to start the new mission of Asitavi.

After Fr Lebel was evacuated, he spent some time in Vanuatu and New Caledonia. Following the war, he returned to Bougainville and worked on Nissan, Torokina, and Tearouki. In 1952, he went to Hahela, on Buka, upon his appointment as Regional Superior.

In 1960, Fr Lebel went to Monoitu parish in Siwai, where he served for 12 years. During his 45 years as a missionary, only twice did he return home to the US. A few days after attending an annual retreat, Fr Lebel died while celebrating Mass. He was 72.

Fr Bishop Leo Lemay SM b: 23 Sep 1909 Portland USA d: 9 Sep 1983 Massachusetts USA

Fr LeMay was professed in 1927, studying in Rome, where he was ordained in 1933, at the age of 23. He received a Doctorate in Theology shortly afterwards.

It was not until Fr Lemay was 42 years old, after working in an American seminary, that in 1950, he left for Oceania, where he ended up teaching in the seminary at Torokina on the west coast of Bougainville. Two of his students went on to become bishops.

In 1954, Fr Lemay became Provincial of Oceania and in 1960, he was appointed Bishop of Bougainville. Lemay was a humble man, seldom seen in full Episcopal regalia. While attending a meeting in Rabaul the newly appointed bishop was admonished by the archbishop about the need to ensure that a Papal flag was mounted on his vehicle. This highly amused Lemay, a situation he shared with staff on his return to Bougainville.

Bishop Lemay's vehicle was a wartime Jeep with access to approximately 25 km of dirt tracks pockmarked by enormous potholes disguised by large pools of rainwater. These roads wound between three mission stations; the girl's school at Tarlena, the Congregation of the Sisters of Nazareth (CSN) novitiate at Chabai and the parish at Hantoa.

Bishop Lemay let it be known that his primary objective was the creation of a national priesthood, an achievement he could feel proud of. Despite a civil war, as at 2023, 35 priests serve in the Diocese of Bougainville. Of these, 24 are diocesan priests from Bougainville and 12 are from religious congregations. In addition, several Bougainvillean priests work in other parts of PNG and overseas.

Bishop Lemay provided strong support for the growth of an Order of local nuns (CSNs) which grew in numbers and strength, providing great support to many people throughout Bougainville, especially during the Crisis, a ten-year civil war with PNG.

The Brothers of St Joseph who resided beside at Tsiroge mission obtained similar support. Sadly, their accommodation was destroyed during the Crisis and arguably as a result of the war and the destruction of the mission infrastructure, their numbers greatly reduced.

When The Garamuts Beat

Leo Lemay resigned his post in 1974, to enable a Bougainvillean, Bishop Gregory Singkai, to take his place. Bishop Lemay passed away aged 73.

Editor's note: Much of this information was kindly provided by Daniel Doyle, a lay missionary who spent some years teaching in Bougainville.

Fr George Lepping SM b: 19 Oct 1909 Philadelphia USA d: 26 Aug 2005 Washington DC USA

Fr Lepping was professed in the Society at Staten Island in 1933, and after seminary studies in the Marist College, Washington DC, he left that same year for Bougainville.

Fr Lepping was posted at first to Lemanmanu on Buka, and then to Nila in the Shortland Islands. It was in Nila, he was taken prisoner by the Japanese, along with Fr Maurice Boch, on 30 March 1942.

Fr Saris' account of George Lepping's war experience is in the Appendix.

After the war, Fr Lepping went on to serve at Torokina, Tearouki, Hahela and Hanahan, helping with the reconstruction and rehabilitation of missions. He also served as Regional Superior. His final posting was to Tungol on Nissan Island.

In 1988, Fr Lepping retired at Kieta, but due to the outbreak of the Bougainville Crisis, he returned to the US in 1990, having spent 51 years of mission life on Bougainville. Fr Lepping died at the age of 95.

Fr Emmet McHardy SM b: 27 Jun 1904 Taranaki New Zealand d: 17 May 1933 New Zealand

Three members of Emmet McHardy's family joined the Marist Society. Fr McHardy was professed in 1923, arriving in Bougainville six years later, aged 25, the second New Zealand Marist to work in the Pacific.

Fr McHardy founded Tunuru station, and ran a catechist school in south Bougainville. Despite the relatively short time he spent on Bougainville, Fr McHardy worked 'with great zeal', journeying into the rugged and mountainous interior. After contracting TB, his career on Bougainville ended in 1932. Fr McHardy died the following year, aged 29. His letters to family were collated into a book, *Blazing the Trail,* published in 1935.

Fr Adam Müller SM b: 10 Jan 1900 Cologne Germany d: 21 Jul 1979 Vunapope PNG

Adam Müller was professed in the Society in 1923, after his Novitiate at St Olav's in Glanerbrug. He arrived in Bougainville in 1929 aged 29, where he worked for 50 years at Turiboiru, Kunua, Torokina and Manetai. Fr Müller mastered many Bougainvillean languages, translating scripture, prayer books, and catechisms, including the writing of dictionaries and grammar.

In 1943, Fr Müller was interned by the Japanese, but he escaped in 1945 and was evacuated to Australia. The last 16 years of his life were spent in the Carterets, before he retired to Tabago mission in south Bougainville.

Fr Müller was known for his droll sense of humour, and spoke in a deep voice that lent a certain gravitas to his memorable quips.

Rudi Dreyer, a lay missionary working in Bougainville at the time, remembers when Fr Müller was based at the Carterets. These are a remote group of islands, 86 km north-east of Bougainville, and subject to the vagaries of isolation, the weather, and irregular shipping services.

Fr Müller must have been waiting for the mission boat to bring much-needed supplies, as when he went on the radio for his usual communique 'the sked', his message to the Catholic diocese office in Buka was very clear, 'If you don't send food today, you can send coffins tomorrow.'

There was another occasion where Müller needed a new hat. In the early days missionaries favoured hard hats much like the 'troppa' pith helmet. Once again, on 'the sked' with the diocese office in Buka, the person in the office asked Fr Müller how many hats were needed. Müller replied: 'I only have one head, so one hat will do.'

Another time, Fr Müller was walking through thick bush when he tripped on thick vines. He badly split open his nose, leaving a large flap of skin hanging open. When he returned to the house and saw the damage, with the aid of a small mirror, needle and thread, he stitched up the wound (pers. comm. Moore: 2022).

Fr Müller died of cancer in Vunapope hospital, aged 79 years. The parishioners of Tabago arranged for his body to be returned to their station so he could be buried near the Tabago church.

Fr Richard (Dick) O'Sullivan SMb: 4Mar 1902 Cooktown Australia d: 3 Sep 1972 Brisbane Australia

Dick O'Sullivan was one of the few Marists to be ordained in the college chapel, at St John's Woodlawn, on the outskirts of Lismore, in New South Wales. He was ordained on Monday 11 July 1937, aged 35.

Fr Miltrup wrote of Dick O'Sullivan and his propensity for guns when he considered them necessary. Rudi Dreyer recalled an incident at Koromira, 'Fr O'Sullivan was desperate to get a message to the diocese office, and as he looked out to sea, there was the mission boat motoring passed. Not one to waste time, Fr O'Sullivan ran back to the house for his shotgun—BANG! BANG! He fired off a volley across the bow of the ship.' The startled skipper soon got the message to call in to the mission.

Another time, Fr O'Sullivan wanted to go home for medical treatment, but Dr Furst told him it would be too cold in Australia for him. Dick respectfully explained to the good doctor: 'I don't tell you what the climate is like in your country, and I don't want you telling me what it is like in mine.'

'That was the end of the consultation,' recalled Harry Moore. Fr O'Sullivan died at the age of 70 in Brisbane, Queensland.

Fr Jean-Baptiste Poncelet SM b: 24 Jun 1884 Namur Belgium d: 29 Dec 1958 France

After his formation in Belgium and France, Fr Poncelet arrived in Bougainville in 1913, aged 29.

Nearly all his missionary life was spent in the Buin district. Fr Poncelet was first appointed to Mugai in 1916, then Turiboiru in 1919, which he founded. He held the position of parish priest there until his return to Belgium in 1949. He remained in south Bougainville for almost 30 years.

During his long time in Turiboiru, Fr Poncelet was closely associated with the Congregation of the Sisters of Nazareth (CSN), which was founded in Turiboiru (Saris: 2008, p. 64).

Robert Stuart wrote of Fr Poncelet in his book titled *'Nuts To You!'* Mr Stuart visited Fr Poncelet in 1926 while he on a recruiting trip to Buin for plantation labourers. Stuart mentioned Fr Poncelet, an entomologist, being financially well off due to his discovery of the rare butterfly Victoriae Regis or the Queen Victoria Birdwing, only found on Bougainville.

The butterfly at that time was purportedly worth £500, but Fr Poncelet was quick to point out that any money a priest made, had to be donated to the church. It was due to this discovery that Fr Poncelet had the funds to build a large church complete with a 'carillon of bells, and comfortable quarters for himself and his nuns,' (Stuart: 1977, p. 62).

His living room was festooned with cocoons and out of these emerged moths and butterflies whilst we were talking. The butterflies and moths were caught as soon as they emerged and placed in a bottle containing some chemical which instantly killed them, after which they were pinned to a board with their wings spread out and then placed in a glass case ready for shipment (Stuart: 1977. p. 62).

In 1937 Fr Poncelet was named Pro-Vicar of the Vicariate. When Bishop Wade was evacuated at the beginning of the Second World War, Fr Poncelet was placed in charge until his imprisonment and subsequent transfer in 1942 to an internment camp in Rabaul.

While he wrote a diary, which he gave to P. O'Reilly, he wanted to forget this time of his life as much as possible and never talked about it (Saris: 2008, p. 64).

The buildings, and airstrip built by the Japanese at Turiboiru, were destroyed during the war. Fr Poncelet returned after the war to rebuild the station. In 1949, he returned to Belgium before becoming superior of the Scholasticate in Differt, Belgium.

Fr Poncelet was also named Delegate-Provincial for Belgium, Luxembourg, and Holland, a post he held for ten years. Fr Poncelet died in France, aged 72.

Fr Pierre Schank SM b: 23 Feb 1887 Luxembourg d: 12 Apr 1957 Sydney Australia

Pierre Schank was professed in the Society in 1912. After his ordination, Fr Schank worked for four years in Holland before arriving in Bougainville in 1920, aged 32. Most of his missionary life was spent in the Buin area of southern Bougainville.

In 1942, Fr Schank was captured by the Japanese and remained a prisoner for the duration of the war. After two years recuperating in Australia, he returned to Bougainville for ten years. He was appointed master of the Second Novitiate in Sydney. Fr Schank's health was not good however, and he died in Sydney shortly after, aged 69.

Fr Josef Schlieker SM b: 14 Jan 1901 Olfen Germany d: 25 Sep 1965 Münster Germany

After Josef Schlieker's formation in the Netherlands and Germany, he was ordained in 1926, aged 25. He taught for four years in Meppen, Germany, before arriving in Oceania in 1932. Starting in the Shortlands, Fr Schlieker spent the next 33 years serving in many stations throughout Bougainville. He died of cancer whilst on a visit to Germany, aged 64.

Fr Charles Seiller SM b: 9 May 1876 Alsace France d: 25 Jun 1951 Bougainville

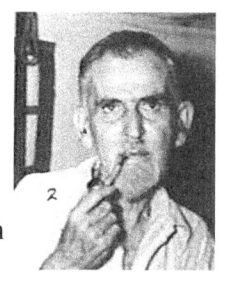

Charles Seiller was professed a Marist in 1901, and arrived at Poporang, headquarters for the new mission in the Shortlands Islands, in 1903. He was 27.

In less than two years, Fr Seiller was posted to Kieta on Bougainville, where he experienced considerable hostility, requiring a guard day and night at the station.

In 1942, when the Japanese occupied Kieta, Fr Seiller was placed in a prison camp until 1945. With Frs Grisward, Lebreton, Junker, two sisters, they escaped to behind the American lines, linking up with Fr O'Sullivan who then took care of them. After his release, Fr Seiller travelled to Australia for medical treatment, remaining there for two years before returning to his old station in Kieta for three years.

Apart from a short period at Koromira, Fr Seiller spent all of his missionary life at Tubiana mission in Kieta. He worked with a diocesan priest and then with the Marist Brothers who had come to establish Rigu High School. There were big celebrations for his 50 years of Profession in January 1951.

> In June he was taken by the Saint Joseph to Tearouki. He was paralyzed at this time After a short illness, there he died, aged 75 on 25th June 1951. P. Hogan at Asitavi, and Rondeau at Tinputz, came with some of their parishioners to the funeral, which P. Lebel celebrated that same day (Saris: 2008, p. 71).

Bishop Gregory Singkai b: 12 Mar 1935 Koromira Bougainville d: 12 Sep 1996 Vunapope East New Britain PNG

Gregory Singkai was ordained a priest on Saturday 17 December 1966, at St Michael's church in Tubiana, after which he was appointed chaplain, of St Joseph's Rigu High School, the following year.

In the late 1960s, Fr Singkai studied in Rome, gaining a license in theology before his appointment as rector of Bomana Major Seminary outside of Port Moresby.

On Sunday 24 November 1974, Bishop Gregory became the first Bougainvillean bishop, having served as a priest for nearly 30 years. He was bishop for another 21 years before his passing.

During the Bougainville Crisis, Bishop Singkai was appointed for a time as Education Minister in Bougainville's Interim Government, before being evacuated to Honiara and then to Australia for medical reasons. He returned to Bougainville following treatment (Niesi, P. *Post Courier:* 19 Sept 1996).

During the Crisis, Bishop Singkai played a role as 'special mediator' between the PNG Government and Bougainville Revolutionary Army leader, Mr Francis Ona (Callick: 1989).

A Requiem Mass for Bishop Singkai was attended by an estimated 1,000 people at the cathedral in Vunapope, before his body was returned to Bougainville (Niesi, P. *Post Courier:* Thur 19 Sept 1996). People say he died of a broken heart due to the stress of the Bougainville Crisis.

Aloysius Tamuka (Noga) from Tabago in Buin and **Peter Tatamas** of Lemanmanu Buka, were the first Bougainvillean priests.

Rev. Peter Tatamas was ordained to the priesthood at Hahela, Buka Island, on 20 December, 1953. A beautiful altar was especially built for the occasion by Br Xaverius and Mr Joseph McGann (The Advocate Melbourne: 1954, p.14). Aloysuis Tamuka was ordained on Sunday 6 December the same year, at Turiboiru near Buin.

Aloysuis Tamuka left the priesthood some years later, changing his last name to Noga. After becoming President of the Buin Local Government Council in 1968, Mr Aloysuis Noga went on to lead a public life in Bougainville's political affairs (UC San Diego. 2021).

Amongst other interests, Mr Noga was a Director with the Bougainville Development Corporation Ltd from 1975 to 1989.

Fr Bernard Tonjes SM was a pilot during WWI, and was likely ordained after that war. He came to Bougainville in 1929.

Seeing the need for the missions to own an aircraft, given their scattered and remote locations, Fr Tonjes persuaded Bishop Wade to contact the German mission aviation association (MIVA) to assist with funding and the purchase of an aircraft.

Tonjes initially wanted a sea plane, but MIVA despatched a Flamingo D 1400, in September 1934. The light aircraft arrived in packing cases aboard the MV *Malaita*. A pilot came out with the aircraft, along with a small film crew, to record its flight. Airstrips were built at Rigu, near Kieta, and Tarlena, in north Bougainville.

The Australian government refused permission for the plane to operate, and ordered that Bishop Wade return the plane.

Tonjes and the pilot thought they'd do a test flight and film it before packing the aircraft up, but the pilot misjudged the landing strip at Rigu, and landed on the beach, flipping the plane over. Fortunately, no one was seriously injured (*BCL Concentrate*: 1973).

After the War, Fr Tonjes was stationed at Sovele. He left Bougainville around 1948, eventually resigning from the priesthood.

Fr Herman To Paivu b: 1912 Tapo village East New Britain PNG d: 12 Feb 1981 Port Moresby PNG

Herman To Paivu was ordained a priest on Sunday 15 November 1953. On Monday 1 July 1974 he was appointed Auxiliary Bishop of Port Moresby and ordained as Bishop Tuesday 29 October 1974. The following year on Friday 19 December 1975, Bishop To Paivu was appointed Archbishop of Port Moresby. He spent 27 years as a priest and six years as bishop (*Catholic Hierarchy*: 1996).

Fr Florent Wache SM b: 26 Jan 1876 Metz France d: 10 Dec 1943 Kieta Bougainville

Florent Wache was professed a Marist in 1906, and arrived in Bougainville about 1910. He was 34 years of age. He served the Vicariate in the Shortlands, Bougainville, and Buka. Just before the Second World War, Fr Wache was posted to the new mission of Nissan Island located north-east of Bougainville.

Suspected of communicating with the American forces, the Japanese imprisoned him in Kieta at Tubiana. Fr Wache was killed in 1943 at the Tubiana camp during an American bombing raid, the same day his confrère Fr John Conley from Nissan, was beheaded in Kieta by the Japanese. Fr Wache was 67.

Bishop Thomas Wade SM b: 4 Aug 1893 Providence Rhode Island USA d: 11 Jun 1969 USA

Thomas Wade was ordained in 1922, aged 29, and arrived in Bougainville shortly after. In 1930, he was ordained as the first bishop for the Vicariate of North Solomons. The following is extracted from Phyllis V. Campbell's *Marist Missions North Solomons* 1943:

He founded the first general school for catechists at Burunotui. Previously the Fathers in each station used to train their own catechists...From 60 to 70 lads from different parts of the islands trained there. They learnt Catechism, Gregorian Chant, reading, writing and arithmetic. The course extended over three years. Successful candidates departed to work as catechists in their own villages. Some even volunteered to go to the wild men of the interior. They summoned the priest to dying people, baptised infants and the aged who were in danger of death. They were in fact, the Missionaries' greatest asset. For five years Father Wade built up and consolidated this work. He was then moved to Lemanmanu. After two years in that district he was summoned to Sydney. To his surprise and dismay he was appointed the first Vicar Apostolic of the North Solomons. He was consecrated at St. Patrick's church, Sydney, on the feast of Christ the King, 1930, by the Apostolic Delegate, Archbishop Cattaneo (Kronenberg & Saris: date unknown, p.94).

Several articles on Bishop Wade's war experience can be found in digitised newspapers of the time. He was eventually rescued from the island and became the Military Delegate for the US Armed Forces in the South Pacific.

After the war, Bishop Wade oversaw the reconstruction of the missions in Bougainville. He began a seminary and ordained the first Bougainvillean priests. Ill health forced his retirement in 1959, when he returned to the US. Bishop Wade died aged 76.

Marist confrères

Fr Wilhelm Weber SM b: 21 Mar 1905 Gelsenkirchen Germany d: 8 May 1945 Manetai Bougainville

Wilhelm Weber was professed in the Society in 1929, and ordained a priest in 1932.

In 1935, he left for Oceania, having been appointed to the mission on Bougainville. An extensive article was written by Fr Joe Lamarre SM on Wilhelm Weber's life as a Marist in Bougainville, and what happened to him in the end as a consequence of the war. Refer to the Appendix for more on Fr Weber.

Fr Wilhelm (Willi) Wöeste SM b: Osnabrück 1921 Germany d: 2005 Meppen Germany

Willi Wöeste, and his brother Herman, became Marist priests, whilst two of his sisters became religious sisters in The Society of Mary. After serving in the military during the war, Willi Wöeste was professed in 1948, and ordained in 1951.

Fr Wöeste was based at Tunuru, and Deomori, on Bougainville, where he experienced difficulties with a cargo cultist movement, led by Damien Damen. He was subsequently based at Hahela where he served as Regional Superior, followed by time spent at Manetai, Marai, and Torokina.

Due to ill-health, Fr Wöeste returned to Germany in 1989, where he died aged 84. He was 57 years a Marist.

§

The photographs used in this section are sourced from: The Society of Mary in Rome, The Australian War Memorial, Christine Leonard's family collection, and the Late Hendry Saris SM.

When The Garamuts Beat

Marist consœurs

In the Catholic tradition, as in other traditions, taking a new name symbolises entering into a new place in one's life. In congregations named after Mary, it was common to include 'Mary' as the first part of a sister's religious name (A Nun's Life Ministry: 2010).

These biographies are of some The Missionary Sisters of the Society of Mary (SMSM) mentioned in Fr Miltrup's memoir. Their publications and the inclusion of photographs along with selected stories in the Appendix was approved by The Missionary Sisters of the Society of Mary.

In the case of sisters living, any personal details included, are with the individual's permission. Baptismal names are shown in brackets.

> The vocation of our first sisters was clarified through their faithful living in response to the inspirations of the Holy Spirit and the guidance of the Marist priests with whom they worked in mission (SMSM: 2014).

Sr Marie Blaise SMSM (Helene Bodinier) b: 1913 Nantes France d: 9 Dec 2021 France
Sr Blaise arrived in Bougainville in 1937. In 1942, she was evacuated by submarine to New Caledonia with other evacuees, and then sent by troopship to New Zealand in 1943. She remained in New Zealand until her return to Bougainville in August 1946.

Sr Blaise was transferred to Piano in 1952, where she served until early 1967. After serving in various stations on Bougainville, in March 1972, Sr Blaise left Bougainville for France, where she died at the grand age of 108 years and ten months.

Sr Marie Gisèle SMSM (Antoinette Christine Chaverot) b: 14 Feb 1912 Ancy Rhone France d: 27 Oct 1994 Killara Sydney Australia
Sr Gisèle arrived in Bougainville in 1935, and remained there until 1989. With other evacuees, she left Bougainville in early 1943 on an American submarine, USS *Nautilus*, bound for New Caledonia.

Sr Gisèle wrote an account of her war experience, titled, During the War in the Pacific which is included in the Appendix. Sr Gisèle returned to Bougainville in August 1946, remaining there until in 1989. She died at Killara in Sydney in 1994.

Sr Mary Hortense SMSM (Marie Jeanne Dagenais) b: 3 Dec 1903 Lawrence Masachusetts USA d: 8 Dec 1998 Waltham Massachusetts USA
Sr Hortense arrived in Bougainville in January 1936, and worked there until 1971. She was evacuated during WWIr in 1943, on an American submarine, and taken to Guadalcanal and then to Noumea in New Caledonia,

before a troopship took her and other evacuees to New Zealand.

Sr Hortense was then assigned to Makogai, in Fiji for the duration of the war. She returned to Bougainville in 1946, and was stationed at Piva, Torokina, from 1949 to 1957 at the mission hospital for the Hansenide

Colony (Leprosarium).

> Piva Clinic, Bougainville, was Bishop Wade's project, subsidised by Government. Maintained for over twenty years by Sisters Hortense and Michael, Piva cared for small groups of lepers alongside a general and maternity clinic. Happily, as new treatment was used, the numbers of Hansen's patients diminished. In 1976 Piva closed (O'Brien: 1989, p. 144).

Sr Hortense retired to Tubiana before leaving Bougainville on Saturday 21 July 1973.

Sr Mary Lidwina SMSM (Catherine Didelot) b:1885 Germany d: 5 Sep 1963 Koromira Bougainville

Sr Lidwina arrived in Kieta, Bougainville, on Wednesday 23 July 1913, aged 28. She worked at Koromira until 1934 when she was transferred to Tinputz. Three years later she returned to Koromira, remaining there until December 1942.

Sr Lidwina was taken prisoner by the Japanese in 1942, finally escaping in April 1945, when she walked overland to Torokina, before being evacuated to Sydney.

She returned to Koromira in August 1948. In December 1960, Sr Lidwina was treated in Tearouki for a severe illness, and at her request in 1961, she returned to Koromira, where she remained until her death.

Sr Mary Fabian SMSM (Catherine Doherty) b: 7 Oct 1905 Donegal, Ireland d: 26 Jun 1982 Sydney Australia

Sr Fabian arrived in Bougainville in January 1938 on the same ship as Fr Miltrup, and worked in Bougainville until 1973.

During WWII in 1943, Sr Fabian was evacuated with other SMSM sisters on the USS Nautilus to New Zealand. After the war in February 1947, Sr Fabian returned to Bougainville. She left Bougainville in 1973, remaining in Australia until her death in Sydney.

Sr Marie Martial SMSM (Marie Fardeau) b: 2 Oct 1888 Maine-et-Loire, France d: 29 Dec 1973 Tubiana Bougainville

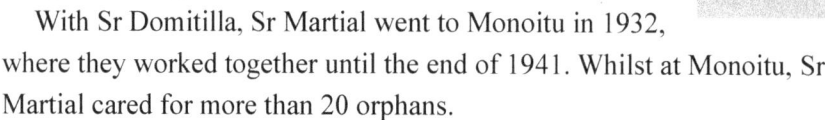

Sr Martial was a trained nurse before taking her Orders, making her the first medically qualified sister on Bougainville, upon arrival in March 1919.

With Sr Domitilla, Sr Martial went to Monoitu in 1932, where they worked together until the end of 1941. Whilst at Monoitu, Sr Martial cared for more than 20 orphans.

> Encouraged by Bishop Wade, and aided by Government funds, their clinics became centres of communication for local women, quick to learn improved ways of health and child care... Martial was stationed at Kieta, and later, in Faisi. For most of her long life, Martial's special concern was for babies. In early days, infanticide was common. Ignace recorded that an unwanted infant was sometimes thrown on the fire, or to the pigs. Others were commonly buried alive: Of twins, one was habitually abandoned. Thus evolved the custom of 'nurseries' where missionary sisters cared for these tiny ones, till they were old enough to be claimed (O'Brien: 1989. pp. 96, 136).

When the Japanese landed in Bougainville, Sr Martial was caring for infants and orphans at Monoitu mission in South Bougainville. She was eventually evacuated with Srs Ignace and Aldalberta on the American submarine USS Gato to Guadalcanal, and then transferred to a troopship, which took her and other evacuees to Noumea, and on to Australia in 1943.

Sr Martial returned Bougainville in 1946, and was at Tubiana mission near Kieta until her death. An autobiographical account of her wartime experience is in the Appendix.

Marist consœurs

Sr Marie Adalberta (Helena Jaspers) b: Hanover, Germany d: 1971 Tubiana Bougainville

Sr Adalberta arrived in Bougainville in October 1914, aged 26. She was evacuated in 1943 by submarine to Guadalcanal, and taken to Noumea, and ultimately Australia. Her story is included with others in the Appendix. Sr Adalberta returned to Bougainville in 1946, remaining there until her death, in 1971.

An article on the evacuation from Bougainville:

Submarine Comes For The Nuns

In between coast watching, Read arranged by radio for the evacuation of a number of civilians - many of whom had earlier been given a chance to leave Bougainville and refused - and a party of sixteen Marist mission Sisters, Americans. A U.S. submarine ran the enemy gauntlet into Teop Harbour on the last night of 1942.

Read describes the scene: In silent procession the Sisters in their flowing robes, the only clothes they had, moved off for the beach an hour away. I admired them as they waded through mud and water, and stumbled over treacherous logs in the uncertain light of the hurricane lantern; yet with never a murmur of complaint.

Read feared that civilians, if taken by the Japanese and tortured, might divulge vital information, including the whereabouts of radio posts. He was glad to see them go (Sunday Herald: 1953, p. 10).

The person named 'Read' is Lieutenant W.J. (Jack) Read DSC who, prior to his transfer to Bougainville in 1941, was a district officer in the Australian administration, based in Madang. Jack Read was stationed at Buka Passage sub-district, becoming a Coastwatcher, reporting to Lieutenant Commander Eric Feldt throughout the war.

Sr Bernadette Kavanagh SMSM b: Victoria Australia
Sr Bernadette was a teacher before joining the SMSM. She went to Bougainville in 1974, becoming involved in teaching and catechetical work at Asitavi.

In 1976 she moved to Tunuru to do catechetical work there and in Arawa. In June 1979, Sr Bernadette returned to Australia for further studies, becoming involved in spirituality courses and retreats in Sydney and Queensland. In 2005, she left the Congregation.

Sr Mary Michaeline SMSM (Irene Medzihradsky) b: 17 Apr 1921 Ohio USA d: 17 Mar 2020 Massachusetts USA
Sr Michaeline was professed in 1948. She worked in finance and administration in Jamaica and in the USA until 1968, after which she went to Bougainville.

After teaching for one year at Moratona, in 1970, Sr Michaeline was assigned to Kieta parish working in finance and administration for the Congregation and the diocese, as well as catechetics in the parish.

Sr Michaeline took up studies in the Philippines after which she returned to do pastoral work at Tunuru until the outset of the Bougainville Crisis. She left Bougainville in 1990, returning to the US to continue her service, where she died in 2020, aged 98.

Sr Marie Crescentia SMSM (Elizabeth Monning) b: 1892 Münster Germany d: 1988 Bougainville
Sr Crescentia was professed in France in 1914, and left soon after for Bougainville at 22 years of age.

She was stationed in Buin at Muguai mission, teaching women and children in Telei, the Buin language. After being held as a prisoner in the Japanese-run camp at Ramale, in New Britain, for three years, Sr Crescentia was finally rescued. She went to Australia, but returned to Bougainville in June 1946, where she served until her death aged 96.

Sr Mary Ludovica SMSM (Fransiska Mosner) b: 1886 Germany d: 10 Feb 1963 Tearouki Bougainville

Sr Ludovica arrived in Bougainville at 26 on Monday 12 February 1912.

With Sr M. Ursule, she opened the first station on Buka, at Burunotui mission. In 1928. Sr Ludovica reopened Banoni (Torokina) and went on to work in Tarlena, and Muguai. In 1938, she moved to Koromira. Sr Ludovica was still at Koromira when she was taken prisoner by the Japanese in December 1942.

After escaping with assistance to Torokina in April 1945, she was evacuated to Sydney. Sr Ludovica returned to Bougainville in October 1946. During the post-war period, she worked at various mission stations, such as Torokina, Piva, Tunuru, and Mamaregu, until she fell ill in 1952. From 1954 to 1962, Sr Ludovica worked in Hantoa in the north of Bougainville before retiring to Tearouki, where she died the following year.

Sr Marie Domitilla SMSM (Lucie Pedrault) b: 1903 France d: 29 Nov 1944 New Britain PNG

Sr Domitilla arrived in Bougainville in 1927. She went to Monoitu in 1933 to take charge of the girls, but in December 1941, she travelled to Rabaul for medical care. Whilst in Rabaul, Sr Domitilla was taken prisoner by the Japanese, and eventually died of illness at the Ramale prison camp on Wednesday 29 November 1944.

Sr Wendelina's account in the Appendix explains in detail life as a POW for Sr Domitilla, and how she met her end.

Sr Mary Dolores (Mary Quigley) b: 1 May 1894 Silvertown, London England d: 29 Dec 1972 Koromira Bougainville

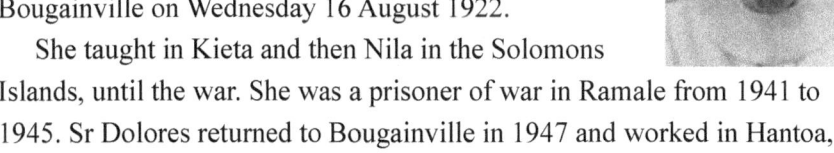

Sister Mary Dolores was professed in Ste. Foy-les-Lyon, France, on Saturday 25 March 1922 and arrived in Kieta, Bougainville on Wednesday 16 August 1922.

She taught in Kieta and then Nila in the Solomons Islands, until the war. She was a prisoner of war in Ramale from 1941 to 1945. Sr Dolores returned to Bougainville in 1947 and worked in Hantoa,

Tearouki, Kieta and finally Koromira where she died on 29 December 1972.

Fr Harry Moore SM made Sr Dolores' coffin when she died. He remembered her as, 'a very proper English woman, who always carried around a small bar of soap in her pocket. I believe it was a habit she picked up after her time in the prison camp. The other thing was, she had no toes. What Sr went through we can't imagine.'

Sr Marie Wendelina SMSM (Marie Richter) b: 1903 Metz, Moselle, Germany d: 2 Oct 1992 Sydney Australia

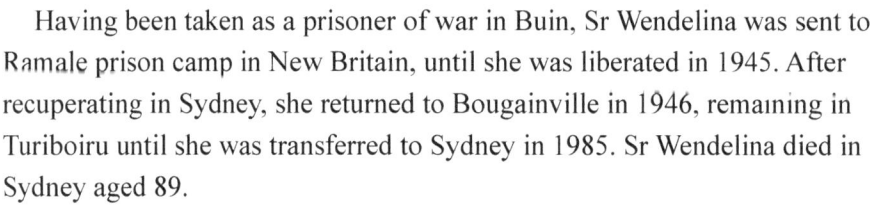

Sr Wendelina was professed in 1924, and left France for Bougainville two years later, aged 33.

She served most of her time in Turiboiru, in Buin, and as a consequence, was proficient in Telei.

Having been taken as a prisoner of war in Buin, Sr Wendelina was sent to Ramale prison camp in New Britain, until she was liberated in 1945. After recuperating in Sydney, she returned to Bougainville in 1946, remaining in Turiboiru until she was transferred to Sydney in 1985. Sr Wendelina died in Sydney aged 89.

Sr Wendelina wrote a moving account of those war years which are in the Appendix. It is a first-hand account of events covering the years between 1942 and 1945, as a prisoner of war in East New Britain.

Sr Mary Juliana SMSM (Florabelle Marie Roper) b: 20 Aug 1919 Louisiana USA d: 23 Oct 2020 USA

Sister Juliana joined the Marist Missionary Sisters on Saturday 2 August 1941, making her profession on 2 February 1944.

Sr was trained as a teacher before travelling to Bougainville on Friday 30 January 1948, where she taught for 20 years at Tunuru, Sovele and Turiboiru. Sr pronounced her final vows in Bougainville on Thursday 2 February 1950.

In 1968, Sr Juliana became a supervisor of teachers, based in Tubiana. After 1970, she began to do social work with the women in Sovele, Tearouki and Torokina.

From 1978, she devoted herself to catechetics in Tubiana, and later taught new converts in Tunuru, until she left Bougainville in 1988. After working in the Solomon Islands, and later American Samoa, Sr Juliana returned to the US, where she remained until her death.

Sr Marie Ignace SMSM (Madeleine Schaal) b: 25 Feb 1874 Alsace d: 8 May 1959 Turiboiru Bougainville

Sr Ignace (sometimes known as Ignatius), at 25, was first sent to Samoa in 1899. She was one of the first two sisters to go to Poparang Island in the Shortlands in April 1901, before moving to Bougainville in 1904.

Across the passage from Buin, at Poporang, in the Shortland Islands, two Marist fathers, Englert and Flaus, started a mission station in 1899, under the jurisdiction of Bishop Broyer of Samoa. Sister Ignace, who was two years in Samoa beforehand, arrived at Poporang in early 1901, with Sr Claire Rochette. In that first year, everyone at Poporang suffered with malaria, the heat, prickly heat rash, and lethargy. Sister Ignace wrote:

> The Bishop became ill while building the house. The Fathers were sick too, flat on their backs, and both of us were not so well. I thought we would all die, and that the first mission of North Solomons would end before it had a chance to get started (O'Brien: 1989. p. 93).

Sr Ignace was by now fluent in the Alu language of the South Solomons, and quickly learning Telei (O'Brien: 1989, p. 94). In 1904, along with Sr Boniface, she and some Alu catechists, sailed on a five-day journey to Kieta.

Fr Laurent had a small house built in preparation, complete with table, chairs, pots and pans. He even arranged to get some chickens for the sisters to raise, in promise of much needed protein some time in the future.

With Sr Boniface, Sr Ignace was often assisted by Dr Bruno Kroening, the German administration doctor who was based in Kieta from 1905. Taking a supply of medicines they visited villages, treating sores, minor injuries and newborn babies. Their medical kit consisted of quinine, castor oil, rhubarb, bandages. iodine and a good supply of aspirin. Along with Sr Placida, Sr Ignace later established a dispensary in the Buin area. (O'Brien: 1989, p. 135).

In 1922, Fr Jean-Baptiste Poncelet welcomed Srs Ignace and Crescentia to Turiboiru. In their visits to nearby villages, they were often greeted by Chief Mege, whose daughter, Poetsi, grew very close to the sisters. (O'Brien: 1989, p. 95). In 1933, Sr Ignace beganformation work with the first Bougainvillean sisters, the Order being the Sisters of Nazareth.

During the Second World War, in 1943, Sr Ignace was evacuated by submarine, on the USS Gato, to Guadalcanal, and then by troopship to Noumea and Australia. She remained in Australia until her return to Bougainville in August 1946. Sr Ignace died in Turiboiru in 1959.

Sr Mary Sevarina SMSM (Louise Visco) b: 2 Feb 1916 USA d: 7Apr 1958 Turiboiru Bougainville

Sr Sevarina, known as a 'New Yorker', entered the Order on 2 August 1938, making her first profession on 2 February 1942, in Bedford Massachusetts, USA.

Arriving in Torokina as a trained nurse in October 1946, her skills were soon put to use in Bougainville. From October 1947, Sr Sevarina was placed in charge of the hospital at Tunuru until she transferred to Tearouki in January 1950.

Sr moved down to Turiboiru, working in maternal and child health at mission hospital that was run by the two Drs Furst, and soon learnt to speak Telei fluently.

By all accounts Sr Sevarina was a very outgoing woman, open to fun and blessed with a heightened sense of humour. She referred to the ruffle framing her face as her 'cigarette holders' (Phillips: 1993).

When delivering the baby of the government medical officer's wife, 'Sister Severina [sic] enlivened the situation by placing bets on the sex of the baby as the head was crowning.' She was teaching a man to ride her motorbike when it slipped and fell on her, rupturing her spleen (Phillips: 1993, p.70).

Sr Sevarina's untimely death was keenly felt.

Sr Margarete Wöeste SMSM (Margaretha Christina Wöeste) b: 1935 Germany

After being professed, Sr Wöeste studied dentistry in Milwaukee, Wisconsin, USA.

She arrived in Bougainville in 1969, where she worked as a dentist in various places, including taking up the government position of Provincial Dental Officer from 1974 to 1979.

Sr Margarete left Bougainville in 1988. After living in Sydney for some years she returned to PNG in 1993, to Boset in Western Province. After leaving PNG finally and working in Germany for an extended period. At the time this book was printed Sr Margarete was ministering in the US.

When The Garamuts Beat

Afterword

Friedel Miltrup visited his uncle in Germany prior to his death in 1996 when Fr Miltrup had plenty of time to think about the past and the next chapter awaiting. Seeing the sadness in Friedel's eyes, Fr Miltrup told his nephew about his plans.

'I will spend my time dusting the wings of angels,' he declared in a voice that was losing its strength. Friedel asked his Uncle Franz what he meant by that, to which the old priest explained, that whenever he heard the sisters' confessions, he imagined he was dusting the wings of angels.

When The Garamuts Beat

Appendix

This section includes published and unpublished accounts written of and by the SMSM and SM missionaries of personal experiences during WWII in Bougainville and in East New Britain. These first-hand narratives and articles were written by the person directly affected or someone close to the subject.

They provide a broader perspective of events of the era covered in Fr Franz Miltrup's memoir, including the traumatic experiences at Ramale and Vunapope in East New Britain between 1942 and 1945.

Readers will get a deeper understanding of what actually happened and what it felt like for those involved.

Lest we forget

The Marist consœurs are listed alphabetically according to their birth names, as are the Marist confrères.

The Missionary Sisters of the Society of Mary have approved the inclusion of the consaurs' stories in this book. The Provincial Bursar and Councillor for the Oceania Marist Province approved the publication of Fr Joe Lamarre's story about Fr Wilhelm Weber.

Sister Marie Gisèle SMSM gave a copy of her story to Merle Wall MBE in the early 1970s, while both were living in Bougainville. This is the Late Sr Gisèle's own story. Who typed and transcribed it is not known—it could have been Sr Martial SMSM.

When The Garamuts Beat

Antoinette Christine Chaverot (Sr Marie Gisele SMSM)
Some data of Kieta S.M.S.M.

During the War in the Pacific

When the war between Japan and the U.SA. broke out on the 5th December 1941, we were five at Kieta: Mother M. Wendelina, Regional, Srs M. Adalberta, Melanie, Hortense and Gisèle. Three Sisters of Nazareth had also arrived from Buin to care for orphans from various Stations, mostly from Monoitu and we also had two little girls in Kieta, one from leper parents at the colony and one from Eivo.

Most of the European women left by the next steamer that came from Australia and some weeks later, the Government gave the order to leave to those still on Bougainville, but letting the sisters free to go or stay. We chose to stay with our people. Anyhow, there would not have been time for those of outer Stations to come and catch the ship, just two days after notification.

However, Bishop Wade was worried about the safety of the sisters, as the Japanese were advancing. Early January, he sent Sisters Denisia, Josephine and Agnes back to Buin, with most of the orphans, and on the 17th it was our turn to get on board the Ludwig and sail to Buin. On the beach at Tubiana, Bishop, the priests and the brothers were very moved to say goodbye. We were very sad! For the first time since the sisters came to Kieta in 1904, the convent would be closed! The ship left the harbour and we sailed for a while, then the engine stopped.

From the hilltop, some missionaries were watching us go, and stop! Promptly two smaller boats were sent to the rescue. We transferred to the Gabriel with the babies, Brother Henry being on board and we continued our trip southwards to arrive about midnight at Patupatuai, Buin. We installed ourselves as best we could in the house left vacant by the nurses of the Marist Medical Mission.

Fr O'Sullivan was away, so there was no Mass in the morning and dispersion began: Sr M. Adalberta took the road to Muguai; Sr M. Hortense walked to Piano, enroute to Monoitu. Sr M. Gisèle would go later to Piano after a few days at Turiboiru, where Mother M. Wendelina and Sr M. Melanie were to stay. A large group of school children, with two sisters had come from Turiboiru to get us and the babies. The whole group started off

Appendix

about noon under torrential rain which lasted most of the four-hour walk between Patupatuai and Turiboiru. There we were received warmly by the sisters and Fr Poncelet, the priest-in-charge.

A week later, the first bombs were dropped over Kieta by the Japs. Then they came to North Bougainville and Buka to stay. In March, a European Planter was killed and Fr Hennessy taken away. This Boston diocesan priest was not heard of again.

On Easter Sunday, a group of Japanese coming from the Shortlands landed at Patupatuai for the first time. They searched the houses but did no harm to Fr. O'Sullivan. The very next day, he and Brother Henry and all the schoolboys left: they returned to their district, except two from the Kieta area, while Fr O'Sullivan and Brother went to Piano, where Fr Miltrup welcomed these new refugees. Some days later, the Japanese returned to Buin, this time setting fire to all the houses of the mission, except the little church. They also burnt the government buildings at Kangu. From then on, the Japs came and went every day between Faisi (Shortlands Is) and Buin. So, we lived in fear, especially when they started walking inland towards the mission.

During July, Bishop Wade was 'prisoner' in his residence in Kieta. After six weeks of it, during an Allied bombing of Japanese ships in Kieta Harbour, he succeeded to get away. We were very happy to hear from him.

On 9 September, we heard from the Coast Watchers and the people, that Japs had definitely landed and were settling in about 5 hours' distance from us. The next day we could hear the dynamite explosions they used to uproot the huge trees of the jungle. Hundreds of Telei people were forced to work to help cut the bush to make an aerodrome.

Saturday, 19 September 1942, we heard that the missionaries of Muguai had been taken to the beach by the Japanese: Fr Schank, Br Bruno, Srs Crescentia and Mary, of the Sacred Heart.

Monday 21st, it was the turn of the Turiboiru missionaries to be brought to the beach H.Q. of the Japanese, all except Sr M. Ignace who pleaded to stay because of her old age and sore legs—she had elephantiasis, but, in reality, it was to be with her Sisters of Nazareth and the children they cared for. The walk to the camp was a very long one, it took seven hours.

Sr M. Andrea was sick and had to be carried some of the way by our brave Solomonese. These were chased away by the Japs after the group arrived at the camp.

The six newcomers shared one house with the four missionaries from Muguai, and for ten days there would be many a lecture of cross-questioning of the group, or individually, to try and find out where the Coast Watchers and soldiers were, in the bush, promising freedom if they gave information. No one did, so the missionaries were put on board a ship bound for Rabaul, on the 1st October. (These informations [sic] from Mother M. Wendelina's post-war narrative of their 3-year internment: Buin—Rabaul—Vunapope and Ramale camps.)

When the missionaries of Piano and Monoitu heard of what happened in Muguai and Turiboiru, the two priests-in-charge promptly took the decision that their sisters were to leave Piano immediately to go further inland, to Nagovis and possibly further. On 23rd September, Srs M. Blaise and Gisèle left for Monoitu on two old bicycles, to rejoin Sr M. Hortense who had gone there on a medical errand.

On this Siwai station, Sr M. Martial was very busy with medical work and bringing up many little orphans. Her companion, Sr M. Domitilla, had gone for medical care to Vunapope, Rabaul, the previous year, but war prevented her return. At this stage, Srs Fabian and Adalberta were her companions.

After a few days at Monoitu, Fr Schlieker thought it would be better for the newcomers to continue to Sovele, farther inland, in the Nagovis district. So off we went: Srs Hortense and Blaise using the ladies' bicycles, while Sr Gisèle was given a man's bike because she was the tallest and could more easily handle it! Some of the bicycles had no brakes, which meant walking in gullies and difficult spots. We went so slowly that we did not reach Sovele that day and slept in a village. Next day we arrived at noon to Fr Tonjes' parish and he made us welcome. As there was no sisters' house at Sovele, he vacated his own for us and took abode in the sacristy of the church.

During our five weeks stay at Sovele, Fr Henry Fluet and Fr O'Sullivan passed, coming from the north-east coast, sent by Bishop Wade, with directives for his missionaries of South Bougainville, who were still free. He had heard of the tragedy on Guadalcanal, besides learning of those in Buin taken to camp by the Japs and nothing was known of Frs Boch and Lepping at Faisi, in the Shortlands.

After our departure from Piano, Fr Miltrup had asked Sr M. Ignace and the Sisters of Nazareth to come. Fr Fluet now brought them a message from Bishop; the Little Sisters were relieved of their Promises and should return to their own people, while Sr M. Ignace should move to Monoitu. It would be safer for all. By that time, Fr Miltrup was sick and he finally arrived in Sovele, carried in as he had black-water fever.

Fr O'Sullivan also arrived back and came to organize our trip to the east-coast for an eventual evacuation. By now, Sr M. Fabian had come from Monoitu, as also Br Henry. Our group of four Sisters, Br. Henry and Fr O'Sullivan, left Sovele on November 2nd taking only the merest luggage: one set of clothes! This first day was an 8-hour walk to a village where the good people gave us hospitality for the night, after a good meal of local food.

The next day was much more difficult, up and down slopes as our guides were avoiding beaten tracks, for fear of the Japs and we were terribly stiff from the previous day's long journey. Our leader had picked good, strong men to help the sisters in crossing rivers, climbing slippery paths, and how grateful we were for the needed help! Very soon on our trip, we were given a name: Ship No. 1 to Sr Fabian who was always ahead; then Sr M. Hortense came 2nd; Sr Gisèle was 3rd only, while Sr Blaise was 4th and last. She was very, tired and slow, so we would go at the pace of the last ship, and for the remainder of the journey in the mountainous jungle, the stoutest of the men was assigned to help her, in case she needed to be carried.

One evening, we came to the top of a mountain, overlooking the ocean on both sides of Bougainville! What a glorious view! The sea coasts were far away on either side. We were given a full day's rest in that village, Moronei, [sic] if I remember correctly. It was very cold at night and we had to sleep close to each other to keep warm. It is also in this area that copper was found. It is now the Panguna Mine.

Next morning, we resumed our walking, struggling up and down gullies, slopes and rivers. These had slippery stones, which made our helpers all the more necessary. Rain seemed to fall in torrents every afternoon, often with an electric storm and deafening claps of thunder. We looked forward to changing into our 'one and only' set of dry clothes at the next stop, while accepting the fact that our wet clothes had to be worn again next day, as we never succeeded to dry them, up besides the little fire that cooked the rice for the meal. It is another wonder of the Lord's protection that we didn't get bad colds.

One day we came to a rather large house, built of bamboo and sago palm. It was the 'hide-out' of Wong You's family, a Chinese trader of Kieta. They had six children and Wong's sister had six also, so it was a big group to look after and keep clear of the Japanese. The good man gave us a cup of tea and then, we resumed our walk. Later in the day, we came to another house, this time it was at Mr Roche's home, a gold prospector. He had chosen to stay when the government evacuated the white population. He kindly offered us hospitality for the night. We thanked him sincerely next morning, hoping and praying that he would be safe. But it was not to be. Some months later, the Japs found him and beheaded him by the river. The Wong You family was also found, but were taken to Kieta, prisoners for the time of the war.

As we continued our way, now helped by 'Highlanders' who were with Mr Roche, we came to a large river spanned by a large tree trunk—but nothing to hold on. These men helped us across, holding us firmly by the hand on either side. When I reached the opposite bank and looked back, I saw with amazement that one single Highlander was carrying Sr Blaise on his back, advancing carefully over the round trunk. I turned away in terror at the thought of a possible fall into that crocodile-infested river. Thank God! he made it, regardless of his small stature. He must have thought that time was too pressing to wait for the return of another to guide Sister across. How often we felt God's protection during this and other future trips.

At long last, we reached Manetai, about the 10th of November, where Fr Mueller [sic] made us welcome to his station. Here we rested three days and tried to clean our clothes, but they remained greyish. Br Henry was very tired; the crossing of the mountains had been hard on him.

Fr O'Sullivan made arrangements with some villagers on the beach, for a large canoe to take us to Asitavi at night. One evening, we walked to the beach some miles away and boarded a big outrigger canoe in the dark. It was a very tiring trip, sitting-up, back-to-back, at the bottom of the canoe, arriving in Asitavi just before dawn. There was Fr Henry Fluet, the pastor, receiving yet another group of refugees!

Appendix

Four Sisters of St Joseph were here already, having moved from Hanahan, Buka, many months ago. Bishop Wade was very relieved that we had made it.

The sisters took us in their community and it was so good to be at last in a home! We needed some medical care, our legs and feet were very swollen. Sr Fabian had lost her shoes, worn out on the way. Bishop gave her his own shoes as they fitted well her very sore and swollen feet. Sisters Irene and Hedda were nurses and quickly saw to our needs, while Srs Isabelle and Celestine helped in other ways to quietly return to normal living after the trying times in the jungle. These sisters were less than two years in the mission and had been uprooted also. Good Fr O'Sullivan went away— mission accomplished, like a scout keeping his contact with various peoples in danger.

Early December, a small boat took us eight sisters to Tinputz at night, arriving there about 2 a.m. and made our way to Tsipotavai village, to a hide-out in the bush which had been prepared for the missionaries, in case of need. Fr Lebel had organized that, but the three sisters of Tinputz were still at the station, near the sea. Besides Srs M. Elie, Cecilia and Francois-Xavier, there was also old Fr Allotte and two German brothers who worked at the sawmill, Bros Gregory and Karl.

The personnel of Tarlena had already arrived at Tsipotavai: Frs McConville and Morel, Srs M. Henrietta, Claire and Remi and the Pitt Family of seven. Bobby and Margareta Pitt had three girls and two boys, the youngest was a baby yet. This group had been brought out of Tarlena by Fr Lebel's daring efforts at night, the expedition lasting three days. Srs M. Claire and Remi had to be carried as they were unable to walk.

From now on, Fr Lebel would be trudging along between Tinputz and Tsipotavai, a walk of two hours, almost every day to make sure of food and safety. At last, he had his three sisters moving to the hide-out before Christmas. Fr Lebel went down to his station on Christmas Eve, in case he could say Mass for his people, but he saw a Japanese ship anchored in the bay. Hastily he returned to Tsipotavai that night, arriving at the end of Midnight Mass, celebrated by Fr McConville. Very moved, he told us all that we had to leave immediately for the bush, each one taking his or her little baggage and follow our guides. We had been told about this possibility some days before and we knew what to take along.

So, into the night we walked, following one another in the bush, down and up gullies, until dawn! The schoolboys had come with us too—they were a great help in various ways. We halted in a glade and rested as best we could, sitting on the ground. By then, Fr Lebel was truly exhausted; his feet were bleeding and we all felt very sorry—and grateful to him.

During the day some Australian soldiers visited us—a strange group in the middle of nowhere! That evening, as we settled ourselves to sleep on banana leaves, under the stars, we sang all the Christmas carols and hymns that we knew, led by the beautiful voice of Sr Francois-Xavier. There was Latin, English, French, Nasioi, Telei, etc... It was Christmas night—a day of great joy to people of goodwill, in our hearts we were at peace, regardless.

Next morning, we were told we could return. The Japs had gone away and there was an expectancy of something to happen soon. So we went back to Tsipotavai—this time it was daylight. How easier it was, going down. For the exciting experiences of the next ten days or so, I refer you to Chapter 8 (eight) of Lonely Vigil, from pages 106 to 127, written by Walter Lord, on the Coast Watchers of the Solomons. It is a most interesting write-up of our evacuation on the U.S. Submarine Nautilus.

4 Jan 1943: when all 29 people were on board the sub chaser, the engines went full speed to get away from the meeting place. What a different atmosphere on that ship. There was fresh air aplenty now and we enjoyed it till late morning when we arrived near Guadalcanal and big ships were around. We transferred to a huge transport, the Hunter Liggett, where U.S. Army troops were disembarking to the shore.

Later, lots of Marines came on board. The poor men looked sunburnt, sick and growing beards—truly needing the leave they were going to have South, after their hardships on Guadalcanal. The Chaplain talked to us and the 'boys' were sorry for us too! They made a collection which would help with the education of the three girls: Margaret, Theresa and Josephine Pitt. A very thoughtful gesture.

5th; Second day on board. Our ship had embarked about two thousand Marines by now and she joined four other big ships in a convoy. We started off in the evening, zigzagging, surrounded by destroyers and a plane ahead. As days went by, we lost the other transports, each going to different countries. We headed for New Zealand.

Appendix

12th; Auckland, late afternoon. We are warned about secrecy to safeguard our Allies in the Solomons. The US Navy put us under Bishop Liston's care. His Secretary Fr McKeafry came to meet us as we disembarked between sailors at attention. Then we were taken to the Convent of the Dames of the Sacred Heart for the night.

13th; Bishop Liston came to say Mass for us and we met him afterwards in the parlour Mother M. Carmella arrived too, having come from Wellington to get sisters from the South Solomons, Srs M. Antonia, Brigitte and Loyola, brought by the same ship some weeks earlier. She now finds ten SMSMs more to take along as well as three young girls. After dinner, we said goodbye to our companions, the four Srs of St Joseph, who would return to the U.S.A. later.

We took the train for Wellington where we arrived the next morning, to go to Aurora Terrace. Ten sisters from Tonga were there, refugees too. Other Convents kindly took them in, as we needed warm clothing right away: we were freezing in our cotton whites, almost threadbare by now, Hence we had to be in our convent! What headaches we must have given to M. M. Theophile and others. The Red Cross made a donation to buy our clothes and shoes. All helped.

Some months later, Srs M. Hortense and Gisèle went to Fiji, to help at Makogai where about 700 patients were treated for Hansen's Disease, staying over two years till Bougainville could be re-opened. This happened in 1946.

§

When The Garamuts Beat

Marie Fardeau (Sr Marie Martial SMSM)

War Tim e Travels—exodus during the war 1942-1945
By Sister Mary Martial, SMSM

Translated from the French manuscript with preliminary information and some slight additions to clarify the text. This is Sr Martial's own story.

We were three sisters at Monoitu, this Christmas of 1942, but my two present companions were 'war refugees' from other Stations. Srs M. Ignace and Adalberta. Our pioneer Sister Marie Ignace had come from Samoa in April 1901, to begin the line of Missionary Sisters in the Solomons.

When the Pacific War broke out, Sister was stationed at Turiboiru, Buin, in the south of Bougainville. Within a few months the Japanese occupied the main points of the big island shores. In September they began raids inland to our stations, up in the bush and marched the missionaries to their beach H.Q.—to captivity. Those of Muguai were taken on the 19th September and two days later, it was the turn of the Turiboiru staff.

Sr M. Ignace dared the Japs' pistols and because of her age, no doubt, was left behind, alone with her charges! the Little Sisters of Nazareth and a number of young orphans. After a few weeks, Fr Miltrup persuaded sister to move to his station at Piano. This young German Missionary had promptly ordered the 3 Sisters of Piano to get away to Monoitu and further on, after the Turiboiru raid, lest they be 'collected' by the Japs also. Some weeks later, higher orders arrived from Bishop—then around Tinputz, and Sr M. Ignace said goodbye to her little sisters, who had to return home, and Sister made her way to Monoitu.

My second companion was Sister M. Adalberta—in the Mission since 1914—who had been evacuated from Kieta in January. After some months in Muguai, Sister was assigned to help at Monoitu, thus unknowingly escaping from the Japs.

It was with Sr M. Domitilla that I had opened Monoitu in 1932, and we had worked together until the end of 1941. Sr M. Domitilla had charge of the schoolgirls, gardens, etc, while I had the nursing and care of orphans— over 20 at that time, and other domestic work. Sr M. Domitilla had to leave for Vunapope for medical care in December 1941. She was unable to return to Monoitu as the war interrupted the transport service and Sister shared the

Appendix

fate of the Sacred Heart Missionaries when the Japanese occupied New Britain. After three years of internment under the Japanese, Sister died in Ramale camp in November 1944.

Sr M. Hortense had come to help at Monoitu in January 1942, when the sisters left Kieta and was replaced a few months later by Sr M. Fabian, who remained until the end of October. Sr M. Fabian was told to join the Piano sisters at Sovele, and the group of four sisters would walk over the mountains, to the east coast at Manetai. The steady flight from one place to another had started and no one really knew what would happen next. Bishop Wade was trying to have the sisters evacuated since news of the death of four missionaries on Guadalcanal had reached him, bayoneted by the Japs.

Now to begin on our exodus.

Sr M. Ignace, Sr M. Adalberta and I left Monoitu on Monday morning, 26 December 1942, the day after Christmas. Fr Schlieker, priest-in-charge, was waiting for us on the road with three boys who would accompany us.

Father gave us each a walking stick to help us on the journey and said goodbye. We started our march on a rough road and crossed several large rivers on the way. In the evening, we arrived at a small village and were quite tired. The villagers brought us some sweet potatoes to eat, then we laid down to rest and sleep, but the night was a restless one. Fear of the Japs excited us.

The next morning we resumed our journey with our bundle and the three boys, until we reached Sovele. We stayed three days there, resting and then we moved on again, climbing high, huge mountains, but we couldn't walk down the steep slopes! so we sat down and let ourselves slide down to the bottom, getting hold of the grass and plants on our track. It is there, in the bush, that good Father O'Sullivan came to meet us.

It was raining in torrents and we finally arrived to a hut where Fr Weber (P.P. of Tunuru) was waiting for us. We were drenched to the skin, so changed clothes. Father lit a large fire but it was not very bright because of the heavy rain. Our dresses couldn't dry, but we had to put them on again in the middle of the night—a Tunuru boy came to tell Fr Weber, 'The Japanese are asking for you. They left a letter on the table and we are bringing it to you.'

We left again next morning and walked all day. In the bush, on our way, we found Wong You (a Kieta Trader) and his family: twelve children. He was taking care of his sister's children besides his own. He kindly gave us a cup of tea and an umbrella to each one, for it was raining—and we made tracks again.

During the afternoon we made another stop in the bush, this time at the house of a gold prospector, Mr Roche, an Australian. He kindly offered us hospitality for the night. There was a loaded gun in each of the four windows and Sr M. Ignace told me, 'I don't want to sleep near these rifles!' My reply was, 'Let me take this room.' Mr Roche was very kind to us, as we were so tired we stayed a day in his home. Being restless, I felt like taking a short walk and about ten minutes from the house, I came up to a river and bathed my feet at the edge of the water.

There was a native man nearby, looking towards the other side of the river and he exclaimed, 'Sister, look! a Japanese!' *Oh! what were we to do?* He had seen me. I could not run away. I was pleading with all the saints in heaven as we waited. The native man said suddenly, 'He is making signs to us. Do not be afraid, Sister, it is Bishop Wade!' We stood waiting till he had crossed the river and came close to us. There were tears in our eyes.

'Sister, I come to get you; where are your two Sisters?'

'They are at Mr Roche's house,' I replied.

We all spent the night at this hospitable home and the next morning we had Holy Mass and were able to receive Communion, to our great Joy. After breakfast, Bishop took leave of us saying, 'Continue on your way with Fr O'Sullivan, for myself, I am going to Sovele.' On his way, he narrowly escaped from a band of Japanese who wanted to take him. Instead of Bishop Wade, they captured Wong You and his family at Kopei [sic] and brought them to Kieta. (for good Mr Roche, he was later taken too and put to death near the river).

To come back to our party—we continued our way to Manetai, where Father Mueller [sic] was. We rested one day there and during the following night, we walked to the seashore to take a canoe and go to Asitavi with Father O'Sullivan. While at sea, our rowing canoe passed a Japanese boat at a short distance, but our Guardian Angels watched over us and in the morning we arrived at Asitavi, where we found Fr Henry Fluet.

We spent a few days at Asitavi, but then, we got news that the Japs were arriving. We fled into the bush. They arrived at the Station, took Father's stove, the refrigerator, our towels and killed the fowls…to eat them,

Appendix

no doubt. After they had gone, we returned to get our things. They had left the house all upside down. We left and went up into the bush, to a native hut where a woman had died a few days before. Sister M. Adalberta set to work to clean it while I went to the river to wash our clothes.

I was given charge of the cooking, but with what, or of what? I had nothing, not a saucepan either. So I went alone to some villages, as my two sister-companions were sick. I bought some taro with a few coloured beads that I had, and then asked one of the young girls to accompany me to the house and teach me how to cook our food in bamboo. As she was afraid of the Japanese she didn't stay with us and ran away.

One day Fr Fluet told us, 'I am going down to Asitavi with a few boys to get a pig.' However, the Japanese were there, so poor Father had to hide in the bush until the Japs departed. Father and the boys returned at last and Father asked me to cook the pig. While I was cooking it, natives arrived saying, 'Father, the Japs have found your track—they saw the smoke and they are coming!' So we quickly put the fire out and carried the meat to safety. I then ran to the two sisters who were near the river. After a few hours of waiting, Father sent the Natives to call me. 'Sister, Father is calling for you to cook the meat and the fat.' Now we had something to eat.

A few weeks later, Fr Lebel (of Tinputz) sent word to go to a certain place (Kotoita, near Inus?) that he would meet us there and bring us in readiness for evacuation by a U.S. Submarine. So we took our belongings and started off. That evening we were at the place of the rendezvous. Late that evening, Fr Label arrived and he arranged for our departure with Fr O'Sullivan who had been accompanying us all along to watch on our safety.

We started out next morning. Two stretchers had been prepared to carry Sr M. Ignace and Sr M. Adalberta, while I walked with two boys. Two police constables were following us, as we were protected by the Australian soldiers, who were giving us some of the food parachuted to them by planes. While trudging along with the boys and through the rivers, I lost my shoes that had become worn out. Sr M. Ignace, who was coming after me noticed it and, ever charitable, said, 'My poor Sister, you can't walk like this!' As she was carried on a stretcher, she took off her shoes and passed them to me. I was pleased, although they were rather big for my size. The boys suggested that I put leaves in them, so they would hold on my feet.

After walking all day on a bad road, we were so tired! It was night but there was moonlight and we sat near a river; we couldn't go anymore, I felt so tired that I lay down on the veranda of a Protestant teacher's house. He kindly said to me, 'Sister, come to rest on a bed.' Fr Lebel who had been searching for me to get the party going again, querie,: 'Sister, you are really tired?'

'Yes, Father,'

'Well, if you wish, we'll spend the night here.'

'No, I'll try to go further, Father.' He then gave me something to drink that gave me fresh courage.

In the wee hours of the morning, we arrived at a small house on a hill between Teop and Tinputz (probably Guadapavi). There were only two beds in the house and as I was going to install myself on the floor, Fr Lebel said, 'No, Sister, we'll prepare something for you to sleep on...' We felt at ease in that little house and we had Mass every morning, said by Fr Lebel. Fr O'Sullivan had remained with Fr Fluet in the bush. I was able to do some cooking as there was a small stove. From time to time we had the visit of Australian soldiers who were looking after us.

After a few weeks here we were told that a U.S. Submarine was waiting for us near Teop, but two Japanese ships were nearby, so we couldn't embark. This we were told at the time set to leave. We waited until the next day and that afternoon, we walked down to Tearouki with five Australian soldiers. This was the 28 March.

At 6 pm a big fire was lit on the seashore—this was the signal for the submarine to come to the surface and for the small boats to get ready. We boarded canoes and they took us to the submarine. With the help of two soldiers, we went down the coning tower; it was pitch dark: no lights, so they helped us to set foot on the rungs of the steel ladder that went down, down.

There we were taken to a room that had no furniture, just a square of steel, where we remained standing and in silence. When everyone was in the room, the door was closed and we were then taken to another room, red like fire where there were machines and soldiers with helmets on. We passed then to another room, a clearer one, where we were given something to eat. Then we went to sleep in the officer's cabin. There were two beds for the sick sisters. I slept on the floor, but it was so hot that I could not sleep and finally got an enormous abscess.

Appendix

In the morning, an officer came to get me to take care of the 24 Chinese children that were on board: their mothers were all sick. They were well looked after. They got everything that they wanted but they were not to cry. We remained in the Submarine, U.S.S. Gato for a night and a day, till we arrived somewhere in the British Solomons. I forgot the name of the place. We boarded a ship that took us to Guadalcanal.

American soldiers prepared a tent for us and we stayed there several weeks. But we were not tranquil there; the siren was sounding the alarm continually and we had to go down a big trench and lay down on bags of sand. Poor Sr M. Ignace was terribly frightened and would pray aloud; 'My God. Have pity on us!' Japanese planes would pass overhead, shelling and bombing, so that our tent was riddled with holes. We have been well protected. God guarded us.

For the poor sick soldiers who had to be taken down into the trench, it was not easy. One got killed right in his bed, so it was not prudent to remain here anymore. The Australian soldiers got busy about us. A big ship had arrived, bringing soldiers for Guadalcanal. An officer came to tell us that we would get on that ship immediately. The Chinese woman and their children and ourselves boarded the ship bound for New Caledonia.

On board ship, we were wonderfully well taken care of. An American Chaplain, Fr. O'Neil, gave me charge of the Chinese children again. When we arrived in New Caledonia, we went to our sisters in St. Louis, staying there three weeks. Then we left on a warship for Australia, together with Margaret Pitt and her two little boys (her 3 daughters had been evacuated to N.Z. some months before—in the 1st Submarine). Soldiers also came along.

On 5 May 1943, we arrived in Melbourne. The nearby Convent of the Good Shepherd was phoned and the Superior came to get us—we were warmly welcomed. The sisters did their best to dress us up, as we had little enough left, and they comforted us as best they could. Margaret and her two boys stayed with us.

Three weeks later, we received a letter from Mother Mary Rose, inviting us to come to Villa Maria, Sydney. The Director for the Propagation of the Faith paid our trip to Sydney. Mother M. Rose and Sr M. Eustslle were awaiting us at our arrival in Sydney. We were at last in safety!

After six months of recuperating and working, I went to the New Hebrides to help the sisters at Montmartre and at Melsisi. Mother M. Alexis and the sisters were most kind to me and I was very happy there. I stayed in the New Hebrides until the end of the war; or rather, until Bishop Wade called on his scattered missionaries to return to the North Solomons. I travelled back to Australia in February 1946, in readiness to return when we would be allowed back in the Islands.

Permission to get back to Bougainville was finally obtained and in a first group of six sisters, we sailed from Sydney on the 14th June 1946. The Ormiston disembarked us in Rabaul and we waited six weeks at Vunapope for means of transport to Torokina. The troops had gradually left but for a few soldiers at Torokina Base, and transport was now a problem... Bishop Wade finally found a plan to take us across.

All the mission Stations had been destroyed by the war and Japanese occupation and all had to be rebuilt. I went back to Monoitu in April 1947. It was hard work to get everything built anew, houses, church, etc. We got down to work again, it was hard, but we were happy to be back in our beloved mission!

§

Appendix

Fr James (Jim) Gerald Hennessy

The following is extracted from Saving the Solomons—From The Diary Account of Rev. Mother Mary Rose SMSM.

On March 9, 1942, nine Japanese warships arrived off the coast of Buka. Father Hennessy was visited and questioned but not otherwise molested. Shortly afterwards he went north to the neighbouring mission station to warn Father Lamarre and his assistants, giving a detailed account of the two-hour Japanese visit, and concluding with the words, 'The next few days will tell. If they return soon. I'm finished!'

'Why not seek safety in the mountains of Bougainville?' someone suggested. Father Hennessy's reply was typical of his courage and heroism. 'By Bishop Wade I was placed in charge of Lemanmanu. There I will stay, cost what it may!'

Early next morning he returned to his mission to offer Mass for his natives, and continued to serve them with his usual zeal and kindness until St. Patrick's Day 1942, when the Japs returned, made him captive, and took him by cruiser to Kavieng, a port town on the north coast of New Ireland. During the voyage he was tried by court-martial and condemned to death.

The captain of the warship on which he was tried had been working along the Bougainville coast as a 'boat carpenter' for some years before the war, and Father Hennessy had been kind to him. Probably this son of Nippon now remembered that kindness. At any rate, Father was granted a reprieve.

Two months had elapsed since his capture when he and a number of civilians were transferred to Rabaul, a town at the east end of the neighboring crescent-shaped island of New Britain.

There he remained for nearly a month with more than a thousand other prisoners, among whom were three priests, Father D. McCullagh, M.S.C., an Australian missionary; Father Brennan, M.S.C., also an Australian; and Father V. S. Turner, S.J., Chaplain to the Australian Force at Rabaul.

One of them had a Mass Kit so that each was able to offer Mass in turn. Frequent prayer and occasional talks on spiritual subjects did much to sustain the courage of the Catholic group. News of Allied victories picked up by prisoners employed to repair Japanese radios also helped to boost morale.

Finally, at 6.00 am about June 22, 1942, 850 soldiers and 210 civilians, including Fathers Hennessy, Brennan and McCullagh, were ordered to embark on the *Montevideo Maru* bound for Hainan, an island off the coast of China. The vessel had reached a point north of Luzon, Philippine Islands, when it was torpedoed by an American submarine with the loss of all on board (Decker: 1948, pp. 89-91).

Appendix

Fr George Lepping SM
Fr Saris' account of George Lepping's war experience

They spent the next five months under house arrest. Although they were not allowed to perform mission work, if locals came to the Mission church, the Japanese permitted them to say Mass and perform Sacraments. One day, the Japanese came and told them to pack up a few things to go to headquarters, claiming they would return the next day. However, they would be gone for three years. While Frs Lepping and Boch spent a few days at headquarters, the Japanese occupied the Mission, converting it to a military base.

Lepping and Boch were put on an old Japanese destroyer and taken to Rabaul, the big Japanese military base on New Britain. They spent the worst six months of their imprisonment at a Japanese Prisoner of War camp there. Along with two Sacred Heart Fathers, two Marist Fathers and a Brother and four Marist Sisters, they endured terrible food, no permission for Holy Mass, and hard manual labor [sic].

The 11 missionaries were all sick and weak, but after six months, in March 1943, they were taken to a Mission Prisoner of War camp at Vunapope. The Mission had a doctor, medicine, food, and houses, which probably saved the lives of the missionaries.

They lived fairly normal lives at the Mission, until the Allies began bombing it in February 1944, completing destroying it. Until the war ended the Australian and New Zealand Air Forces on Bougainville used Rabaul as a training area for their young pilots, at the same time keeping the Japanese quiet. War planes were always over the area from 8 a.m. until noon, but afternoons would be free of aircraft, allowing the prisoners to spend some time outside. Some of the larger planes returned at night for nuisance raids which lasted till dawn.

Fr Lepping was released from the P. O. W. camp in September 1945, and although he volunteered for mission work in Japan, he returned to the Nila Mission. He lived in a room of the bombed-out house, doing pastoral work on the weekends in the villages.

In one village, Fr Lepping met his former station teacher, Dionisio, who asked him to baptize his first child. Dionisio and his wife wanted their son to have an American name and insisted on naming him after Fr Lepping.

The young George was educated by the Dominican sisters in their school at Nila. Later George obtained two Certificates of Agriculture from Vudal and Keravat, Rabaul, and a Masters of Agriculture from Reading University in England. He became a good athlete and won silver medals in the triple jump.

George Lepping went on to become Minister of Agriculture, then Minister of Finance, and finally, Governor General of the Solomon Islands: Sir George Lepping (Saris: 2008, p.48).

§

Appendix

Sr Marie Wendelina SMSM (Marie Richter)
OUR EXPERIENCES UNDER THE JAPANESE
by Sister Mary Wendelina S.M.S.M. P.O.W.
1942-1945 War in the Pacific.

The declaration of war between Allies and Japan in December 1941 came as a thunderbolt to trouble the peace and serenity of our Solomon Islands and our missionary life! Alas! Absolutely nothing remains of our stations and of the nice churches that His Lordship Bishop Wade had built during the last years preceding the war.

Materially our Mission of the North Solomons is completely destroyed, but the people who convert and strengthen in their faith remain, and while our health is improving here at Killara, under the kindly care of Mother M. Rose, we hope and pray that God will let us take up our work again in Bougainville very soon. We also hope to return with a large group of young Sisters who will help us and replace our dear sisters who have died.

I was in Kieta when the war between the European and Asian races broke out in December 1941. A few days later the European women on Bougainville left for Australia on board the Malaita. A few weeks later, the Government gave order to leave to those who were still there, but left the sisters free to go, at government expense, or to stay. We answered that we wanted to stay with our Natives; anyhow, there would have been only the five of us in Kieta and the three sisters in Koromira who would not have had time to get on board the two small ships that came to get the ladies. Two days after notification had been received, at 6 a.m.

On 6 January 1942, Bishop came to tell me that the three Little Sisters must return to the Novitiate of the Sisters of Nazareth at Turiboiru, which is about ten miles inland of the Buin District. The Japanese were advancing rapidly and Bishop feared the Japanese would not respect black Sisters. They left that very day, taking along nine little boys of the orphanage who were from the south of Bougainville.

A week later Bishop communicated to me the decision he had taken to have us leave also, as he was very worried about us, the Japanese were coming nearer and nearer. So we started packing up all we could and early on the morning of the 17th, we said goodbye to Kieta. We were very sad!

When The Garamuts Beat

For the first time since the beginning of the Mission, Kieta would be without sisters. Priests and brothers were very moved too and His Lordship could hardly say '*au revo*ir' after a last blessing in the workers' little chapel at Tubiana Beach.

The Ludwig glided proudly away from the nice Kieta Harbour, a bit too proudly perhaps as, after twenty minutes, the engine stopped and absolutely refused to get going again—and this was the largest of our mission ships! A small boat was approaching from the south and for a few painful moments we thought it was a Japanese pinnace. Soon we recognized it as being the Rosa. A brother was on board and seeing our distress, came to the rescue. With a big rope, the Rosa began to tow us back to Kieta. However, from the hill-top, the Fathers were watching and a quarter of an hour later we saw two mission schooners coming to our help. It was the Gabriel and the Theresa.

At sea we boarded the Gabriel. We were five Sisters and also had five babies from the orphanage, whom we had been unable to place in Kieta. Our luggage returned to Kieta and all the other boats while we continued our trip on the Gabriel to arrive late at night at Patupatuai, Buin. We installed ourselves the best we could in the house left by the nurses of the Marist Medical Mission—just for the night.
The mosquitoes were dreadful and we were pleased to find the two large beds of the nurses still there, with their big nets reaching to the floor.

Dear Sisters, I hope not to scandalise any of you in saying that we managed to fit all ten of us under the two nets! The sisters fitted on the beds the best they could after having tucked the little children underneath. In spite of all these precautions, we spent a sleepless night... and there would be many another in the future. The next morning there was no Mass, Fr O'Sullivan being absent.

During the morning we began to disperse and make our way to various stations; Sr M. Adalberta took the road to Muguai, Sr M. Gisèle would go to Piano after a few days rest in Turiboiru, so she stayed with Sr M. Melanie and I too walked to Turiboiru, Sr M. Hortense went to Piano, enroute to Monoitu. The Superior of Turiboiru, Sr M. Placide, together with Sister Denisia and a large group of school boys and girls, had come to get us. We started off about noon under torrential rain, which lasted the four hours' walk between the beach and Turiboiru. I was so happy to arrive at my old 'home' where Sr M. Ignace and Father Poncelet received us warmly.

A week later the first bombs were thrown over Kieta by the Japs and then we heard they were in the north of Bougainville, at Buka and Tarlena. On Buka a European planter was killed and Fr Hennessy taken away in March.

On Easter Sunday the Japanese landed at Patupatuai, Buin, for the first time. They searched all the houses but did no harm to Fr O'Sullivan who, the very next day, left the place with all his school boys. A Japanese officer had taken Father aside and told him in English, 'Father, get away as quick and as far as you can!' He was most likely an honest man and we think that it was Tashiro, a Japanese who had worked at the Mission in Kieta before. Father O'Sullivan did not know him, but we learned later that he was in that particular group who had come from Faisi. In New Britain also, he saved the life of several priests of the Sacred Heart Mission.

The Japs did not remain at Patupatuai that day, but they returned four days later and this time set fire to all the houses of the Mission and of the Government at Kangu, leaving only the little church. From that day on Japanese soldiers came and went continually between the Shortlands (Faisi) and Patupatuai, Buin, so we lived in an atmosphere of constant fear, one night especially when Fr Poncelet sent us word to hide the parachutes given us by Australian soldiers some weeks previously, as the Japs were halfway up to the Mission. Around 11 pm. Father came to tell us we could go to sleep: the Japs were returning to the beach.

During July, Bishop Wade was prisoner in his residence in Kieta. After six weeks of it, during a bombing of Japanese ships in Kieta Harbour by the Allies, Bishop Wade succeeded to get away and we were very happy for him.

On the 9th September, we heard from the Coast Watchers and from the Natives that the Japanese had definitely landed and were installing themselves in Buin at about five hours distance from our station. The following days we heard dynamite explosions they were using to uproot the huge trees of the jungle. Hundreds of Natives were forced to work to help them cut the bush to make an aerodrome.

The Australian radio transmitter was near the Mission, but after the Japanese landing, the men went further up in the bush and from the top of a mountain could observe all the activities of the Japanese Navy. Before too long, American planes made their apparition in the blue sky, and from afar we could see the small clouds of smoke sent up by Japanese anti-aircraft guns. Then on Saturday, 19 September 1942, we heard that the Missionaries of Muguai: Fr. Schank, Brother Bruno, Sr M. Crescentia, and Sr M. of the Sacred Heart had been taken away by the Japs, but were due back after 'regularizing' their papers with the new government. On Monday, 21 September we were in front of our convent when suddenly two Japs came running to our side; pointing their pistols to our chest they shouted in English' 'You stop!'

We did not move and I said, 'Well, we stop.'

Fr Poncelet having seen them running to our place came over and the two Japs ordered us to go up into the house in front of them, with their guns still pointed at us. Our school girls ran away into the bush, but Father's boys and many natives followed Father to our place; however, the Japs chased them away with their pistols.

Then they started telling us we were spies, that they were going to kill us and they had already cut Sr. M. of the Sacred Heart's neck. One of them drew up his long sword and pointed it on Father's chest, shouting that he was a New Zealander and a spy. All of a sudden he changed tactics and ran up to Father like a madman, with a rope to tie his hands. Two of us placed ourselves between him and Father, but the irate individual grabbed Father by the throat over our shoulders, pressing strongly to strangle him.

At last he seemed to calm down a bit and let go, still continuing his yells of hate against the whites and his threats of prison and death. He was still gesticulating when another group of five men arrived. One spoke English and told us not to be afraid, he was coming to help us but he had orders from the Commander to bring us to their camp to sign papers and that we would return in a day or two.

Sister M. Ignace was permitted to stay as she was old and would not be able to walk the long road. In reality, Sister was not pleading so much for her age and her poor legs, but she thought of the native sisters whom she did not want to leave alone. Alas! A few months later she would be obliged to leave them all the same.

Appendix

Prisoners of war 21 September 1942

We left Turiboiru under pelting rain with hardly any clothes to change. The villains! As we had entered our rooms to take some clothing, the Japs were already in our trunks and suitcases, taking what pleased them and throwing the rest pell-mell on the floor: cornettes, collars, etc. everything got it.

I took one of my dresses hanging and one of the Japs pulled it from my hands; I pulled too and took it away—never shall I forget this departure! Our hearts were heavy and I had the presentment that we would not return. Some of the less frightened girls had come up from the gully where they had been hiding; the poor children were crying. The Little Sisters were also crying and we ourselves had such a lump in the throat that we found it impossible to say a word of encouragement or hope to them.

While three Japanese marched us to a house abandoned by a Chinese trader, about ten minutes from the Station, the rest of the band searched our house—this we learned from the natives who, after two hours of waiting, had to accompany the Japs and carry all they had stolen in our place. The poor men had to comply, but did so reluctantly, and all the way gave vent to their indignation in words that are not easy to put down! The roads were bad and the night was falling; fortunately, the moon was giving some light through the branches of the forest. We walked two hours in mud to our ankles and sometimes we would sink to the knees in pig holes. Sister M. Andrea could walk no more, so our brave Solomonese carried her a good part of the way. After walking seven hours we finally arrived at their aerodrome and their camp.

Our guards chased the natives then and we were led to the seashore, to a tent where we underwent a first questioning. They took us then to a little house opened to all winds, where we would remain until 1 October.

After half an hour that same evening, we were taken again before the authorities for a second and more difficult cross examination. They lined us up under their tent, then one Jap made us move back, traced a line on the sand saying we were not to pass beyond it. The tent was for the Japanese not for whites. This was the first of many humiliations that were to follow.

After answering a lot of questions and giving information on our 'person', our country of origin, etc. they took us back to prison but only to call back several of us for a new complicated cross questioning. They wanted especially to know where the Australians operating the radio transmitter were. They were intercepting their messages every night—however, they were unable to decipher them. But we were far from betraying our friends who had often visited us at Turiboiru. During other questionings the following days, they offered us our freedom if we would lead them to the Aussies. We refused to guide them or to give information regarding them.

American planes were coming regularly around 10 or 11 a.m. daily, to bomb the Japanese ships in the harbour. The zig-zag movements of the warships alerted us of the approach of danger. During the night American planes would come to throw bombs on the airfield where we were. We trembled with fear in our exposed jail as we had no trench to hide in.

On a particular night it was really terrible: the bombs were falling very close and an officer came to tell us to go a few hundred yards to the rear, that it was dangerous and the Americans were coming. We spent the rest of the night in the chapel of an abandoned native village. Dawn finally arrived but no Americans!

The Japs then took us to a house at the end of the village and burned down all the other huts and the chapel as well. The following night bombs fell very near our miserable hut; the cries of the poor wounded and dying were pitiful to hear. In the moonlight we could see them carrying their dead and the wounded—and the ten of us were without a scratch! During all that time we were guarded by three Japanese sentries, bayonets in hand and we were absolutely forbidden to go out. At our slightest movement, the torchlight would be flashed on us. We couldn't take one step outside during the day, or the night, without being accompanied by a guard! In spite of all these troubles, we could not help smiling at the silliness of it all at times.

On 1 October, an interpreter came to say that a ship was about to leave for Rabaul and the Commander gave us order to go. We begged him to let us return home, to our natives—as we had already asked on previous days, but it was useless. The interpreter, who had an Irish name in spite of his Nippon face, seemed to understand our distress: 'It is better to go without replying, the Commander is getting more and more furious, and say a Hail Mary for me sometime.' We saw the brave man again five months later in Rabaul. There his first greeting was: 'Oh! How thin you have become!' and the next day he sent us a few tins of milk.

Appendix

We embarked on 1st October, 1942. We were ten altogether: four from Muguai station and six from Turiboiru. Fr Poncelet was from Belgium, Fr Schanck from Luxemburg, Brother Bruno and Sr M. Crescentia from Germany; Sr M. Dolores and Sr. M. of the Sacred Heart were from England; Sr Mary Placide, Sr M. Andrea and I were from France.

For want of a gangway to climb aboard ship, we were placed on some sort of loading platform and then lifted up onto the ship, together with a band of Japanese who were well well-behaved, they even tried to help us with small gifts. During the night we could stretch on the floor and during the day we tried to sit as best we could—we had permission to go up on deck even, but the sun was burning hot.

On 3 October, during the morning, we arrived in the port of Rabaul. For the rest of the day and the next day also, the Japanese disembarked the wounded they had brought from Buin. No one seem to worry about us: however, towards evening, we were permitted to go ashore which was a great relief for us; American planes were continually flying overhead without dropping bombs, happily. We were very scared because the ship was terribly shaken by the firing of her anti-aircraft guns.

A soldier led us to a house about a hundred feet from the sea. For a while, I had hoped to find more freedom in Rabaul than we had in Buin, but this hope was soon frustrated as a sentry planted himself in front of us with fixed bayonet. Shortly after we had to climb into a truck and we were taken for a drive in the streets of Rabaul, stopping here and there to search for someone, whom they never seemed to find. Imagine the sight: two priests, a brother and seven sisters seating on the boards of the truck and a guard with bayonet standing on the foot board, riding through the streets! It was like the chariot of Louis XVI—we thought our last hour had come!

At dusk, we were taken to a little house measuring about 7ft by 18ft and the Japs started immediately to nail barbed wire to the two windows while the sentry stood at the door. We stretched on the floor to rest but couldn't find any good position; we had neither blankets nor pillows and the mosquitoes kept buzzing around. At each change of sentry the new one came to count us. We were so close together that no one could move without waking her neighbour: the ten of us stayed four days in that small house.

We had to undergo two questionings; at the end of the second, they made us clean our dungeon, and one Father not being quick enough for their liking received brutal blows from the sheath of their Samurai sword. Once more We were trembling with fear — what were they going to do with us?

Rabaul Camp October 1942 - 28 February 1943

We climbed into a lorry and ten minutes later we were in front of the military prison. With heavy hearts we came down before three houses surrounded by a large fence of barbed wire and we caught sight of the kind faces of Rev. Fr Boch and of young Fr Lepping, this latter smiling as ever. (Those two Marists had been taken from Faisi, Shortlands and brought here six weeks before.)

Other prisoners came to greet us and began to share with us some of their meagre belongings— all that they could spare, one even brought a sheet to us to make a dress! Among them them were three Fathers of the Sacred Heart in this camp, two of whom were to disappear mysteriously three months later. I shall never forget their kindness towards us.

A poor old priest of 72, Fr Neuhaus, had managed to bring his mattress into the camp; he made me open it to take some of the cotton out to make some small pillows for ourselves. We were given the house in the center, which was the one of the guards; however, they had the good idea to separate our quarters from theirs by a curtain and to leave us in peace. One Sergeant came to invite us to dance, but we politely excused ourselves and they left us alone.

The prospect of having a real rest on a good bed was such a cheering thought Our fellow-prisoners had given us some mosquito nets, and copra sacks stretched on a wooden frame were inviting for a rest. It was such a long time that we had only the floor for body, and such dirty floors sometimes! Alas! About 10 pm. the sound of an American plane startled us; she threw a flare directly behind our houses, turned back and returned to throw her deadly load.

Bomb splinters flew into our room while outside there were cries of wounded men. The hum of the plane drew near a third time and we tried to dash outside to a small trench, but the sentry pushed us back into the room, bayonet in hand. At that moment, Father Boch came running to our door to give us a last absolution. Then in a resolute voice he said: 'Sisters, follow me!' This time the guard let us go and scarcely had we arrived in the trench when the bombs fell.

A part of our shelter collapsed, half burying Father O'Connell, N.S.C. who was handcuffed and could not help himself. The other prisoners pulled him up from under a heap of soil and board. We spent the rest of the night sitting on the ground or standing in our hole. The bombs continued to rain down but not as near as at the beginning of the night.

At 6 am next day, we were allowed to come out and the Japs lined us up to be counted. Imagine the sight: Everyone was half dressed, the sisters were in petticoats and minus cornettes—and the Japanese standing in front of us to count how many we were, and they graciously asked if no one was dead or wounded.

Our houses were half demolished and on the hill opposite, the Japanese continued to carry their dead until noon. Once more we were all safe while the Japs suffered very heavy losses. A single bomb behind our houses, wounded or killed 170 Japanese. During that day the prisoners repaired our houses, or rather, what was left of them, as well as they could while we sisters did some patching on what remained of our mosquito nets and dresses. Everything was full of holes: houses, beds, clothing, nets, but what we regretted most was the water tanks. The most expert in the trade among the prisoners immediately went to work on them, trying to solder and patch them. The very evening the tanks were ready to receive the first rain that would fall.

Subsequently, there were many bombardments, especially at night. How many hours of anxiety and fear did we spend, sitting in the trench for hours, sometimes whole nights! At the most dangerous times, we were happy to have the priests with us; almost every day we received a general absolution, trying to profit from the moments of bombing for confession, because we were not permitted to speak to them outside, however, later on, we succeeded in receiving the Sacrament of Penance early in the morning before the guards were up.

There was a sentry guarding us day and night, it is true, but if he watched us, we were watching him still more, and only once did a sister get caught in 'very serious conversation' (confession) with Father. We used to do it standing, so as not to draw the guard's attention.

The reception of the Sacrament, almost regularly, was a great consolation to us, but we could not receive Holy Communion, of course, since the priests were not allowed to celebrate Mass, not even on Christmas Day. They had made a special request to obtain this favour, but a flat 'NO' was the answer.

Christmas Day 1942

That Feast of Christmas I shall never forget it! On the evening of the 24th, the Sergeant told us that he knew Christmas was a very great feast for us and because of that, we would not be sent to work. So we promised ourselves a very happy day in spite of the barbed wire and the miserable meal of rice three times a day. At that time we still had a few native vegetables, but from Christmas onwards, we were given only rice.

Rice without salt was not very nice, especially when there was only a cup of hot water to help swallow it. Anyhow, we had promised ourselves a happy Christmas feast! And then, in the middle of the night, instead of going to Midnight Mass, the Americans came bringing their presents to the unfortunate Japanese who were sleeping quietly since it was Christmas for the Whites!

I was awake and the humming of a heavy plane put me on the alert; it passed overhead, then passed a second time, but no alarm went, no siren from the Japanese. I was beginning to quieten down, thinking it was a plane of theirs when several terrific explosions made us jump out of bed and run to the trench. Hardly were we all in safety when the guns of the Japs began their midnight concert: too late, happily, for the noise of the American plane was fading away. But near us in the harbour, the sirens of ships in distress were calling for help. It was an ominous sound to listen to, and we thought of the unfortunate men who, at this moment, were struggling and wrestling with death.

It was midnight and Christmas! The Blessed Night in which the Angels had sung. 'Peace on earth' What irony! In the morning, the guards who had gone to get their food returned in a furious mood. After breakfast, they came to our house and chased us out saying, 'Quick to work! The Americans have no Christmas; they have killed many of our sailors, you will have no Christmas!'

Appendix

I made some resistance, saying that the Sergeant had said we wouldn't work since it was Christmas. It was useless. 'Blue-beard', as we had nicknamed this particular guard, chased us with a big stick after having showed me how one must obey the Japs by giving me a few slaps on the face that I still felt a week later. So we spent our Christmas day cleaning up the streets of Rabaul. During the afternoon though, they let us have a little respite, because of a poor American pilot whom they had just captured and this diverted their attention from us.

The poor pilots! When they were brought into the camp they would always be hand-cuffed, blindfolded and the Japs held them with a rope tied around the waist. They would lead them thus everywhere they needed to go, just like it is done for dogs—and it was so sad to behold. Most of them disappeared mysteriously as well as the other civilian prisoners.

Life in Rabaul Camp

Days and weeks and months passed by so slowly. We had the happiness of being able to say our Office. Together with our Profession Cross, the Office book was the only thing left of our religious habit until, three years later, we would arrive at Killara.

Never have I said with so much fervour the Psalms of our little Office: 'I lift up my eyes...' as in Psalm 120, especially, during these long months of waiting in Rabaul. And later at Vunapope, when we could receive our God in daily Communion, with what joy we would sing in Psalm 123: "Blessed be the Lord who did not leave us a prey." Still later, during the destruction of Vunapope Mission, when we were trembling with fear and that hell itself seemed to be let loose around us, we would repeat with more confidence than ever Psalm 124, 'They who trust in the Lord are like Mount Zion...'. We really had around us a rampart of mountains—we were living inside the mountain itself and we felt so strongly that a powerful hand protected us. Our Little Office of the Blessed Virgin was truly a treasure for us.

During February 1943 (we were in Rabaul yet), the bombardments became closer and more dangerous. One morning as we came out of the hole—trench, we found only the skeleton of our house standing. Six houses had disappeared around us; one bomb fell just in front of the opening of our trench and another slightly to the rear. During the morning, high-ranking officers came to visit the ruins; we begged them to let us go to a less dangerous spot. I said to them that Sr M. Placide was 60 years old, to have pity on her age.

They seemed embarrassed and one said, 'I too am 54'.

I replied, 'But you are a soldier! We are only women.' They left and we stayed there. The prisoners surrounded our room as best they could with straw bags and we stayed a few more weeks.

Sister Marie Melanie had been sick for some time and she began to worry us seriously. The Japanese Doctor came to see her but was unable to help. Poor Sister could hardly get to the trench anymore when the sirens gave the alarm for air raids, several Japanese ladies came to see us too; they were actresses and were leaving by plane. One of them showed much sympathy to us and sent us a few tins of milk.

Transfer to Vunapope Mission

At long last, on the 28th February, early in the morning we were told to be ready for 8 o'clock as we were going. We wondered with anxiety if we would be separated from the Fathers, and where they would take us? After breakfast the Fathers too were told to get ready and at 8 am a truck came for us. At the time of departure an officer told us that they were taking us to the Mission of Vunapope. They lined us up, we had to make bows and military salutes and were given a whole list of orders to follow—advice and prohibitions without end.

We were 14 on the truck: 6 priests, of whom two were missionaries of the Sacred Heart, four were Marists; Brother Bruno, S.M. and we seven S.M.S.M. After an hour and a half, we arrived at Vunapope and were given a very warm welcome by the Missionaries of the Sacred Heart, and especially by the Daughters of Our Lady of the Sacred Heart.

We had the great joy to find our Sister M. Domitilla in good health. She had come to Vunapope from Monoitu, Bougainville, for medical care just before the war broke out, and could not return. Alas! We were to lose her two years later in the Camp at Ramale.

Dr. Schouy, the Vunapope Mission Doctor, lost no time in caring for our medical needs. He diagnosed an advanced case of Beri-beri in Sr M. Melanie and promptly administered specific medicine for it. It was his last

Appendix

ampoule, he said, and without it Sister would not have lasted more than ten days. She was so swollen all over that she could not even bear to be touched, but a few days after the injection, Sister became her old self: more like a broomstick!

Fr Muller, M.S.C. the Mission Procurator, was speaking of our arrival in Vunapope a few weeks later and he commented: "it was a cargo of misery the Japs brought me that day!" Good Mother Martha, the Superior of the Daughters of O.L.S.H. quickly set to work to dress us up from head to foot. She gave us the clothes of her sisters and a few days later we got busy making some dresses for ourselves. Mother gave us white material for the Mass dresses and coloured prints for work overalls—prints with green and yellow flowers, etc.

I have just mentioned Mass. Our surprise and joy were great when a sister told us on our arrival in Vunapope that the Blessed Sacrament was reserved in the house and that Holy Mass was celebrated every morning.

We spent some relatively calm months at Vunapope. American planes hummed over the sea and on Rabaul during the night and often the sirens, or the bombs would wake us and we spent hours near the trenches. But on October 11th 1943, it became more serious.

During the morning, just before 10 am we were all assembled around the bed of a sister, who was receiving the Sacrament of the Sick when suddenly, the air was filled with the confused noise of machine guns and the zoom of planes. While rushing to the trench we saw planes diving over the Japanese airfields and huge clouds of black smoke rising between the trees behind the Mission.

Vunapope was encircled by four airfields, three being relatively near and one being on the Mission property. That day the Japanese sustained terrific losses. The attack had been unexpected, no siren had given the alarm and no anti-aircraft had fired. From that day onwards no plane ever took off from this aerodrome nearest to us: it had been completely wrecked by the bombs. 400 American and Allied planes had come that day. During the following days, they returned in the same manner: they seemed to come from nowhere and would disappear likewise. During November, air-attacks became more rare, but a reconnaissance plane would come daily and fly overhead several times.

When The Garamuts Beat

Towards the end of the year, the Japanese built some barracks for their mentally ill, on the right-hand side of our house, beyond the barbed-wire enclosure. The poor wretches! Most of them had become mental during battles and bombings. They had become so for their country, and for their reward they were treated harshly, even beaten cruelly. We could hear them crying for entire nights, especially when the sirens sounded the alarm. When these unfortunate defenders of the Fatherland became too excited, a doctor would go with an empty syringe, give them an injection of air and a few minutes later they were taken away: Dead for their country.

We were given the opportunity to make a good retreat even though we had to make some excursions to the trenches. The Retreat Master was Rev. Father Nollen, M.S.C. for us SMSMs, and he spoke in French. The other Sisters, M.S.C. and the Daughters of O.L.S.H. had theirs [sic] in German and English respectively.

During the year the Japs allowed us a trip to the cemetery every Sunday, during the morning. Later on, they let us go daily between 5 and 6 pm. The cemetery was about five minutes away and on the way we would stop at a Grotto of Our Lady of Lourdes. This was completely destroyed during later bombings. There was a statue of St Joseph on top of the hill, dominating the whole of Vunapope, but it also disappeared during the last bombardment: St Joseph kept guard to the end.

Towards Christmas 1943, air battles began. It was a spectacle, terrible and grandiose to watch the planes pursuing one another furiously while their machine guns rattled noisily. How many planes didn't we see falling in flames or in pieces! We were sad at heart to think of the young men enclosed in these fiery planes. Some pilots succeeded to parachute down. The planes would fall at great speed while the parachutists would come down very slowly, and we would wonder if these brave men were not going to a fate worse than death!

The Americans were losing relatively few planes whereas the Japanese planes were diminishing rapidly. After some weeks the Japanese had neither planes nor ships. While the air fights went on, the heavy bombers continued to come and drop bombs on land and sea. We were on a continual alert and the bombs seemed to fall nearer and nearer.

Appendix

The destruction of Vunapope Camp

Vunapope received its first bombing on 11th February 1944, on the feast of Our Lady of Lourdes. A few days earlier, early morning, bombs had fallen quite near already. So when the siren sounded the alarm on 11 February, we hastened to the trenches: it was about 9.30 am. Sister M. Dolores was sick and could hardly walk, so I led her to a small trench close to the house; other sick and a few old Sisters were in it already.

Mother Martha and I stood in front of the trench with the Sister Nurse when, all of a sudden, a formidable noise of bombers was heard. The Japanese planes went from the airfields nearby and a few moments later we saw the American planes coming straight at us.

Our hearts started pounding and at once hell seemed to swoop down upon us. Bullets from the American machine guns rained from the sky, followed by frightful explosions of bombs. These were minutes that seemed to last hours! When the worse was over, we came out of our holes, still shaking. Oh! What a sight of desolation met our gaze! Houses were in ruins, others were on fire.

Several bombs had landed on one of our trenches and had closed one of the exits. Brother Joseph, S.M. of our North Solomon Mission was killed outright, cut in two. He was a young American Brother who had come to the Mission in recent years. Among the Missionaries of the Sacred Heart, there was one father, two sisters and several brothers who were seriously wounded. The two sisters survived but the priest and the brothers died of their wounds within a few days or some weeks later.

Before our trench, around the houses, even on the roofs, everywhere pieces of human flesh were lying. A bomb had landed in the midst of a Japanese trench and had killed a hundred men, throwing them up in the air in one go. We found parts of them at two or three hundred yards away. About 60 wounded pilots who were in the hospital were killed outright also by a single bomb that fell in the middle of their house. The Japanese had several hundred dead while among us there was only one and several critically wounded.

After the planes had gone, Sister M. Dolores was carried over to one of the main trenches by some of the girls. These trenches were dug right into the hill and were supported by coconut-tree trunks. The little trench of the sick in which we sheltered during this first bombardment was covered only by two feet of soil. The Good God had protected us well: a single bomb would have been enough to send us all to Paradise. We were about twenty sisters in it.

Having installed Sr M. Dolores in safety, I returned to our house: it was still standing, but in what a state! Half of the chapel was gone, the altar, the furniture were riddled with holes like the rest of the house, but the tabernacle was intact! The infirmary, besides the sanctuary of the chapel, was in complete disorder; the bed where Sr M. Dolores had been lying half an hour ago, was broken in two; cupboards were thrown about, full of holes; nets were in a thousand pieces and our umbrellas had completely disappeared.

During the afternoon of the 11th, we went over to see the damages on the side of the fathers and of the sisters M.S.C. The sisters' house was half demolished as also that of the fathers, but the brothers' house had completely disappeared. Sisters and girls were busy trying to save whatever they could, climbing over the debris to get inside of what used to be their convent. It was a very small and miserable 'convent', it is true, but it had sheltered them after a fashion: it was the former little house of the shoemaker! The Japanese had taken all the beautiful buildings of the Mission for themselves, including the Cathedral! Now all the missionaries: fathers, brothers and sisters were lodged in the smaller, secondary buildings and in native houses hurriedly built.

The laundry, the bakery, the kitchen, the infirmary of the bathers, the store, all were flattened out. Boys were busy covering with soil the bags of flour and rice which were smouldering, to put out the fire save what could still be saved.

A new kind of sleeping quarters

Towards evening we received orders from the Japanese police to stay near the trenches for the night. Each one took a blanket and a pillow and we installed ourselves the best we could near the trenches. Some lay down on banana leaves, others on trunks of coconut trees, while the most fortunate had deck chairs. Inside the trench some lay on the ground while others, who did not find enough space to stretch out, slept sitting down on the ground, leaning their head against posts or against the shoulder of the neighbour.

Appendix

From that day onwards we had Holy Mass near the trenches and for several days our main work was to run to the trenches at every warning, but nothing serious happened. We were just beginning to calm down a bit, when on the 18th—a rainy day, the planes arrived very unexpectedly and their machine guns were firing furiously. But this time we got off with only a fright and a few bullets lost here and there, the planes were firing at the surroundings.

Around midnight this same day, we heard the hum of a plane at a distance, then almost immediately the hissing of shells followed by explosions following one another rapidly. It was the batteries of American ships whose guns in action got us out of our slumber near the trenches. A few sisters had returned to the house to sleep and the poor things were running for dear life to the trenches, all out of breath. The cannonade lasted one hour and when we came out of the trenches in the morning, there were unexploded shells everywhere. They were picked up later and buried.

On 25 February, the bombers brought again their load of destruction and death, destroying some more houses and the precious well which Bishop Scharmack had caused to be dug some months earlier, in case something should happen to the piping of the water system. And this had not functioned anymore since the first bombing. Now that the well had also disappeared—a bomb having fallen right into it, we faced a problem which, at first sight, seemed without solution. Towards evening though, some boys risked themselves towards the sea with buckets and came up again with precious water which they had drawn from a very deep hole dug by the Japanese near the sea.

We were 300 in the Camp: Bishop and fathers, brothers, sisters, Dr Schouy and family—bringing the number to about 150; then there were the seminarians, the mix-race school boys and girls, and the boys of the Kunigunan School, so the water rations were measured!

The lack of water was one of the most mortifying sufferings that we endured during three long months. The brothers and boys succeeded in digging a well near our trench, but it took three months of hard work to do it. They had to dig to a depth of twenty meters— about 65 feet deep to find water. Unhappily, after a few weeks, we were transferred to another camp.

During these three months, each one could have about a pint of water to wash. in the morning, there were three basins half full of water, set near the trench in which we 40 Sisters would wash our face in turn. We were full of the dust and ground that fell from the sides of the trench during the night. At this stage we couldn't sleep outside anymore because of the planes that flew all night, throwing bombs anywhere, we had to sleep close to each other like sardines, and no one could move without waking up her neighbours—and no one could go outside either without waking the whole lot!

Anyhow, let us return to events. The next day: 26th February 1944, the bombardments destroyed all that was left of the once beautiful Vunapope Mission headquarters of the Sacred Heart Mission in New Britain. The sirens did not give the alarm anymore and, at this stage, everyone's nervous system had beached such a degree of tension that the mere noise of planes made us tremble with fear! On this particular morning, our hearts pounded hard when we saw a large formation of bombers coming straight towards us. As so many times in the past, Fr Hoehne gave us general absolution in the trench and calmly began the Sub Tuum and then, as usual, the rosary.

Hardly had we started it that the most terrible of bombardments began, such as we had not experienced yet. The earth shook as in a violent earthquake, the lamps went out in the strong draught created by the exploding bombs. We held on to one another while continuing to say and repeat our acts of confidence in God and in the Blessed Virgin. I do not know what saints in heaven we did not invoke to our aid during these dreadful moments, especially when, after a lull of about ten minutes, another group of planes was announced! This time it would be the end, at least, we thought it would be the end.

It would be impossible to describe what happened in our trenches during these few minutes of agony: the children were crying, calling out and even the sisters and fathers were crying out, crying from sheer fear at the same time as praying their acts of confidence—be it to live or to die! The shocks came without interruption and were so violent that we had to help ourselves together not to be thrown down; the draught took the veils off our heads. when the noise of these frightful deadly machines became distant, we tried to light our lamps again, but the air was too dense! and they wouldn't light.

After emerging from our trenches all we could do was to thank God for being alive! Right in front of the two main entrances to our tunnels, there were five enormous craters dug by torpedo bombs; a sixth crater blocked the third exit and there were many others all over the place. Of Vunapope there was left only half of the cathedral and the small house where Doctor lived for a few months. A few coconut trees were still standing; everything else: trees, banana trees had disappeared, this we noticed with dismay.

The openings of our trenches which used to be completely hidden by the large banana leaves could now be seen from far away.

However, the boys succeeded to camouflage them with coconut palms. So a great 'thank you' went up to God from our grateful hearts. His special protection had been so evident! If those brave pilots had released their bombs half a second later, we would have been all shut up alive in our trenches with 65 feet of ground over us.

On the 27th, we got another bombing but not as heavy, and from then on the bombardments continued all around us. Vunapope would receive only a few bombs which finally destroyed what was left of the cathedral. As the Doctor's little house was still a target for bombs, Bishop Scharmack had it uncovered which seemed to satisfy the Allies. One day, however, the bombers returned with incendiary bombs so that all the decapitated coconut trees lying about caught fire, including those that were hiding the entrances of our tunnels. They did succeed in smoking us thoroughly, but we got out of this with no other harm than red and burning eyes.

For three and a half months life continued for us inside, or around, the trenches, without shelter from either the sun or the rain. Some of the boys were posted on top of the hill to observe far away and warn us of danger, relieving the watch every hour. Other boys worked with the fathers day and night, and even on Sundays to dig and enlarge our underground 'dwelling'.

Holy Mass was celebrated 20 metres inside the hill and 20 metres under the hill. Every day a different priest was the Celebrant. It was very moving when, at the moment of Communion, a priest went along the trench from one to the other with the ciborium, accompanied by a sister who carried a small lamp. Often during that time, planes would be humming and machine guns going but in our hearts, it would be peace and calm as the priest gave us the Author of Peace—the One Who, with one word, calmed the agitated sea.

When The Garamuts Beat

Humourous moments of dark hours

There would be so much to say about these bombings in Vunapope! But I fear to bore you. One day a sister got two broken ribs in the rush to get into the trenches! She fell and as at such times the order of the day was, '*Sauve qui peut*!' or 'Every man to himself!', the others passed over her: the mixed-race boys were so frightened that they would even jump over our shoulders.

This reminds me of another such case later, in Ramale camp, where for the same reason a sister got a broken rib. I can still picture her, laying at the entrance of the tunnel, shouting with all her strength, 'They are killing me, they are killing me!' while others were passing over them, I say 'them' because at the moment I arrived, they were three on top of each other while others still continued the stampede. Afterwards, regardless of her aches, the poor Sister had a good laugh with us: the picture had been so comical!

Another day, it was at breakfast time. In the precipitation towards the hole which was the only safety in those days, someone spilt his cup of cocoa over a missionary's back and, at that moment, bullets were whizzing by, while machine guns made their non-stop racket, the poor father thought he was their victim, and he cried with all his might, 'I am hurt. I am wounded!' Well, he felt something hot and thought that blood was running down his back but it was only the hot cocoa. It was even stolen cocoa! During the bombardments, the Japanese had run away into the jungle and our good boys profited from it to scrounge all they could. It seemed at this time that stealing was a virtue. Good Father Lepping had given us an 11th Commandment: 'Take all you can from the Japs!'

One day all the available cooking pots and boilers were filled with roasted chicken, pork, beef and even goats—all victims of the bombs that had rained down the previous day. Everything was cooked, and our poor stomachs being seldom satisfied in those days, we were looking forward to the prospect of a good meal. Alas! At the signal of danger, our saucepans stayed outside with their precious contents. When we came out of our hiding place to appease our hunger, the pots with the roasted meats had disappeared. A bomb had disposed of it all! How we did regret our chickens! Sister Fabiana O.L.S.H. told me in a disappointed tone. 'And I had taken so much pain to roast them, I with my broken ribs!' Once more we had to go without a meal.

Appendix

During May 1944, the Japanese notified Bishop Sharmack [sic] of their intention to evacuate us from Vunapope to send us into the jungle. This did not appeal to us very much. At Vunapope we had our solid trenches and being close to the sea we always hoped that our friends would soon come to rescue us. We had even made several placards with large letters in red and black, reading, 'Catholic Mission—Civilians only'. These were to be placed at the entrances of our tunnels in case of an attack. But the Japs forced us to leave. Bishop Sharmack [sic] asked them to give us a place near water and that it would not be too far from the gardens of sweet potatoes and tapioca, and he asked also that the Americans be notified of the exact place of the new camp. The Japanese agreed to the first two points but refused to send a message.

Exodus to the new camp Ramale, June 1944

Some fathers, brothers and boys went to prepare the chosen spot and from the first day set to work to dig tunnels in the hill. A second group went on the 3rd June and this time a few sisters went along. A third group followed on the 6th June in the early morning, and in the afternoon of the same day. The aged and the sick missionaries were transported by trucks. The trips were very dangerous because planes were flying overhead day and night. At the moment of departure of the first group of sisters, a few bombs fell close to the camp and our Sister M. Placide came back running to the trench to leave only on the last day.

A few days after we had moved to Ramale, Vunapope got an unexpected bombing. The Japs suspected us of communicating with the Americans, so they came to the camp in a rage, searching for a radio, which we didn't have, of course.

The native sisters had not been interned with us. They were living in community at about four hours' distance from Vunapope. They were forbidden to come to see us or to speak to us. During the bombardment of Vunapope, the Japs, including the police had run away to hide in the jungle; the Little Sisters profited from their absence to come and see us and to bring us some food. They were happy to be able to receive the Sacraments. The term of their Vows had expired for some of them and they renewed them after Holy Mass, during which they sang hymns.

A little mixed-race girl made her First Communion in the trench also and the sisters sang appropriate hymns for the occasion. Several new-born babies were also baptised and the dying received the Annointing of the Sick. Ceremonies such as these taking place 'under-ground' were very impressive and they reminded us of the first Christians and the Catacombs.

The local sisters showed their utter devotedness during the days of our transfer to Ramale. They carried on their back most of the things that were left to us. It was wonderful to see them at the task: they really were our greatest help. Our new camp was inland, two hours' walk away and situated in a deep valley, at the foot of a steep hill. These generous sisters made the journey back and forth twice a day, and they did it with such a willing heart! When going down the steep gully of Ramale, we wondered when we would have the happiness of climbing it up again. It was to be only fifteen months later!

We were 40 sisters to share the cover of a roof about 15ft by 30ft, and this was to shelter us from the rain. We needed no protection from the sun since the huge trees of the virgin forest were preventing us from even seeing the beautiful blue sky and the sunshine. We were absolutely forbidden to cut down any tree, but the dense undergrowth of the jungle could be cleared.

We thought we were in a safe place when exactly five days after our arrival, several bombs landed right in the midst of our camp. You can imagine the amazement of everyone! This time again no harm was done but for the fright. The Japanese had laughed at the brothers who started to dig tunnels before building houses, but now they laughed no more. Brothers and boys were working hard to get everybody sheltered, but especially to lengthen the trenches. The sisters themselves took their part of the task by removing the soil as the men dug it out, taking turns hourly.

One after another we found a little space to shelter for the night, but here the tunnels were very damp, water was oozing in several places and it was impossible to lie on the ground like we did in Vunapope. Then the boys, brothers and sisters started making small beds with bamboo canes.

When the work in the trenches was finished, the tunnels measured 600 metres in length, about two metres for each person since we were 300. Each one had about six feet along the trench to sleep, the other side being the passageway for free circulation. The tunnels were about 4 ft wide and there were ten of them, each having its own entry outside. They were so efficiently planned and made that all ten tunnels communicated by joining the main one at the far end, inside the hill. This larger tunnel had an opening at both sides.

Appendix

Our underground domain was shaped somewhat like a crescent, the outer line being the main tunnel.

We had more room than in Vunapope, but as there was nothing for support, we were always in danger of being buried alive. During those fifteen months there were about twenty landslides inside, but as providence was ever on the watch, we never had any serious accidents.

During the first months, we had small oil lamps with coconut oil to light our underground domain, but one day the poor boys who made the oil and also boiled down seawater to procure salt for us, were killed by bombs. They died victims of their devotedness: they knew quite well that in making a fire they exposed themselves to the danger of drawing the attention of the planes.

The double deprivation of light and salt became almost unbearable, as our food in the new camp was really miserable: a few roots of tapioca morning, noon and night was our daily menu. The last cows had been killed by bombs a week after our arrival in Ramale. The native sisters devoted themselves to collecting leaves and vegetables in the bush for us. Three brothers had also obtained permission to stay in the mission plantation with a few workers: it was they who sent the tapioca and sometimes sweet potatoes. As the food arrived in quite an insufficient quantity, Father Procurator made inquiries to the brothers through the Japanese police and he learnt that half of what the brothers sent disappeared on the way. Once more the native sisters volunteered to get our food themselves.

The Mission also had a large plantation of bananas, but as they were continually exposed to Allied bombs because of the Japs machine-guns and anti-aircraft guns placed in them, the workers refused to go and get the bananas. These brave sisters went, and collected the bunches of bananas and brought them to us on their backs. After a few weeks, Bishop obtained permission for the boys to go twice a week to the sea to get water, and this improved our menu a bit. However the sea was two hour's walking distance and the quantity of salt water was always inadequate.

Towards the end of our captivity, the boys started again to make salt for us. The Japs let them have a trench near the sea where they boiled the water day and night. Naturally, the boys had also a guard keeping watch over them: whoever was of the mission was suspected of being a spy. At last, Bishop discovered a new method to make oil without boiling, solely by fermentation.

Thus, after a long deprivation of light in the tunnels and of oil for the food, our admiration for our good Bishop Scharmack, M.S.C. was now increasing daily. It would be impossible to say all that Bishop Scharmack did and invented to protect us and to improve our conditions. How many painful hours didn't he spend holding out his firm stand with Japanese authorities or their Police, who were continually stirring up troubles for us.

From time to time they would make new laws and proclamations, and it was often very difficult to understand what they meant. But we could understand well enough that if we did this thing or the other, our heads would be cut off; and we 'were not to think our own thoughts anymore', nor should we 'make our own acts', this being the way they expressed themselves in their best English.

Two months after our arrival in the new camp, when the work of the tunnels was well advanced, the boys began to clear up a piece of land about fifteen minutes away from the camp, and everyone who was able had to go work in it.

Bishop obtained permission from the police for the aged sisters to be exempt from outside work. The Japanese showed themselves understanding enough for the sisters, provided some of them went to work. But we did not feel too safe outside, because the planes continued to bomb all around and in the gardens where there were no trenches.

We went to work in several groups, each having the company of a Japanese guard. At a given signal, we had to walk to the door of the enclosure and there wait for the sentry. He counted us as we filed out of the gate, and he would count us again when we returned. It happened several times that having hardly arrived in the garden, the rain would surprise the sisters, and they had to stay for hours working under torrential rain. Once out, no one had the right to return to the camp without the guard, and he had a tiny house to shelter in.

New stringent laws for Ramale internees

After the fathers and sisters of Nakaro Camp in Buin, had escaped (April 1945), new rules were made for us, but we knew nothing of their escape at the time. These new laws enforced that the prisoners going out to work were counted in groups of ten, each group having an appointed leader among the prisoners who was responsible for his group and who would pay with his or her life if anyone ran away.

Furthermore, three other prisoners were appointed to take charge of three different gardens: these being responsible for all their workers including the leaders of the group of ten. Rev. Fr Moene M.S.C., the Superior of the seminarians, proposed one of his boys be in charge of our garden. He said that John would be the first one wanting to escape and this way, no one would bear responsibility for him. Our gardens were such a success that during the last months of our captivity we had enough to eat. Our health began to improve and when the Australians came, we were in fairly good health.

In Ramale Camp as in Vunapope, we had Holy Mass every day, In ordinary times, flour hardly keeps good for three months in our tropical isles, but then, it remained in perfect condition during four years! We consider this miserable. The fathers were careful to use very little wine for the Consecration and used water for the absolutions. The Brothers also built a small chapel and we took turns for adoration in half-hour relays.

From the outset, there had been a necessity to find a place to make a cemetery. The Japanese did not allow us to bury our dead outside the enclosure. In spite of the limited space of our camp, we found a nice little spot to bury those who could not resist the hardships of so many privations, especially the lack of medicines.

It is there, under the shadow of a large Christ on the Cross carved by one of the Seminarians, that Sister Marie Domitilla is resting. During the month of November 1944, while making a short retreat of three days, she became sick and right away we realized that she was very ill. She herself told me, 'This time I will not get up again!' Because of the continual bombardments we were obliged to let her die inside the tunnel, and she suffered a lot from the want of air to breathe freely. She received the Anointing of the Sick on the third day and the following day, at 9 p.m. she went to Heaven after a short agony.

During the day she was still singing hymns to Our Lady. Towards evening she said to the priest who was assisting her, 'I am going,' and Father asked her, 'But where are you going?'

She replied quickly, 'Oh! but to Heaven!' The next morning, we wrapped her in coconut palms by way of coffin, and while the sisters and the mixed-race girls and boys were singing '*Libera Me*', the Japanese Doctor, who we had called, arrived.

In 1945 the Japanese became intractable with us and exceedingly cruel towards the natives. Some of our boys were even tortured under pretext that someone had come into the camp during the night. They also tortured some of the local sisters under the pretext that they had spoken to the three brothers who worked in the plantation. At this time, the Little Sisters were living nearer to us, but outside the camp enclosure. During the night they molested them with guns and bayonets, but they remained firm and faithful to their promises. The missionaries of Vunapope can be proud of their Little Sisters—'Daughters of Mary Immaculate.'

The great news!

Our Nippon Masters never gave us any news. They did not even mention the end of the war in Europe. According to them, Germany was still victorious everywhere in the month of July 1945.

Towards evening on the 16th August 1945, the interpreter, who had drunk a little too much, came to see us and said that he had great news but he could not tell it to us! The next morning, we were told to go to the gardens without guards. For two or three days now, the bombings had stopped. We began to draw some happy conclusions when, on Sunday morning, 19th August, we were officially told that the war was over!

We were all in jubilation until, a few days later, Bishop was notified that we were not to pass the limits of our enclosure, that it was not very sure that the war was finished. Those days too, some civilian prisoners of Rabaul were brought into our camp. The Japs gave the news that in a few days, their executor would come into the camp.

We did not suspect their malicious intentions and we thought that it was to visit the camp, as so many officers had done in the past. It is only after our deliverance that we learnt that the day of our execution had been fixed for 24 August.

You can imagine our disappointment when the Japs again took our freedom away. During the week we learned that there was trouble in the camp of the Indian prisoners. Exasperated by the bad treatment they received, they had taken revenge by killing some Japanese. We were told that it was because of that we were interned again.

The month seemed to drag on much longer than the others, but one day, before noon, someone in the camp shouted, 'The Australians. The Australians!' To say what happened then inside us and in the camp would be impossible! To see these big and strong men coming down the hill almost running—the Japs looked like dwarfs beside them, it was an explosion of joy on our side. There were bursts of laughter and of tears as all of us, with one accord, rushed towards our liberators. Then there were questions without end: we were really hungry for news. And the soldiers told us how happy they felt to see us so happy!

Among these five officers, one was the Military Chaplain, Rev. Fr. Holland, a Redemptorist. At their own risks, they had come to bring us freedom, because they had to pass the Japanese lines, who still had their arms and numbered one hundred thousand (100,000) in the Rabaul area.

During the afternoon another group of Australians arrived and the next day, it was the General-in-Command himself who came down to our valley. We gave him a little entertainment of songs and thanks. The Javanese soldiers had come with their brass band and at the sound of the National Anthem of the King of England, the Australian flag was hoisted by an Australian sister and a German brother. The General said that all of us, Allied or Germans, were all free and could go where we liked. We were so happy for Bishop Sharmack [sic] and his Missionaries who were nearly all Germans. They had been so good to us during these two and a half years in Camp.

As the General climbed up the hill again, the mixed-race girls sang the Australian National Anthem. The Japanese, our masters of past days, were observing us with spite, but they could not do anything to us anymore and were obliged to leave Ramale that very evening. Before going, one of them came to tell us, 'Now we know that you really were spies!' *Oh! How happy we were to see them go!!*

Two days later, seven trucks arrived loaded with provisions. But of all the good things these brave Australians sent us, it was the cup of coffee that was most appreciated. For a long time now, we had only a cup of boiled water to wake us up in the morning. The Red Cross immediately made arrangements to evacuate the sick and a few days later they went by plane to New Guinea and then to Australia.

When The Garamuts Beat

Meeting again the Marist family

Bishop Sharmack [sic] hastened to send a cable to Bishop Wade S.M. on the first day of freedom. A few days later, Fr Holland came down into the camp and asked Bishop Scharmack if he would give hospitality for the night to an American Officer. They were talking together when the Officer, who was none other than our dear Bishop, came down the hill. You can imagine our emotions, and how happy we were! What a welcome he received among us!

Two weeks later, to show our gratitude to our liberators, an appropriate little concert was organize. Officers and soldiers were impressed by our gratefulness; they had been so sick and tired of military life in the tropics.

At long last on 4 October 1945, we left Ramale for Rabaul where, for several days, two nurses cared for us as if we were Queens. By a happy coincidence our hospital was on the same spot where we had suffered so much three years before. We went to visit our trenches, this time accompanied by Australian soldiers. From there they led us to a little chapel where, at 6 pm a chaplain was just beginning to offer Holy Mass. He gave a beautiful sermon on little St Therese and the missions. Many soldiers received Communion then, at dusk.

On 8 October, the anniversary of our arrival in the military camp and of the terrible bombardment three years previously, we went on board ship, the *Ormiston*. We passed one day at Torokina, Bougainville, where Fr O'Sullivan SM, also an army chaplain, came to see us on-board ship. Officers from the Red Cross brought us some clothing and a pair of brown shoes for each one of us. After 24 hours near our dear Mission of Bougainville, where the volcano, Mount Bagana, was 'smoking its pipe' as always, we sailed for Australia.

There were 700 happy soldiers on board and how thrilled they were to return home! In his address to the men, one of the officers warned them that there were ladies on board and they were not to say 'big words'. The soldiers were most kind to us and gave us lots of sweets and chocolates. When the *Ormiston* arrived in Sydney on 18 October, the soldiers received a noisy welcome.

For us, we were greeted by our kind Mother Mary Rose and Sister M. Florence who had come to meet us. What a wonderful welcome it was! A few minutes later a special car was put at our disposal by the Red Cross and we went to Villa Maria to see the Sisters. The Fathers and Brother Bruno

Appendix

stayed at the Monastery and we continued our way to Lourdes, Killara where another group of Sisters gave us a warm welcome. It was almost dinner time and, naturally, there was a grand *Deo Gratias*.

During the afternoon, we parted with our improvised habit, to be transformed back into the looks of S.M.S.Ms. Each one in Lourdes hastened to bring a bonnet, or a dress, etc. to fit one or other of the newcomers. As we all assembled in the chapel for Benediction of the month of October that evening, a very fervent *Magnificat rosé* towards the Queen of Heaven and of Oceania.

Killara, February 1946.

PS

We have just read in a newspaper that on a small island near Bougainville the bodies of almost five hundred English soldiers have been found. Examination of them has shown that the poor men have been killed after the armistice. They will not tell about the Japs' atrocities: they have closed their lips forever. Some of them were beheaded, others were shot in the head.

We the prisoners of Rabaul, who knew that these young men had been sent to the Solomons. They had been taken prisoners at Singapore. Eighty of them were kept near Vunapope and M.S.C. Brothers gave them food secretly until they were watched so closely that no one could get near them anymore. They all died of misery and starvation with the exception of one.

Today we are asking ourselves 'how' and 'why' are we still alive? It is probably thanks to the fervent prayers offered for our intentions.

(Signed) Sister M. Wendelina
(Translated from the French M/S) 1968

§

When The Garamuts Beat

Fr Wilhelm Weber SM

Fr Silas included in his book Bougainville and its Missionaries the following account of Fr Weber. The writer Fr Joseph Lamarre, was stationed at Mabiri in 1965 when he wrote this. The final paragraph has been added in more recent years.

Fr William Weber, a young German Marist Priest, arrived in the mission of the North Solomons at the end of 1935. He was appointed to the station at Tunuru, which had been founded by the late Father Emmet McHardy. When Father Weber arrived at Tunuru, he lived with Father Albert Lebel who was then making preparations for the starting of a new Mission Station at Asitavi, some 35 mile up the coast. In January of 1937, Father Lebel left Tunuru to take up residence at Asitavi and Father Weber remained in charge of the mission until his death.

It is beyond the scope of this account to tell of all the work done at Tunuru by Father Weber. But a few lines about his work are not out of place. Father McHardy had founded the Station at Tunuru, Father Lebel and others in their short time there had cleared the ground, but it was Father Weber who who did the building. The present writer was a neighbour of Father Weber for two years and knows well the work done by him in this new Station.

With the help of Brother Xaverius, a large and very beautiful church was erected, schools and other buildings went up. But Father Weber's work was mostly pastoral. He established a large school at the station and in spite of many difficulties, kept it well filled with children from the mountain villages, and those children were well instructed in the faith. A good part of Father's time was spent travelling up and down the mountains, from village to village, baptising the babies and ministering to the needs of the people.

Father Weber was a good religious and a zealous priest who did not spare himself but gave his all for the people. He instructed and baptised hundreds of them. One year he had a record number of 365 baptisms. What then comprised the District of Tunuru, is now divided into three large Districts. He trained his helpers well with the help of some faithful Catechists. Tunuru became one of the flourishing Stations of the Mission.

At Easter time, 1942, the Japanese invaded Bougainville and put small garrisons at many places and large concentrations of troops at Buka, Buin,

Appendix

Kieta, and Numa Numa. Father Weber, like the Missionaries, received fair treatment in the beginning, that lasted until August 1942, when the Americans landed on the Island of Guadalcanal.

Then the Father was under constant watch for some time. As the Americans were getting closer to Bougainville, Father Weber was arrested by the Japanese Military Police. The police brought him to the Eivo District some 15 miles north of Tunuru. There he was allowed to go around the villages and minister to the people, accompanied by guards.

On 1 November 1943, the Americans landed at Torokina, on the west Coast of Bougainville. That changed the whole situation for the Missionaries. Those that had remained free were put into concentration camps. In 1944, and in the beginning of 1945, many escaped through the mountains and made their way to the American lines. The Native Soldiers came and carried others to Torokina. It seemed that these actions carried the death sentence for those who were still in Japanese hands. Fr Franz Miltrup was warned by a Japanese friend and escaped the night before he was to be beheaded.

For Father Weber it was different. Mr Robert Stewart [sic], a planter on Bougainville, who was then in the Civil Australian administration at Torokina tells this story. Native were sent over the mountains to Father Weber, telling him to escape. Father refused and replied that he wanted the native soldiers to come and carry him away. He did not want to escape of his own accord for fear of reprisals on the people he lived with. The native soldiers never came or came too late.

Father Weber continued to minister to the people, and in June 1946 were found records of Baptisms performed by him as late as 28 April 1945.

In early May 1945, Father came down from the mountains and arrived at the village of Tarara, on the beach, about three miles south of Mabiri. He found some men to carry his Mass Kit and his bags and headed north. He wanted to say Mass for the people at the village of Teporoi, near the Numa Numa plantation. Joachim Mateagu and William Matepa accompanied Father on the road while other people who carried his belongings walked along the beach.

After walking the miles of road through Mabiri plantation, he was stopped by the Japanese soldiers close to the boundary line between Mabiri and Kuruwina Plantation. The Japanese told him that he had to report to the Headquarters, a little further into the jungle. The natives were told to continue on through to Kuruwina and wait for Father at Arigua.

By that time the people who went by the beach caught up with the party and all the people went with Father's bags. They saw Father being taken to the Headquarters, a little distance into the jungle, between the Barurubiri and Kasipava rivers, two small rivers that join just before reaching the sea, on the Mabiri plantation, close to the Kuruwina boundary.

Joachim, William and the other people carried Father's bags to Arigua and there waited till nightfall. Then they were told by the Japanese to leave Father's belongings there and return to their village because the 'Kristo' (as they called Father) was being taken to Buin (the Southern tip of Bougainville) that night by motor Boat. The people did not believe the story but there was nothing else for them to do but follow instructions and return home. They never saw Father alive again.

Some time later, the people saw a Japanese wearing Father's watch. Others were seen with clothes that had been in his bags, some found the Mass Vestments from the Mass Kit torn to shreds. Then one day a Japanese appeared at Bove, close to the village of Tarara, with Father's Breviary from which he tore out pages to roll his cigarettes. The people report that the day after his arrival at Bove, the Japanese collapsed and died. By that time there was not the least doubt in the mind of the people that Father Weber had been killed.

August 1945 saw the end of the war. As soon as the Japanese were gone from the surroundings, the people decided to investigate. Joachim Mateagu and Tomuai, the faithful Catechist of Bove, went with a small party to the spot where they had last seen Father. From there they visited all the small camps of the Japanese and found the Headquarters.

The Jungle growth was reclaiming the ground, the Japanese makeshift houses were falling to ruin and close to one group of houses they found a cemetery, and then a few yards from the cemetery, a lonely grave, close to a large tree. (A canoe tree for people to make their canoes). That was it.

The people dug and at about the depth of two feet, they found the body in an advanced stated of decomposition, the head resting on the chest. They recognised Father by his hair, his glasses, clothes. Shoes and his Rosary. Even his walking stick had been thrown into the grave.

There was not the least doubt in the mind of the people that they had discovered the body of Father Weber. They covered the remains with a sheet

Appendix

of corrugated iron from a nearby camp and reburied him.

The Japanese veterans insist Fr Weber was shot, not beheaded. Mr. Yokoyama and Mr. Kimura were eye-witnesses. Their story is as follows:

> The officer told Fr. Weber that they had to execute him. Then when Fr. Weber asked what was the reason for the execution. He was told by the officer that they had received the order that they had to obey. Then Father asked to It is timegive him time to pray. He continued his prayer for a while told, and was then was told, 'It is time now to be executed.' He was shot in the back of the head and died instantly. His body was buried with respect at a Japanese graveyard and a cross erected on his grave and flowers were put there by Japanese soldiers.

Thus far the story of the eye-witnesses. The Missionaries returned to the East Coast of Bougainville in June 1946. Father Muller was appointed to Tunuru. The people who had been without a priest for so long. Immediately rose to the occasionand rebuilt their churches and village chapels. Now was the time for them to fulfil their duties towards Father Weber.

A group of people, headed by Joachim Mateagu, the faithful Catechist Tomuai, the Catechist Paul Uwa and others returned to the grave, exhumed the remains, placed them in a Japanese ammunition box and brought them to Tarara. There they placed the box under the altar in their little village chapel. A delegation was sent to notify Father Muller at Tunuru. There with all the prayers of the Church, the remains of the valient and zealous Missionary were buried in July 1946.

Fr Weber's bones rest a short distance from where he worked so well for so many Catholic people.

Since the main concentration of Japanese troops was at Arigua, it was always said that Father Weber was executed and buried at the back of Arigua. Mabiri did not count in those days.

A few years after the war, the Mabiri plantation was bought by Bishop Wade. For some years Mabiri was the site of the Novitiate of the B.S.J. Brothers. For the past two years the buildings of the native brothers have been occupied by the Catechist Trainees while waiting for their own building to be completed.

Having known Father Weber well and having been his neighbour for two years, I got interested in the site of his execution. During the month of September 1965, I questioned William and Joachim about the spot 'in the back of Arigua' Plantation. They emphatically denied that it was in the back of Arigua. They claimed it was on the Mabiri property, close to the Kuruwina boundary. Brother Patrick and I obtained all the information necessary before starting the search.

So it was twenty years later, on the 3rd of October 1965 that Brother Patrick with Joachim and William, some Catechist Trainees and other people went out in search of the grave. The jungle had grown, the roads had disappeared, a part of the ground had been cleared for a new coconut plantation. But the two small rivers had not changed; they were the guide-posts. First Brother and the people located the large 'Canoe Tree', the debris of the Japanese camp, then the little Japanese cemetery, and finally the open grave from which they had removed the remains of Father Weber. All recited prayers for the repose of his soul and returned.

The following day a larger party of people from Tarara, with the Catechist Paul Uwa, together with the catechist trainees, accompanied me and Brother Patrick to the site. The trainees cleared the spot, and there was the open grave and the place of execution of a real Marist Missionary. Close to the grave was the sheet of corrugated iron that had covered his body. Prayers were said for this Marist Priest who sacrificed his life rather than abandon his flock.

The Brothers of St Joseph have since placed a large cement slab over the grave and a erected a large white cross bearing Father's name. Soon a brass plate will be placed on the grave with the proper inscription. This hallowed spot is only half a mile through the bush from the buildings being erected for the new Catechist School.

Father Weber's bones were removed to Tunuru, but his flesh decayed in a lonely spot near the Barurubiri River on Mabiri. The Catechist Trainees have adopted this place as a revered grave that they must keep and cherish as befits the ground that has drunk the blood of a true priest of God.

Appendix

The Kagawa—Bougainville Association and the Japan— Solomon Association donated a hall at Mabiri *Ministri Skul* in honor of Fr Wilhelm Weber. The hall was blessed and opened on Wednesday 4 August 2004 in a ceremony attended by representatives of both Associations, the Japanese Consul General, government officials, church personnel and people from the area. Also a Reconciliation ceremony for healing of memories was held.

Silas

Most of Fr Lamarre's 43 years as a missionary in Bougainville were spent on Buka Island. It is not clear where or when a neighbour for two years. At Kieta or Asitavi? Asitavi is 60 km 'as the crow flies', an interesting definition of neighbour! The intermediate Stations at Manetai and Mabiri were not founded until 1948 and 1958 respectively.

When The Garamuts Beat

Abbreviations

BCL	Bougainville Copper Limited
Br	brother
BSJ	Brothers of St Joseph
CRA	Conzinc Rio Tinto
DC	District Commissioner
DDT	dichloro-diphenyl-trichloroethane
Fr	father
Lt	Lieutenant
Mgr	Monseigneur
MIVA	Missionary Vehicle Association
NAB	Novarsenobillon for the intravenous treatment of yaws
OLSH	Our Lady of the Sacred Heart
Pers. comm.	Personal communication
PNG	Papua New Guinea
PS	post script
RANVR	Royal Australia Navy Voluntary Reserves

SM	Society of Mary commonly known as Marists is attributed to the male clerics of that society
SMSM	Sisters of the Society of Mary refers to the sisters or nuns of the Order
Sr	Sister
TB	Tuberculosis
USA	United States of America
USS	United States Submarine

Glossary and added notes

English and religious terms

alb	a full-length, long-sleeved, usually white liturgical vestment
Beriberi	a disease caused by a vitamin B1 deficiency, also known as thiamine deficiency.
ciborium	a receptacle shaped like a shrine or a cup with an arched cover, used in the Christian Church to hold the Eucharist.
copra	dried flesh from inside the coconut. The flesh is usually smoked or dried before it can be exported.
leguan	a large amphibious monitor lizard generally found in Africa (https://www.thefreedictionary.com/leguan). Large monitor or goanna type lizards were on Bougainville in the early days, but anecdotally, people don't see them anywhere now. Perhaps they are endangered if not extinct on the island.
novena	an ancient Christian tradition of devotional prayer, that may be said privately or in public and repeated for nine successive days or weeks. Marian prayer dating to the 250 AD century (Ref Wikipedia)

Sub tuum praesidium

an ancient Christian hymn and prayer. One of the oldest known Marian prayers and among the most ancient preserved hymns to the Blessed Virgin Mary still in use (Ref Wikipedia)

When The Garamuts Beat

Tok Pisin

Comments on spelling: Where there is a repeated word such as *liklik* or *kaikai*, these adjectives and nouns can be spelled as two separate words, with and without a hyphen, or as one word.

Much of *Tok Pisin* relies on phonetics to spell words, hence spelling varies frequently.

PNG currency uses toea and kina. Fr Miltrup refers to a toea whilst speaking of German currency. It was likely a force of habit.

bello	lunchtime, midday
bosboi	foreman, supervisor
bulmakau	cattle, bulls, and cows
garamut	a large wooden slit drum used to call people to meetings or to send out messages. Their beat can be heard for miles.
giamanim	to fool, tell a lie, play a trick or joke,
guria	earthquake, earth tremor, to shake
hausboi	man servant. If spelled as two words it can mean a house for single men
haus kuk	kitchen
haus kakaruk	chook house
haus kiap	the kiap's house
haus lotu	church, chapel, place of worship
haus paia	cook house, bush kitchen, more likely a smoke house to smoke copra
haus pekpek	bush toilet
haus sik	health centre, aid post, hospital
kaikai	food
kakaruk	chooks, poultry

Glossary and added notes

kalabus	prison, if used as a verb it is to hold captive or imprison
kapul	possum
kastam	culture, tradition
kaukau	sweet potato
kiap	derived from the German word Kapitan (captain), refers to representatives of the colonial government, taking on political education, policing and judicial roles Kiaps were known formally as district officers and patrol officers, holding wide-ranging authority, including the completion of censuses Refer https://en.wikipedia.org/wiki/Kiap
klaud	cloud
kulau	green coconut
kastam	tradition, culture
Laplap	sarong that wraps around the waist old person, elderly
lapun	young
liklik	small, not much,
limbum	palm tree that the trunk is split for house flooring
luluai	village chief in the Kuanua language of the Tolai people of East New Britain, ref: https:// www.pngattitude.com/ 2018/04/luluai-to- councillor-the-evolution-of-local-government- in-simbu.html
	The system of *tultuls* and *luluais* was created by the German administration in New Britain, and was continued by the Australian administration up until WWII https://madfornewsblog.wordpress.com/2021/03/27/tultuls-and-luluais-from-the-territory-of-new- guinea/).
masta	white man, boss. Can also used by a PNG woman when referring to her husband but it is less common today
mausgras	facial hair, beard, mustache

When The Garamuts Beat

meme	goat
meri	woman, girl, female,
mimis	a form of shell money
mipela	us, we
missus	white woman
nogat	no, a response in the negative
no gut	not good, bad,
paiarup	fire-up, to get mad, burst into flames, explode
papa bilong graun	male landowner. South Bougainville is patrilineal while most other areas of Bougainville are matrilineal
pas	letter, message. Has other meanings depending on the grammar used with the word
patere	Father as in a Catholic priest
pikinini	small child, infant. Can also refer to one's adult child no matter the age
ples balus	airport, air field
police boi	native policeman
pukpuk	crocodile (pronounced pookpook)
raus	get rid of, throw out,
ren	rain
saksak	sago palm leaves
singsing	traditional dancing, usually to celebrate a special occasion
taim bipo	a long time ago, olden days
tok ples	Indigenous language or local dialect

toktok	gossip, discussions, speaking
tultul	chief's assistant or second in command. The term originated from Kuanua, spoken by the Tolai people of East New Britain. Ref: https:// www.pngattitude.com/2018/04/luluai-to- councillor-the-evolution-of-local-government- in-simbu. html. This position was a construct of colonial administrations.
waitpus	old Pidgin word referring to the white band on the luluai's cap. It was a title of respect. Waitpus Makis of Aku village was a paramount chief, senior in rank to luluais who were often village chiefs.
wantok language	relative, friend, compatriot, a person from the same group
wiliwil	bicycle

Telei — languange of Buin people

ekio	month
kaikai	speaking
mekai	medicine man
moi	galip tree, one year
monale	road
murugeinu	loyal friend or very good friend
nkoma muruge!	my heart!
nkio	penis
pogusere	mad, intellectually disabled

Added notes:

1. South Solomons referred to in the text, is the independent nation of Solomon Islands. North Solomons is the Autonomous Region of Bougainville.

2. Visale station where Fr Miltrup called into on his way to Bougainville in 1938, on the MV *Malaita*, was the headquarters of the Marist South Solomon vicariate (Decker: 1948, p. 112)

3. A little information on Paramount Chief Makis: extracted text from Patrol Officer reports for Buin district 1950-1953, p. 53

> The outstanding personalities of the area are:-
> 1/ MAKIS Paramount *Luluai* who lives at AKU Vil
> lage. He is a pre-war appointment, in his late 50s and
> keeps a keen interest in his area. He is respected by all,
> natives and Europeans alike, and his judgement is sought
> in all problems In the area. Surprisingly active MAKIS
> rides his bicycle around his area at least once every two months.
>
> 9 March, 1951.
> District Commissioner,
> Bougainville District, SOHANO.
> PATROL REPORT - BN 4 of 1950/51
> It is pleasing to note the progress made in this area since
> the late war. MAKIS the Paramount *Luluai* is evidently
> an excellent man and should be encouraged. Items of
> interest to other Departments have been passed to those concerned.
> (I. F. Champion) ACTING DIRECTOR. (p. 63)

4. Buin people follow a patrilineal system, unlike most other areas of Bougainville, which are matrilineal.

5. There is a Bougainville custom of non-verbal language, and that is, to raise one's eyebrows, means 'yes', to protrude one's bottom lip means 'no' (Miltrup: 1989).

Glossary and added notes

6. Miltrup's memoir originally stated the Kroenings were interned in New Zealand, but records in the National Archives of Australia confirm the Kroening's internment was at Tatura in Victoria. After the Second World War, Dr Kroening returned to Bougainville. He is buried on Sohano Island in Buka Passage.

7. When Fr Miltrup refers to an Australian soldier called 'Slim' this could have been Edward Douglas 'Slim' Otton, one of two Australians assigned to Lt. Paul Edward Mason, Coast Watcher.

8. The catechist, Mege, had a daughter called Poetsi. Fr Miltrup mentions her:

> When Sr Wendelina arrived in 1927, young Poetsi asked her if she might become a Sister too. Indeed six years later, Bishop Wade presided at the first profession of Poetsi, Noela and Gabriela, vanguard of the Congregation of the Sisters of Nazareth (CSN). They would continue the pioneer Sisters' work among women. Already Christian family life was thriving (O'Brien: 1989, p. 95).

9. Fr Miltrup mentions Tashiro, a Japanese resident of pre-war Bougainville. Tashiro is mentioned in several books on Bougainville during the Second World War era.

This would be Tsunesuke Tashiro, a young Japanese who still in his teens, travelled to the New Guinea Islands shortly after the First World War in 1917. Tashiro is said to have traded in copra and trocus shell, working on boats which meant he also likely worked for the missions at different times.

In March 1941, Tashiro returned to Japan on a business trip and was conscripted to serve as a gunzoku (civilian) in the Japanese Navy Civil Administration. This is how he came to play a role during the war.

Prior to the war, Paul Mason and Tashiro knew each other well, and despite the war putting these men on opposing sides, there is conjecture that Tashiro could have taken a much more hostile approach Mason's activities (Wright: 2009)

10. Regarding the Japanese Jesuit Matusmora: some years after the war, Fr Adam Muller visited Japan and tracked down Matsumora's mother. They wept in each others arms (pers. Comm. Moore: 2022).

11. The Japanese interpreter at Fr Miltrup's trial, Shimabukuru, was a school friend of Matsumora.

12. Japanese and Australian sources suggest an estimated 845 military personnel and up to 208 civilians lost their lives in the sinking of the MV Montevideo Maru by the American submarine USS Sturgeon (available online at the AWM).

13. The chief loyal to the Allies was Barosi Toroke, Paramount Chief, from Sirovai village. Forced to dig his own grave, Chief Barosi was beheaded in Kieta in January 1943. Barosi is the man Fr Charles Seiller stood with, as witness to his brutal end.

14. St Mary's Asitavi Secondary School for girls located in Central Bougainville, was founded in 1956 by the SMSM.

15. Fr Miltrup met *kiap* Bill (WT) Brown, then a District Officer, when he was transferred to Kieta from the Sepik, to assist with the problems associated with CRA's prospecting activities. In January 1968, Brown was Deputy District Commissioner at Kieta when Des (DN) Ashton took over as District Commissioner, Bougainville.

When Ashton moved district headquarters from Sohano to Kieta in August 1968, Brown continued as Deputy District Commissioner until November 1969, when as District Commissioner (Special Duties), he became responsible for the areas that involved CRA activities: exploration, prospecting and mine construction areas, and the future port, towns, roads, power lines, tailings etc.

Ashton remained in charge of Kieta and the majority of Bougainville until March 1971, when Brown replaced him. (Pers. comm. Brown: 2022).

In March 1968, the administration concluded negotiations for the purchase of Marist mission land known as St Michael's. The area was surveyed to become the suburb of Toniva, about five minutes' drive from Kieta town (Brown: 2017).

16. The Gilbert Islands referred to in the memoir gained independence in 1979, becoming known as Kiribati, while the Ellis Islands gained their independence in 1979, and is now Tuvalu.

Glossary and added notes

17. The Bougainville Crisis signalled ten years of conflict and warfare between the Bougainville Revolutionary Army and the PNG Defence Force, and in time, hostilities spilled over to include a guerilla war between opposing groups in Bougainville.

The uprising caught everyone's attention with the sabotaging of BCL equipment and infrastructure in late 1988. Initially the civil unrest was viewed as a fight over grievances between landowners affected by environmental damage to land and waterways caused by the mine's operations, as well as the financial compensation and other arrangements, negotiated between BCL's parent company and the PNG national government. These issues remained at the core of dissent and provided a catalyst for the rebellion, but there were other factors at play which have been eloquently described and analysed by experts in other writings.

Simply put, some of those factors include the rapid and negative societal change that felt all encompassing to many Bougainvilleans; a sequence of events unfolded as unrest continued, seemingly bringing all points towards a 'perfect storm' and the longheld aspirations by many to be independent. These were just some of the contributing elements that helped mobilise more of the population to join, if not support, a broader pan-island fight for secession.

The violence that ensued saw the collapse of civil and public institutions, and a catastrophe for human life, leading to the deaths of an estimated 20,000 lives.

When The Garamuts Beat

Maps and selected photographs

1 Map of Bougainville, available online at *http://www.bougainville-copper.eu/bougainville- maps-2.html*

2 Map showing Catholic stations in the North Solomons (Bougainville) and dates of occupation (Laracy: 1969, p. 499)

3 Map of Torokina and Piva Forks Battle available online at https://www.nps.gov/parkhistory/ online_books/npswapa/ extcontent/usmc/ pcn-190-003141-00/sec8.htm

4 Tunuru mission, photograph from *Blazing The Trail* p.78 based on *Letters from the North Solomons* by Rev. Emmet McHardy.

5 Mt Balbi volcano

6 Photo taken at Rigu airstrip 1934. L - R: J. Sanson, Dr Kroening (Toberoi Plnt.) talking to Fr Tonjes, R. Diercke (Woskawitz Plnt), P. Berkenheier (camera man). Per C. Diercke in *Una Voce* article Sept 2015, available online at https://pngaa.org/miva-in-north- bougainville-1934-chris-diercke/.

7 Bishop Wade with Sgt Frank Hennessy. Photo from Decker: 1948, p. 83

8 Patupatuai mission waterfront 1950s, Photo from R. Dreyer

9	Church at Tubiana missioni near Kieta built by Br Xaverius
10	Fr Franz Miltrup SM taking Mass in Meppen, Germany, 1985. Courtesy of Mr Friedel Miltrup.
11	Photo: Marist priests gathered at Tubiana mission in Kieta for Sr M. Dolores' Diamond Jubilee. Feedback on who is in the photo pers. comm. Rudi and Pat Dreyer and Harry Moore SM:

L to R: in row behind Sr Dolores—Bishop Leo Lemay, Bougainvillean Brother Thomas of Koromira, Brother Wilhelm Lubbering, Father Willy Wöeste, Brother Pat Thomson (manager of Mabiri farmers' school), Father Kelly Pelletier and Father George Fahey.

Second row: Father Miltrup could be standing behind Bishop Lemay. Bougainville priest looking to the right is possibly Fr Edmund Tsivara.

12	Fr Grisward following his liberation from Japanese interment. Photo taken at Torokina. Courtesy of AWM available online at https://www.awm.gov.au/collection/C69795
13	Fr James Hennessy, photo from Decker: 1948, p. 83
14	Rev Emmet McHardy, copied online from https://teara.govt.nz/en/photograph/3447/father-emmet-mchardy-about-1929
15	Fr Seiller. Photo taken with Fr Grisward after they were liberated from Japanese internment—Torokina. Photo courtesy of AWM. Available online at https://www.awm.gov.au/collection/C69795
16	Marist sisters at Tubiana mission early 1970s.

L to R: Srs Carmen, Barbara, Michaeline, de Lourdes, Concilia, Mary Murray, Kathleen and Theresa (side on). Photo from Leonard family collection.

'Sister Mary Dolores SMSM sitting down. Photo possibly taken at her Diamond Jubilee. Most of the sisters in that photo have since gone to heaven.' (Sr Margaret Tisch SMSM

Bibliography

Begg SM, J: Duffy SM, E. O'Connor SM, M. and Weemaes SM, W.
2020. *National Catholic M onthly*, 'Ma r ist Messenger', available at http- s://www.maristmessenger.co.nz/2020/06/01/death-of-a-marist-7/

Bougainville Copper Limited
1973. *Spanning 40 years*, excerpt by Fr Franz Miltrup, Bougainville Copper Concentrates Vol 3, No. 12 1973

Brown, W.T.
2017. *A Kiap's Chronicle,* ch. 30. Available on https://www.pngatti- tude.com/2021/04/a-kiaps-chronicle-30-tightening-of-the-screw.html

Callick, R.
1989. *Bougainville Facing Military Sollution,* AFR. Available online at https://www.afr.com/politics/bougainville-facing-military-solu- tion-19890606-k3gh1

Decker, C. Ed.
1948. *Saving the Solomons: from the diary account of Rev. Mother Mary Rose SM SM.* 2nd Edition, Digitised 2020. The Marist Missions, Bedford Massachusetts USA.

Feuer, A. B. Ed. & Read, J.W. & Mason, P.
1992. *Coast Watching in the Solomon Islands: The Bougainville Re ports, December 1941-July 1943.* Praeger Publishers, New York, USA.

Fitzgerald, M. Grossin, F.
2011. *Alive in Memory a Biographic Necrology of Oceania Marist Provinces 1836-2011.* Oceania Marist Province, Suva Fiji.

Kronenberg, H. and Saris, H.
Catechists and Church Workers in the Church of Bougainville, Society of Mary Marist Fathers and Brothers available online at https://www .maristsm.org/wp-content/uploads/ 2020/09/11FN11Kronenberg.pdf.

Laracy, H.
1969. *Catholic Missions in the Solomon Islands 1845—1966*, thesis, Australian National University, Canberra.

Laracy, H.
1976. *Marists and Melanesians: A History of Catholic Missions in the Solomons.* p. 107 ANU Canberra

Laracy, H.
1999. 'Maine, Massachusetts, and the Marists: American Catholic Missionaries in the South Pacificl'. *The Catholic Historical Review,* 85(4), 566-590. http://www.jstor.org/stable/25025587

Lockwood, J.
2009. *The Pilot,* 'Effects tell tale of Boston missionary who perished in WWII'. Boston USA available at http://www.thebostonpilot.com/article .php?ID=11135

McHardy, E.
1935. *Blazing the Trail In the Solomons. Letters From The North Solomons* of Rev. E. McHardy SM. Ed. E. Duggan. Dominion Publishing Company, Sydney, Australia

Missionary Sisters of the Society of Mary
2014. Website of the SMSM Rome. Available at http://www.smsmsisters.org/index.php?id=216. Accessed 29 April 2022

National Library Australia
1943. Trove, *Advocate,* 'Bishop Faces Japanese'. Melbourne. pp 4. https://trove.nla.gov.au/newspaper/article/172207706?searchTerm=on%20several%20occasions%20bishop%20wadeAccessed online at
1953. Trove, *Sunday Herald,* 'Submarine Comes for the Nuns', p. 10. Available online at https://trove.nla.gov.au/newspaper/article/ 18510663?searchTerm=sisters%20escape%20submarine%20bougainville.

1978. Trove, *Pacific Islands Monthy* https://nla.gov.au/nla.ob- j-335670856/view?section&partId=nla.obj-335671827

O'Brien, C. SM
1989. *To Celebrate My Son: a history of the Marist Missionary Sisters. SMSM, Sydney.* Available online at https://andrewmurraysm.files.word- press.com/2020/06/obrien_tocelebratemyson.pdf

Phillips, A
1993. *As The Catalina Flies: a Hungarian girl growing up in Bougainvile.* Butterfly Books, Springwood NSW. p. 70

Richter, M. (Sr Marie Wendelina SMSM)
1946. *War experiences under the Japanese 1942—1945.* Translated into English in 1968

Bibliography

Rigotti, Livia (Eds.)
> 2014. *Deutsche Frauen in den Sudsee-Kolonien des Kaiserreichs* (1-4). Bielefeld: transcript Verlag. p. 664 https://doi.org/10.14361/transcript.9783839428368.fm Book DOI: https://doi.org/10.14361/transcript.9783839428368.fm Online ISBN: 978-3-8394-2836-8 © 2014 transcript Verlag. Accessed online 27 Apr'22
>
> Title translated: German women in the South Sea Colonies of the German Empire - Everyday Life and Relations with the Indigenous Population, 1884-1919

Saris, H. SM
> 2008. 'Lists of Marists who served in Bougainville'.

Smith, Geoff P. And Siegel, J.
> 2013. Tok Pisin. In Michaelis, Susanne Maria and Maurer, Philippe and Haspelmath, Martin and Huber, Magnus (Eds.), *The survey of pidgin and creole languages*. Vol. I: English-based and Dutch-based languages, 214-222. Oxford: Oxford University Press. Tok Pisin in Michael

Societas Mariae Provincia Oceaniae
> 1990. *In Memoriam*. Oceania Marist Province, Suva Fiji.

Societa di Maria
> 2021. *Memoriale Societatis Mariae*. Roma, Italia

Stuart, R.
> 1977. *Nuts To You*. Wentworth Books, Sydney, Australia.

University of California (UC).
> UC San Diego Library. *Patrol Reports. Bougainville District, Wakunai, 1968 - 1969.* National Archives of Papua New Guinea, Accession 496. Available online at https://library.ucsd.edu/dc/object/bb45069406

Vaney SM, N.
> 2017. National Catholic Monthly, *Marist Messenger*, available online https://www.maristmessenger.co.nz/2017/01/31/marist-walked-death- fr-richard-osullivan-sm/

Wright, K.
> 2009. *Read, Mason, Tashiro And The Bougainville Mystery*. Available online at: https://asopa.typepad.com/files/read-masontashiro-the- bougainville-mystery.pdf

Other articles accessed online:
Article on the evacuation from Bougainville in the *Sydney Morning Herald,* 23 August 1953 p. 10 'Submarine Comes For The Nuns'.

https://stpatschurchhill.org/about-st-patricks-church-hill-sydney/

https://www.champagnat.org/shared/bau/HermitagetoGermany_English .pdf pp 73-74

https://www.encyclopedia.com/religion/encyclopedias-almanacs-tran- scripts-and-maps/marist-fathershttps://en.wikipedia.org/wiki/Marist_Brothers#:~:text=The%20interna- tional%20Marist%20brotherhood%20is, the%20General%20House%20in- %20Rome

A Nun's Life Ministry: 2020 T*he "Sister Mary" Naming Custom.* Available online at https://anunslife.org/blog/nun-talk/the-%E2%80%9Csister-mary%E2%80%9D-naming-custom

Index

A

Aku village 29–30, 33, 39, 47–48, 86, 90, 288–289

Allotte SM, Fr Francois 21

Apotu, Chief xix

Arawa xxiv, 26, 147, 150–151, 154, 158–163, 165–173, 179–180, 182, 217

Arigua plantation 277–279

Aropa plantation 147, 150, 166, 197

Ashton, Des 154, 291

Asitavi 20, 26, 29, 150, 199, 206, 217, 231, 237–238, 275, 280, 291

Allotte sm, Fr F. xx, 21, 187, 232

B

Barrett SM, Fr Charles 118

Barurubiri river 160, 277, 279

Bata 124

Bau 66–67, 82

Baubake, M. 139

Begg sm, Fr. J. 173, 180, 198, 296

Bernaden 121

Binois sm, Fr A. 13, 123, 188–189

Bledendiek sm, Fr T. 5

Bleischwitz sm, Fr R. 166, 174, 179

Boch sm, Fr M. 9, 15, 105, 189–191, 201, 230, 244, 253

Bogisago village xxiii, 83–85, 92, 95–96

Bove village 277

Brady sm, Fr 118

Brosnahan sm, Fr 122

Brown, W. (Bill) T. xvii, 39, 148, 151–152, 156, 160, 291

Brown, Wallis 39

Broyer, Bishop xviii–xix, 189–190, 220

Brüser sm, Fr A. 144, 174

Buin xiv, xvi, xx, xxii–xxiii, 1–2, 12–13, 19, 21–22, 24–25, 30, 34, 39–40, 44, 46–47, 50–53, 66, 68, 70, 72, 75, 77, 79, 82, 84, 87–88, 90, 92, 94, 98, 107, 109–110, 114–116, 121–122, 124, 130, 134–135, 147, 152, 158, 165, 177, 187–188, 192, 195, 203–205, 207, 211, 217, 219–221, 227–230, 235, 246–248, 252, 269, 275, 277, 288–289

Buka xviii–xx, xxiv, 14, 21–22, 72, 104–105, 110–111, 113, 121, 124, 132, 135, 143, 145, 156, 160, 163, 188–190, 192–193, 195, 199, 201–202, 207–208, 216, 218, 228, 232, 242, 248, 275, 280, 290

Index

Burunotui 188–189, 192, 209, 218

C

Caffiaux sm, Fr P. 21, 131

Chabai mission 21, 143, 194–195, 200

Chaize sm, Fr L. 103–104, 112, 191–192

Clariziaro, Monsignor 122

Clemens 125

Conley sm, Fr J. xxiii, 77, 192, 208, 211

Conzinc Rio Tinto

    CRA 153–155, 158, 291

Courtais sm, Fr E. 11

Croker sm, Fr 102–103

Cyr sm, Fr 120–121, 159

Clemens 125

D

Dapera village 176, 179–180

de Klerk sm, Fr E. 141, 196

Deomori village 20, 132, 154–155, 210

Dowden sm, Fr L. 132

Dubois sm, Fr 6

Duffy sm, Fr E. 150, 157, 193–194, 198

Dynan sm, Fr 103

de Theye sm, Fr A. 103

E

Ekio 47, 51, 62, 108

Elixmann sm, Fr F. 142–143, 154–155, 158, 166, 170–171, 194

Ellis, Mr J. 158

Englert sm, Fr E. xviii–xix, 220

F

Fahey sm, Fr G. 165, 170–171, 176, 295

Fahey sm, Fr R. 135, 139

Fingleton sm, Fr W. 43, 137–138, 145

Flaus sm, Fr K. xviii, 18, 188, 220

Fluet sm, Fr H. 26, 28–29, 31, 55, 68, 137, 139–140, 229, 231, 237–239

Forestier sm, Fr J. xx, 190

Furst 117–120, 203, 221

Franz 276

G

Geers sm, Fr Fr. 146–149

Goedert sm, Fr N. 19

Goldert sm, Fr 180

Gregory sm, Br 20, 232

Grisward sm, Fr J. 25–26, 61–62, 70, 194–195, 205, 295

Index

Germany

    Fürstenzell xxii, 6, 12, 103, 127, 144, 159, 171, 173

    Meppen xxii, 5, 18, 24–25, 127, 144, 146, 159, 173–174, 179, 181, 194, 205, 210

    München 6, 127, 144, 171

    Münster 127, 144, 174, 205, 217

    Osnabrück xxii, xxiv, 5, 28, 127, 140, 144, 194, 196, 210

    Passau xxii, 4, 127

    Steinbeck xxv, 144, 159, 173–174, 179

Gisèle 234

H

    Hahela mission xxiv, 105, 111, 124, 199, 201, 207, 210

    Hanahan village 143, 166, 174, 192, 198–199, 201, 232

    Hannett, Mr L. 153

    Hantoa village 189, 200, 218

    Hennessy sm, Fr J. 21, 101, 195, 228, 242–243, 248, 294–295

    Herbert sm, Fr 129

    Hockenbrink Familly 142, 155

    Hogan sm, Fr T. 142

    Hurley sm, Fr D. 103

I

I

Inus plantation 69, 238

Itanu 149, 153–154

Ignace 66

J

Jaschke sm, Fr K. 91

Jünker sm, Fr A. 71, 75, 79, 95, 101

K

Kahili village xx, xxii, 15, 65–67, 69, 106

Kaitsi 52–53

Kakarikiru village 30, 39

Kangu 15, 30, 60–61, 64, 134, 140, 152, 228, 248

Kasipava river 277

Kato 19

Katuku village 25

Kauro 37–38

Kekemona village 97–98

Kiau 84, 96

Kieta xix, xxii–xxiv, 12–13, 15, 18–20, 22, 24, 31–32, 40, 44, 61, 63, 65, 70–74, 76, 79, 84, 87, 90–91, 95, 121, 123, 125, 131–132, 139–142, 146–147, 149–151, 155–157, 166, 181, 188–189, 192–194, 201, 205–208, 214–215, 217–220, 227–228, 231, 235–237, 246–248, 276, 280, 291, 295

Kikimogu village 83

Klöster sm, Fr A. 18–20

Koch sm, Br X. 20, 24, 71, 79, 97, 117, 140, 142, 146, 148–149, 155, 196–197, 207

Köller sm, Fr G. 156

Koromira mission xx, xxv, 15, 19, 39, 71, 93–95, 98, 142, 150, 168, 177, 180–181, 194, 197, 206, 214, 218–219, 246, 295

Kotoita village 238

Kroening Family

    Dr Bruno 22, 63, 220, 290

    Kroening, F

        Frances 63, 158

Kronenberg sm, Bishop H. 170–171, 187, 198, 209

Kukumaru village 139

Kunka 114–115

Kunua village 21, 110, 202, 211

Kuraio village 110, 112–113, 125

Kuruwina plantation 276–277, 279

L

L'Estrange sm, Fr T. 137

Laguai village 42–43, 64

Lamarre sm, Fr J. 143, 198–199, 210, 242, 275

Laruma 99, 101

Lebel sm, Fr A. 20, 29, 103, 105, 199, 206, 232–

233, 238–239, 275

Lebreton sm, Fr G. 18, 61, 71, 78, 107, 205

Lemanmanu village 21, 143, 160, 192, 194–195, 201, 207, 209, 242

Lemay sm, Fr L. xxiv, 120, 125, 130–131, 140–141, 144–145, 147, 153, 155, 158, 160, 166, 168, 193, 200–201, 295

Lepping sm, Fr G. 1–2, 103, 105, 116, 118, 120, 137, 145, 201, 230, 244–245, 253, 265

Liloki river 98

Loloho 156

Luecken sm, Fr H. 126, 143, 155, 166, 174

Lukauko village 47

M

Mabiri mission 198, 275–280, 295

Mahoney sm, Br F 155

Mahoney sm, Fr D 155

Makis, Paramount Chief 29–30, 33–34, 47–48, 52, 64, 288–289

Mallinson sm, Fr P. 143

Mamaregu village 98, 107–108, 121, 218

Manetai village 20, 61, 123, 188, 202, 210, 231, 236–237, 280

Marai village 147, 149–151, 154, 157, 180, 210

Mason, Paul xxiii, 65, 69, 96–98, 290

Index

Mateagu, J. 276–278

Matepa, W. 276

Matsumora 73–74, 95, 291

McConville sm, Fr J. 25, 111, 126, 232

McGuire sm, Fr 116–117

McHardy sm, Rev Emmet 20, 201, 275, 294–295

McKillop, Francis R (Kip) 154, 158

Mege 68, 85, 221, 290

Meini 47

Meyer sm, P. xix

Mills sm, Fr V. 130

Mirinu, J. 159

Mivo river 29, 36, 103

Moatsi 139

Mogoroi village 82, 95

Moisurui village 121

Molas, C. 160, 167, 173, 176, 178

Momis, John 152–153

Momotoro village 83, 88

Monoitu mission xxiii, 15, 25–26, 29, 34–36, 66, 68–70, 80, 107–108, 118, 122–123, 139, 145, 195, 199, 215, 218, 227, 229–230, 235–236, 241, 247, 257

Montauban sm, Fr Paul 22, 137

Morula village 30–31, 42, 66, 108

Muguai village xxii–xxiii, 15, 30, 51, 60, 66, 80, 93–94, 108–109, 115, 134, 217–218, 227–229, 235, 247, 249, 252

Muisuru village 25

Müller sm, Fr A. 21–22, 71, 74, 76, 79, 83, 90, 100–101, 102–103, 123, 188, 202–203

Murphy sm, Fr P. 153

Miltrup family

Angela 5, 93, 127, 143–144, 159, 174

Franz Miltrup xii, xiv, xxii, xxiv, 10, 183, 203, 214, 224, 226, 228, 230, 235, 289, 291, 295, 296

Miltrup, Friedel xii, 224

N

Nabaku village 44, 47, 65, 114–115

Nakaro village 90, 93, 95, 269

Nakorei village 37

Nerau, P. 138, 169

New Caledonia 4, 6, 68, 199, 213, 240

Noumea 215–216, 221

Nissan Island 14, 22, 77, 137, 149, 192, 194, 199, 201, 208

Tungol 201

Ntuga 39, 149

Numa Numa plantation 76, 89, 115, 132, 276

O

O'Sullivan sm, Fr Richard (Dick) 56, 64, 68–69, 106, 110, 113, 122, 203, 205, 227–232, 236–239, 247–248, 273

Ogan, Dr Eugene 154

Otton, E.D. (Slim) 64, 290

Oude-Engberink sm, Fr Henk 7, 9–10

P

Panguna xxv, 155–156, 171–172, 174, 176, 177–180, 230

Parer, D. 106

Patupatuai mission xx, 24–26, 28, 34–36, 43, 50, 56, 60, 62, 64, 113, 121, 123, 135–137, 139–142, 145, 187, 196–197, 227–228, 247–248, 294

Pelhans Bishop 121

Pelletier sm, Fr Gerard 173, 295

Piano mission xxii–xxiv, 22, 24, 26, 28–41, 43–44, 47–48, 50, 52, 55–56, 60, 62, 64–67, 69, 83, 85, 106, 108–109, 113–115, 118, 134, 144–145, 213, 227–230, 235–236, 247

Pitt Family 232–233, 240

Pius Br J.A. 11, 128, 166, 174, 179

Piva 213–214, 218, 294

Poetsi 221, 290

Pok Pok xix, 65–66, 151–152

Poncelet sm Fr J.P. 21, 25, 37–38, 42, 66–67, 107, 109, 115–116, 118, 203–204, 221, 228, 248–249, 252

Porror river 114

R

Ramale Prison Camp 217–219, 226, 229, 236, 257, 265–270, 272–273

Rausch sm, Fr J. xx, 11, 180, 187

Read, W.R. (Jack) 216

Redman 182

Rigu xix, 139, 148–149, 153, 155, 206–207, 294

Roche, F. 231, 237

Roland sm, Fr D. 112, 125

Rome 4, 6, 9, 32, 53, 127, 140, 146, 168, 173, 186, 195, 200, 206, 210

Rorovana village xxiv, 156

S

Sarai, Chief xix

Schank SM, Fr P. 25

Scharmack, Bishop L. 116, 121–122, 262, 264, 269

Schilder sm, Br B 66, 228, 249, 252, 257, 273

Schlieker sm, Fr J. xxiii, 25, 28, 34, 44, 60, 68–71, 76, 80, 90–91, 95, 118, 126, 143, 205, 236

Seiller sm, Fr C. 18, 71, 77, 123, 147, 205–206, 291, 295

Sharp, Pastor J. 163, 167

Shimabukuru 95, 291

Simmonds, Br H. 66, 68

Singkai, Bishop Gregory xxiv, 168, 179, 198, 201, 206–207

Sipai village 110–111, 191

Sipuru village 70, 98

Sirovai village 291

Solomon Islands 166

> Choiseul 13, 87–88, 122, 188
>
> Faisi 122, 132, 137, 215, 228, 230, 248, 253
>
> Honiara 12, 67, 120–121, 125, 206
>
> Nila 13, 43, 201, 218, 244–245
>
> Poporang xix–xx, 187–189, 205, 220
>
> Shortland Island xviii, 12, 14, 38, 40, 42, 64, 163, 187, 190, 198, 201, 220
>
> Tangarare 196
>
> Tulagi 11
>
> Visale 11–12, 190, 199, 289

Soraken plantation 115, 125, 132

Sorin, Bishop 116, 121, 124

Sovele village 15, 32, 61, 68–70, 91, 99, 154, 171, 194, 208, 219, 229–230, 236–237

Stuyvenberg, Fr D. 12

Suavita 97

T

Tabago mission 139, 145, 146, 149, 202–203, 207

Tack Long, Mr J. 154–155, 173, 182

Tamuka, Fr A. xxiv, 124, 132, 144, 207

Tangan sm, Fr W. 181

Tarara village xxiii, 188, 276–279

Tarlena mission 20–22, 61, 72, 143, 196, 200, 207, 218, 232, 248

Tashiro 70, 248, 290

Tatamas, Fr P. xxiv, 122, 124, 132, 144, 207

Taufa, Rev. 149

Tearouki mission 125, 137, 199, 201, 206, 214, 218–219, 221, 239

The Missionary Sisters of the Society of Mary (smsm)

    Adalberta 69, 216, 227, 229, 235–236, 238, 247

    Bernadette 169, 182, 217

    Blaise 68, 213, 229–231

    Claire xix, 220, 232

    Crescentia 32, 217, 221, 228, 249, 252

    Dolores 218–219, 252, 260–261, 295

    Domitilla 25, 215, 218, 229, 235, 257, 270

    Fabian 10–12, 68, 214, 229–230, 232, 236

    Foott 137

Index

Gisèle 213, 227, 229–230, 247

Hortense 68, 120, 213–214, 227, 229–230, 236, 247

Ignace xix, 66–67, 69, 130, 140–141, 215, 220–221, 228, 230, 235–238, 240, 248–249

Immacula 168, 195

Juliana 150, 219–220

Kevin 44

Leo 137

Lidwina 180, 214

Ludovica 180, 218

Margarete 160, 222

Martial 25–26, 69, 108, 113, 118, 215, 226, 235

Michaeline 164, 172, 217, 295

Noreen 169, 182

Sevarina 36, 132, 136, 139–140, 221

Wendelina 18, 106, 135–136, 149, 219, 227, 229, 246, 274, 290

Tinputz mission 20–21, 68, 187, 199, 206, 214, 232, 235, 238–239

To Paivu, Fr H. 124, 126, 208

Tokuaka 39

Tome 47, 65

Tong Lep 136

Tonjes sm, Fr B. 61, 63, 70–71, 76, 80, 83, 85, 87, 89, 95, 207–208, 229

Toongabbie 102–103, 118, 124

Toroke, Barosi, Paramount Chief 291

Torokina xx, xxiii–xxiv, 16, 43, 54, 61, 70, 88–89, 97–99, 101, 103, 105–107, 109–110, 112–113, 115–117, 120–125, 144–145, 148, 187, 191–192, 197, 199–201, 210, 213–214, 218–219, 221, 241, 273, 276, 294

Torokoi 67

Tsiroge mission 125, 132, 137, 143, 166, 193–194, 197–198, 200

Tsivara, Fr E. 159–161, 295

Tualagai village 47, 52

Tubiana mission xix, xxiii–xxiv, 14, 18, 24, 31–32, 61, 71–73, 75, 146–151, 154, 159, 168, 177, 180, 197, 206, 208, 214–216, 219–220, 227, 247, 295

Tugiogu village 47, 49

Tunuru mission 15, 20, 35, 68, 70–71, 74, 123–124, 132, 159–161, 170–172, 188, 194, 197, 199, 201, 210, 217–221, 236, 275–276, 278–279, 294

Turiboiru mission xxii–xxiv, 15, 25–26, 30, 33, 36, 42–43, 50, 60, 66–67, 69, 87, 109, 115–116, 118, 120–121, 124, 128, 132, 135, 138, 141–143, 147, 153, 158, 177, 192, 194, 202–204, 219–221, 227–229, 235, 246–248, 250–252

U

Uwa 278–279

V

van Houte sm, Fr A. 7, 9–10

Vanuatu

    Espiritu Santo 130–131

    Port Vila 131

von Bennigsen, R. xix

Voyce, Rev. A.H. 15, 61, 106

Vunapope mission 99, 104, 117, 124, 136–137, 166, 168, 196–199, 202–203, 206–207, 226, 229, 235, 241, 244, 256–260, 263–268, 270–271, 274

W

Waché xxiii, 18, 24

Wade sm, Bishop T. xxiv, 18, 21, 24–25, 29, 31–32, 61, 63, 66, 76, 103, 110, 116–118, 121, 125–126, 132, 136, 140, 144, 147, 158, 189, 192, 195–196, 204, 207–209, 214–216, 227–229, 232, 236–237, 241–242, 246, 248, 273, 278, 290, 294

Weber sm, Fr W. xxiii, 18, 20, 35, 60, 68, 70–72, 74, 95, 183, 197, 210, 226, 236, 275–280

Weemaes sm, Fr W. 170–171, 296

Wieschemeyer sm, Fr F. 121, 159

Wöeste Family

    Herman Wöeste xxv, 157, 177, 180

    Margarete Wöeste 222

    Willy Wöeste 124, 132, 154, 166, 168, 180, 210, 295

Wong, You 106, 109, 150, 231

Y

Yamaru village 83, 85, 93

Index

When The Garamuts Beat

www.ingramcontent.com/pod-product-compliance
Lightning Source LLC
Chambersburg PA
CBHW062031290426
44109CB00026B/2588